THE
PRODUCT
MANAGER'S
HANDBOOK

FOURTH EDITION

LINDA GORCHELS

New York   Chicago   San Francisco   Lisbon   London   Madrid   Mexico City
New Delhi   San Juan   Seoul   Singapore   Sydney   Toronto

2 3 4 5 6 7 8 9 0   DOC/DOC   1 6 5 4 3

ISBN: 978-0-07-177298-3
MHID: 0-07-177298-7

e-ISBN: 978-0-07-177341-6
e-MHID: 0-07-177341-X

This publication is designed to provide accurate and authoritative information in regard to the subject matter covered. It is sold with the understanding that neither the author nor the publisher is engaged in rendering legal, accounting, or other professional service. If legal advice or other expert assistance is required, the services of a competent professional person should be sought.

> —*From a Declaration of Principles Jointly Adopted by a Committee of the American Bar Association and a Committee of Publishers and Association*

Library of Congress Cataloging-in-Publication Data

Gorchels, Linda.
   The product manager's handbook / by Linda Gorchels. — 4th ed.
     p. cm.
   ISBN-13: 978-0-07-177298-3 (alk. paper)
   ISBN-10: 0-07-177298-7 (alk. paper)
   1. Product management.   2. New products—Marketing. I. Title.
   HF5415.15.G636 2012
   658.8—dc23   2011018023

CONTENTS

Preface .... *v*

Acknowledgments .... *vii*

Part I: Bedrock Concepts 1

1. THE MULTIFACETED NATURE OF PRODUCT
   MANAGEMENT JOBS AND STRUCTURE. 3

2. LEADERSHIP AND MANAGEMENT COMPETENCIES 15

3. BUSINESS COMPETENCIES. 37

4. INTELLIGENCE GATHERING. 59

5. PLANNING FRAMEWORKS. 105

Part II: Upstream Product Management: Strategic New Products and Initiatives. 145

6. ROAD MAPS, INNOVATION, AND THE FUZZY FRONT END. 147

7. CREATING—AND GETTING APPROVAL FOR—BUSINESS CASES 175

8. OVERSEEING THE NEW PRODUCT PROJECTS 199

9. FORMULATING AND EXECUTING LAUNCH PLANS 219

Part III: Downstream Product Management: Ongoing Life-Cycle Management and Growth 249

10. LIFE-CYCLE MANAGEMENT 251

11. MANAGING BRAND EQUITY. 283

12. MARKETING STRATEGY AND GO-TO-MARKET EFFORTS 303

Part IV: Fine-Tuning 327

13. ESTABLISHING A GLOBAL MINDSET 329

14. GOAL AND PERFORMANCE ALIGNMENT 351

NOTES. 373

INDEX

Preface

This is the fourth edition of this book—and it's aimed solidly at practicing product managers. While the first edition started out simply extending the discipline beyond traditional consumer packaged goods (and was primarily definitional), the next two editions began to add more fundamental tips and tools. During that 15-year period, dozens of consultants, trainers, associations, and (since 2002) LinkedIn affinity groups emerged to capitalize on the growth of product management and to expand on the basic principles. Many focus almost exclusively on an industry or niche emphasis.

So it was time for another evolution—from presenting product management as a fill-in-the-blank, step-by-step process to one requiring more executive, strategic thinking skills. (Yes, there are still templates and tips, but also substantial emphasis on *why* these templates are relevant.) Here are a few of the changes.

- This edition is organized around upstream and downstream product management responsibilities, as indicated in the book's framework. As a result, there is deeper coverage of both new product development (from the perspective of a product manager rather than R&D) and product life cycle management.
- The book was cocreated with customers. End-of-chapter interviews were completed by product managers or by executives who oversee or work with product managers. Several chapters contain business briefs written by practicing product managers, demonstrating principles in use. The majority of these individuals had adapted and expanded concepts from prior editions.
- Instead of a laundry list of items at the end of chapters, each chapter concludes with a single integrative, high-level, thought-provoking challenge. The more experienced the product manager, the more profound and complex the chapter challenge will be.

Throughout the book, I reference several Web sites that contain videos or other explanatory material to provide greater depth of information on the topic at hand. Some of these external sources are provocative, eye-opening, or surprising, and they enable you to create your own learning "package" as you advance your career. Even though I have decades of experience working with thousands of product managers, one of my greatest contributions is my ability to direct you to a variety of knowledge sources beyond myself. And that's what I have tried to accomplish with this edition. Contact me (lgorchels@exed.wisc.edu) if you have any other knowledge sources worthy of sharing with product managers. Enjoy!

Acknowledgments

This book is in many ways a cocreated product based on contributions from many sources. I would specifically like to acknowledge the following. First of all, I want to thank the people who gave thoughtful answers to my interview questions and are featured at the end of each chapter. These include:

- Mark Rothwell, Vice President-Marketing Communications, Dean Clinic
- Scott Davis, Chief Growth Officer, Prophet
- Doug Vaughan, Vice President-Finance, Ingersoll-Rand
- Paula Gray, Anthropologist-in-Residence, AIPMM
- Brad Rogers, Director of Enterprise Integration and Process Excellence, TIAA-CREF
- Dave Franchino, President, Design Concepts
- Kevin Booth, President, The Hines Group
- Laura Farnham, Vice President, Johnson Controls
- Elyse Kaye, Senior Product Manager, HoMedics (part of Black & Decker)
- Greg DiCillo, President, Life Cycle Strategies, Inc.
- Jeff Mikula, Vice President-Global Branding and Marketing Communications, Hill-Rom, Inc.
- Gabriela Saldanha Brink, Global Product Manager, Promega Corporation
- Mark Phillips, Chief Marketing Officer, GE Healthcare Asia-Pacific
- Stan Kopec, Intellectual Property Portfolio Manager, Nortel
- John Luszczek, General Manager, MSS Business Unit, Nortel

Second, I would like to express my appreciation to the product managers who authored success stories to share as Business Briefs, including:

- Gloria Green, Senior Manager-Lean Marketing, Springs Windows Fashions
- Dan Roche, Marketing Manager, Briggs & Stratton
- Wade Whitmus, Product Development Manager, CUNA Mutual

Third, I would like to acknowledge the efforts of the two "advice columnists":

- Mark Phillips, CMO, GE Healthcare Asia-Pacific
- Richard Gesteland, President, Global Management

Finally, I want to thank Knox Huston, Ron Martirano, and the team at McGraw-Hill for their help in creating the final product.

PART I

BEDROCK CONCEPTS

The Multifaceted Nature of Product Management Jobs and Structure

TRUE OR FALSE: Product management is an entry-level position.

FALSE. But there's more to the story. In general, a comprehensive product manager job is *not* an entry-level position. Most product managers with comprehensive positions have had prior experience in diverse areas. However, some companies have jobs such as *assistant* product manager or product marketing manager which are for close to entry-level people. These jobs allow the people filling them to move up to a full or senior position once they obtain experience. The perspective I take in this book is that for a senior product manager. (In other words, someone moving toward the type of position in the tongue-in-cheek help-wanted ad (see Figure 1.1).

YOUR JOB IS UNIQUE—JUST LIKE EVERYONE ELSE'S

Product managers exist in virtually all industries from consumer packaged goods (such as grocery and retail products) to industrial products (such as equipment and components) to services (such as health care and financial offerings). Some product managers emerge from specialized MBA programs (such as the one at the Center for Brand and Product Management in the Wisconsin School of Business at the University of Wisconsin-Madison), but most product managers transition to the role from positions in engineering, nursing, computer programming, and

3

FIGURE 1.1 ➤ Caricature of a help-wanted ad

other disciplines. Not surprisingly there are both similarities and differences in the jobs of these varied product managers—and each manager can learn from all the others.

In working with thousands of product managers over the past two decades, I have repeatedly found several common areas of inquiry. Here are a few of the typical questions and an answer in a nutshell:

- *What are the differences between business-to-business and business-to-consumer product managers?* Business products are generally more complicated than consumer products. The more complex the product and purchase process, the more likely it is that a product manager will need a related technical background. In addition, the go-to-market strategy may be different. Both kinds of product managers, nevertheless, should start with knowledge of the targeted customers.
- *Aren't all product managers product developers?* Some companies separate product management into upstream activities focused

on development rather than downstream activities focused on marketing and life-cycle management. However, the majority of product managers are responsible for both.

- *How many products does a "typical" product manager manage?* There is no standard here. I have worked with successful product managers who are responsible for one complex product as well as those responsible for hundreds—or even thousands—of related stockkeeping units (SKUs).
- *How do product managers work?* The vast majority of product managers function in a matrix organization in which they have to accomplish their goals and execute their strategies through others. This requires significant skill in communication and influence.
- *Where do product managers fit in the organization?* Occasionally, product managers report to engineering, product development, or even product management. But most product managers report to a marketing function.

The product manager's job is to *oversee all aspects* of a product or service line to create and deliver superior *customer satisfaction* while simultaneously providing *long-term value* for the company. Note the critical implications in this statement. First, product managers have *oversight* of the product. They need to accomplish their goals through others. Second, the foundation goal is to deliver customer satisfaction—not just a product or set of features. While engineers and designers might have more insights into whether something *can* be built, product managers should have more market insights into whether it *should* be built. And finally, this must all be done profitably. Successful product managers need a solid business sense from financial knowledge to forecasting to pricing to operational effectiveness.

YES, PRODUCT MANAGEMENT CAN WORK FOR SERVICES, TOO

Product management as an organizational form long ago moved into service companies such as financial institutions and hospitals. Many large banks have product managers for credit cards, deposit services, trust operations, and commercial cash management. Property and casualty insurers have product managers for various lines such as auto and commercial. In fact LinkedIn, at the time of this writing, had over 1,200 members in its Insurance Product Management group.

Hospitals have also experienced success with the product management structure. A study published in the *Journal of Health Care Marketing* reported that hospitals with product-line management outperformed those without it on virtually all performance indicators, including occupancy rate, gross patient revenue per bed, average profit margin, and return on assets.[1] Not surprisingly, the implementation of product-line management increased with the level of competition and hospital bed size. Other health-care studies found that product-line management in hospitals offered the benefits of increased accountability, elimination of duplication of services, and a better market orientation. The limitations included a possible increase in costs (because functional management was not eliminated) and an increased need for more timely and accurate data. While these studies are several years old, product management continues to be a presence in the industry.

It's worth noting that even with services, product managers practice oversight, strive for customer satisfaction, and work to build long-term value for the company. But of course there are some differences. Services are less tangible than products, occasionally making it harder to "prove" claims of quality and superiority. The materials and techniques used to produce a product can often be shown as visible *proof of quality.* Since many services are delivered person to person (rather than produced on a production line and inventoried), it is both harder to show quality before the fact and to control the potential for variability in the outcome. As a result, part of the job of a service-sector product manager is to manage the *evidence* of quality. Customers will use supporting services (e.g., customer service), empathy, trust, and other subtle "cues" to establish a perception of quality—often to a greater extent than is true for physical products. Product managers must work to manage these quality cues to the best of their ability.

AN ENTREPRENEURIAL MINDSET

Product managers who think like entrepreneurs recognize that entrepreneurs view themselves as owners of their products and their own success. They put "blood, sweat, and tears" into the business. So it's important that product managers think like entrepreneurs—or perhaps *intrapreneurs* is the more appropriate word.

Let's expand on this a bit. While people may argue that entrepreneurs have more control over everything than do product managers, the reality is just the opposite. It is the rare entrepreneur who is independently wealthy with easy access to materials, operations, and labor. Most entrepreneurs have a vision for a product or service they are passionate about, but they have to find the resources to actualize the vision. They must craft business plans to solicit money from venture capitalists or banks. This is not unlike the challenges product managers face in developing business cases for new products. The business case is essentially a proposal for an investment of time and resources from the firm. In fact, some firms expect product managers to treat the management team like angel investors who must be convinced of the future value of the product concept being proposed.

After receiving guarantees of funding, entrepreneurs may need to source materials or locate contract manufacturers. They must work carefully with third parties they don't directly manage in order to accomplish the design, development, and commercialization of their envisioned products or services. Similarly, product managers must constantly accomplish their goals through organizational functions over which they have no direct authority. They must use their skills of persuasion and diplomacy to make things happen.

Entrepreneurs often need to work with independent reps or channels to reach the intended market. To help these groups function more effectively, entrepreneurs must provide not just product knowledge but also an understanding of the target markets and the best approach to reach these markets. That's akin to the challenge product managers face when they're training and motivating the sales force. There is a strong need to empathize with the needs of salespeople to advance the sales process.

The common link between the entrepreneurial business plan and the product manager's business case is clarity of customer need. Strong entrepreneurs and strong product managers know the profile, needs, emotions, and purchase drivers of their customers. They don't think exclusively in terms of product features or benefits, but rather how these features or benefits align with customer goals better than competing offerings, as well as what it might take to sell them. They have a strong command of marketing and customer-focused competencies.

Entrepreneurs share several traits that influence the way they think. Entrepreneurs embody traits of risk-taking, passion, focus, product/customer knowledge, and tolerance for failure. Strong product managers share these traits (or elements of these traits) which influence their thoughts and decision-making processes.

Let's carry this analogy one step further. Successful entrepreneurs can grow successful companies. (As an aside, serial entrepreneurs start *several* companies. My focus here is *not* on serial entrepreneurs but rather on those more focused on a single economic endeavor.) As their companies grow, the passion, focus, and connectedness with the product/customer becomes diffused. That's where product managers come in. Product managers can restore the passion, focus, and connectedness with the product/customer for their areas of responsibility. They carry on the role (and spirit) of the original entrepreneur.

THE PRODUCT MANAGER CONTINUUM: FROM UPSTREAM TO DOWNSTREAM

There are two fundamentally different—though related—classifications of product management functions: upstream functions and downstream functions. *Upstream functions* deal with the strategies of product road maps and new product development efforts. This usually includes identifying critical portfolio needs and then providing marketing leadership throughout the development process up until launch. *Downstream functions* deal with ongoing life-cycle management. Some medical device and diagnostic manufacturers (in particular) hire separate people for the two job categories. GE Healthcare, for example, has upstream product managers responsible for global product strategy and launch. The downstream product managers handle the marketing and sales support necessary to manage the profitable sales of products after launch and beyond. Sometimes the downstream product managers are responsible for marketing the products in different countries. Beckman Coulter has similar split positions but refers to them as strategic product managers and tactical product managers.

The split between upstream and downstream is not consistent across industries, either. For some companies, particularly in highly technical fields, upstream activities end *before* commercialization, with downstream product managers taking over at launch. And some companies shift from upstream to downstream at the *start* of a new product project (at the shift from R&D to active development). The "best practice" for a company depends on what works best for its specific circumstances. Long development time, heavy regulatory oversight, and prolonged testing prior to approvals may suggest an appropriate environment for splitting the product management function into upstream and downstream. Without question, however, the vast majority of companies I deal with expect product managers to handle both upstream and downstream functions.

In this book I am presenting the product management function as having both upstream and downstream components. The framework I use addresses both. (See Figure 1.2).

Part I presents the foundation skills required of most product managers. Chapters 2–5 provide an overview of the competencies listed at the bottom of the framework. The next two parts deal more specifically with

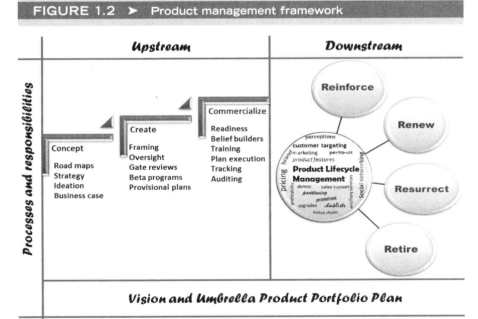

FIGURE 1.2 ➤ Product management framework

Upstream | *Downstream*

Processes and responsibilities

Concept
Road maps
Strategy
Ideation
Business case

Create
Framing
Oversight
Gate reviews
Beta programs
Provisional plans

Commercialize
Readiness
Belief builders
Training
Plan execution
Tracking
Auditing

Product Lifecycle Management
perceptions
customer targeting
marketing   personas
product features
demos   sales support
positioning
promotions
upgrades   checklists
value chain
branding   pricing   profitability   ancillary services   Social networking

Reinforce
Renew
Resurrect
Retire

Vision and Umbrella Product Portfolio Plan

Foundation skills

Strategic thinking | *Leadership & decision-making* | *Competitive benchmarking*
Financial aptitude | *Forecasting* | *Trend-spotting & innovation*
Business planning | *Market research* | *Go-to-market knowledge*
Influence & motivation | *Technical competence* | *Project management*
Team management | *Basic operations* | *Self-discipline*

© Linda Gorchels

processes and responsibilities. Part II covers upstream activities related to strategic new products and initiatives. Part III covers the ongoing life-cycle maintenance and growth of downstream product management. The final part touches on the special issues of globalization and organizational structure.

CHAPTER CHALLENGE

Strive to think like an entrepreneur. Become the spirit of entrepreneurialism for your product line.

INTERVIEW WITH MARK ROTHWELL: THE MANY SIDES OF BRAND MANAGEMENT

Mark Rothwell, Vice President Marketing, Communications, and Community Partnerships, Dean Clinic, Madison, Wisconsin

Mark, you started out in brand management for several consumer packaged goods companies and then shifted to retail and service products. Can you talk a bit about the different brand management "philosophies" you encountered along the way?

Having been fortunate to learn at some of the top brand-management companies in the world (from Coca-Cola to Miller Brewing to Famous Footwear), I've noticed a definite range in philosophies. The main difference is in the commitment to the *art* of brand management and the dedication to creating, maintaining, or accelerating great brands.

I've been asked the following question when shifting from one industry to another: "Do you feel you are at a disadvantage not having experience in X industry?" My answer is simple and consistent: *no.*

Whether the companies are traditional or lifestyle marketers with hard goods, soft goods, or services in their portfolio, there are consistent methodologies that most successful companies in any industry believe. Here is my brainstorm list of those philosophies:

- *Consumer, consumer, consumer (or in B2B: customer, customer, customer):* The organization that intimately knows its target audience and has a differentiated story to tell will ultimately have the long-term advantage in influencing the minds and hearts of consumers.
- *Target memorable:* Those who win in the marketplace are those brands that not only consistently *deliver* on their brand promise, but they *overdeliver*, which makes them memorable.
- *Never be satisfied; always be curious:* Winners are open to trying new things, taking calculated risks, and learning from mistakes. When they make a mistake, they own up to it and make it right in the minds of the consumers.
- *Honesty wins:* We are all fighting for perfection, but when perfection isn't achieved, our brands or companies need to acknowledge, "We were wrong," "We are sorry," or "Here is what we would like to do to make it right."
- *Create brand advocates from bad experiences:* Many research studies show that when brands do make a mistake, those that address it head-on and find a solution create a stable of brand advocates.
- *Success or failure is a click away:* In today's technology age, your consumers are in charge. It is your job to build an active relationship with them on *their terms*. If you can't do this effectively, your brand's demise is simply a click of a mouse away.

More and more health-care organizations are instituting variations of a product or brand management structure. What have you experienced in the industry?

If you scan the various lists of top brands—brands with the highest equity—you won't see many health-care organizations. So visionary health-care organizations are reaching outside the industry for help in creating and maintaining winning brands. A winning brand structure requires organizational commitment from top to bottom. Then it must be populated with great brand-minded people who bring a discipline, curiosity, and tenacity to ensure that the brand is successful. In most cases simply instilling a formal brand management approach is all it takes; when you provide smart people with facts and insights about how to engage consumers with your brand, you ultimately get commitment to this philosophy. Many traditional brand leaders are coming into to health care not only for the opportunity to build something special, but more for the inherent altruistic, "If you do it right, you are helping people" impact. The health-care industry is ripe for a game-changing organization dedicated to delivering an exceptional experience. The organizations that do this first will create a juggernaut brand that patients will never leave and many will seek to be part of. Health care is about quality of life, and brands that can improve a consumer's quality of life in an exceptional fashion will be the true game-changers.

The job of a business-to-consumer (B2C) brand manager is not exactly the same as the job of a B2B product manager. What do you see as the similarities and differences?

Let's start with the similarities. First, both brand managers and product managers should have an intimate knowledge of and connection with their respective target audiences. Whether you are in B2C or B2B, knowledge of your customers is critical to being able to deliver on their needs more effectively and consistently than your competition does. Second, it's critical to create a truly differentiated story on why your brand is the best choice to satisfy the needs of the target audience. To do this, you will need to constantly monitor and anticipate the needs of your target. Finally, you must consistently *deliver* on your brand promise. That means, when a mistake is made, acknowledge it and make it right.

Now let's shift to the differences. There is a different type of customer relationship with different resource allocations between the two. In the B2C world, the resources are focused primarily on the marketing research and communications directed at consumers; marketing is the lead role with consumers, and sales play an important supporting role with channels. In the B2B world, product management, sales, engineering, and support must work together to provide solutions to complex problems with a necessary focus on multiple levels of purchase decision makers. That yields another difference—one between technical knowledge and branding knowledge. In B2B, the brand story and approach focus on the technical satisfiers or more to the *head*, while in B2C, the brand story focuses on the emotional satisfiers or more on the *heart*.

So it sounds as if brand knowledge is necessary for business, consumer, and service-sector product managers. What are a few tips you can provide on this point?

Brand knowledge comes from never losing sight of end customers and consumers, what they desire, and how your brand delivers versus the alternatives. In today's age of technology, segmentation is even more important to ensure you are reaching the right audience with the right message at the right time via the right medium. This is critical if you want to consistently achieve the right result.

I have always approached my product management experience with the mindset that it is *my* brand and I will develop the brand better than it was before I arrived, thus leaving it in better shape for the next team.

Buyers are more fickle than ever before, they have access to more information than ever before, and they can share their thoughts more broadly than ever before. Successful brand managers will be active participants in the lives of their consumers and customers; those who can anticipate their thoughts and proactively provide thoughtful solutions will create a special bond that will result in instant brand star status.

Brands are built every day. The architects or managers who are committed to partnering with their markets will grow over time and will ultimately win in the marketplace regardless of the brand or the company.

What is the best advice you ever received—and what advice can you give to today's brand and product managers?

I think the best professional advice I ever received is, *"Remain curious and tenacious."*

The best personal advice is, *"Always be empathetic."* That's great advice for being a successful brand manager because it ensures that you always view things through the eyes of your customers.

CHAPTER 2

Leadership and Management Competencies

TRUE OR FALSE: Leaders are born, not made.

FALSE. Warren Bennis was quoted in 2006 as saying, "The most dangerous myth is that leaders are born—that there is a genetic factor to leadership, that people have certain charismatic qualities or not. That's nonsense. Leaders are made rather than born." While it's true that some people have more of the inherent qualities associated with leadership than others, the traits can be further developed. And those who have few inherent qualities can gain a fundamental grasp of the basics, thereby improving their leadership competencies. Unfortunately there is also the ironic fact that while leadership can be learned, it cannot be taught (per se). Yes, skills and competencies can be taught, but the actual development of leadership comes from experience and practice. There is no shortcut.

PRODUCT MANAGERS AS LEADERS

Many companies I work with are adamant that their product managers should be leaders. If product managers are leaders, why are they not called product leaders? Actually, in some companies they are—and sometimes they are called product owners or product general managers (GMs). Nevertheless, the fact is that leadership and management are situational and that product managers have to practice both skills. They manage a product or product line, and they lead peers and cross-functional teams toward a product vision. Good product managers approach strategy and tactics, as well as leadership and management, holistically. (Nobody ever said that the job was easy!) So let's take a look at the varied aspects of leadership and management—remembering that one is not inherently better than the other.

In an oversimplified paraphrasing of John Kotter's definitions, management is about coping with complexity, whereas leadership is about coping with change. Managers capitalize on skillful utilization of resources to reach a visible goal. They are typically concerned with the day-to-day how-to-get-it-done issues. Leaders guide and direct a course of action into a changing future, usually by influencing others. They must motivate and inspire others—and often under challenging conditions. There are times when it is most important to make a decision (leadership), and other times when it is more important to make a decision *work* (management). In reality, there is a very blurred line between leadership and management.

Some experts separate leadership into two categories: transformational and transactional. For example, when camera companies (such as Kodak) faced major business model changes in transitioning from traditional to digital photography products, transformational leadership was required. On the other hand, the types of changes needed for modest product improvements are less intensive, requiring more transactional leadership. Most product managers get to "practice" *transactional* leadership before handling *transformational* leadership.

When companies hire product managers to be "change agents," some are expecting the individuals to be transformational leaders, and others expect transactional leaders—but most of the time the company simply wants product managers to move the company toward a growth agenda.

What does it take for a product manager to be a leader? People often think of leadership from the perspective of providing guidance for direct reports. They are expected to remove obstacles and marshal resources for their direct reports and staff. But most product managers have no (or few) direct reports. Rather, they must lead progress toward a product vision. Leadership from a product management perspective requires a capacity to anticipate market requirements, analyze intelligence, make decisions, and execute plans through others. It is somewhat improvisational in terms of leading through trust, influence, and logical persuasion rather than formal authority.

TIPS ON DECISION MAKING

Most people—including product managers—have not had formal training in decision making. So they may seek "best practices" to supplant decision making. Unfortunately, "best practices" don't necessarily teach people *how* to think. In fact, they may make it too easy for people to be trapped by the *adequate* when a better alternative might exist. Effort is required to generate alternatives beyond the obvious ones. I encourage product managers to look for *next* practices in addition to *best* practices as they explore the future for their products. Not doing so results in complacency—and complacency is occasionally fatal (or at the least it yields nonoptimal results).

Let's talk a bit about the decision-making process. (See Figure 2.1.) In general it involves: (1) defining and framing the issue, goal, or problem requiring the decision; (2) gathering appropriate data; (3) generating alternative solutions; (4) evaluating the solutions; (5) choosing an acceptable solution; (6) acting on the chosen alternative; and (7) evaluating the outcome. The way a product manager frames a decision has a significant impact on the remaining steps in the process. For example, assume that a product manager is considering a price increase on a product because profitability is lower than desired. If the decision is framed as *whether or not to increase the price*, different information will likely be gathered than what would have been obtained if the decision had been framed as *how to improve the product's profitability*. Give careful thought to how you frame your decisions.

Once the framing is done, information will need to be gathered and examined. The next two chapters describe how to gather and evaluate various types of intelligence so they won't be discussed here; rather I'll skip to the next step: using the information to generate alternative solutions. Be open-minded on this step. Rather than limiting yourself to one solution hypothesis (that you try to prove with your data), broaden your thinking to consider potentially novel solutions. We as human beings often develop answers to problems before we gather data, and

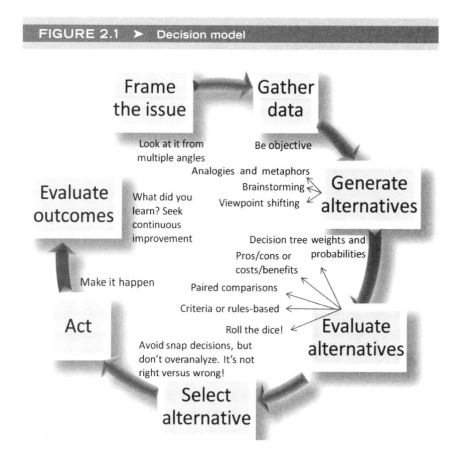

FIGURE 2.1 ➤ Decision model

then we simply use the data to justify or rationalize a decision we have already made. Sometimes that can work, but it should not be your standard modus operandi.

After coming up with a few possible solutions, you have to evaluate them. Different approaches work under different circumstances. Sometimes listing the pros and cons of each alternative can provide insight. As you go through this process, be mindful of implementation issues and possible unintended consequences. For example, if you enter a new market with different channels, what might be the consequence on your relationship with existing channel partners? Another approach to evaluating alternatives could be a simple prioritization including weights or probabilities of outcomes. Using flowcharts and other planning tools described in Chapter 5 might be useful in this situation.

Using these "tools" won't make it easy to select between two *equally attractive* alternatives because you have to "give up" an attractive alternative. The act of carefully evaluating the issues, though, helps prepare you for the challenge of eventually selling the solution to others.

Regardless of how you evaluate the alternatives, you have to choose one alternative; you have to decide which alternative to select. Keep in mind that you are choosing from alternatives rather than between "right" and "wrong." In many situations, making a decision work is more important than making the "right" decision. In these cases, rolling the dice actually may be just as appropriate as in-depth analysis. Relate the speed of the decision to the "permanence" of the outcome; a snap decision may be okay if the decision can be easily reversed but is risky if the decision is permanent. If the impact of the decision affects others or if others are necessary to implement the outcome, include them in the process. You need their buy-in. And this means that you need to establish mutual respect with various stakeholders, as is described later in this chapter.

In the end, not only do you have to make decisions, you must also act on them. Just as carpentry tools in a tool kit will not—in and of themselves—build a house, decision tools will not—in and of themselves—provide outcomes. Product managers have to make it happen. After implementing a decision, be sure to evaluate it and "teach yourself" how to improve it going forward. It's worth remembering that emotion plays a role (sometimes a major role) in all decisions. Product managers should try to understand their own emotions as they relate to the decision as well as the emotions of other stakeholders.

SURVIVING MATRIX STRUCTURES AND CROSS-FUNCTIONAL TEAMS

Planning is just the beginning of a product manager's job. It has to extend to execution. And for product managers, this means that a significant amount has to be accomplished through people who don't report to them.

To become change agents or cross-functional leaders, product managers must establish mutual respect with a variety of stakeholders. A product manager, by definition, is a generalist who must rely on numerous functional specialists to get the product or service to the customer. These specialists can be internal or external to the company. The presence of internal support groups (such as advertising and marketing research) means that product managers can be less skilled in these areas and instead focus on managing the product's success. However, their control over internal groups may be less than it is over an external group because product managers have no direct authority over an outside group. A good starting point is to list all the functional areas you deal with. Then create a simple table with columns describing what you expect from them and what you think they expect from you. Validate these expectations by sharing your list of expectations with your colleagues. Do they agree with your perceptions? Understanding and dealing with these expectations can help establish mutual respect.

INTRODUCING THE STAKEHOLDERS

Let's now discuss some of the typical relationships within an organization. Figure 2.2 shows the results of a proprietary survey that asked product managers to indicate the extent of contact they have with a variety of functional areas on a scale from 1 (no contact at all) to 5 (very high level of contact). The groups with which product managers had the greatest level of contact were sales, research and development

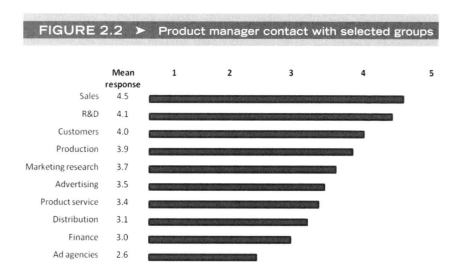

FIGURE 2.2 ➤ Product manager contact with selected groups

	Mean response	1	2	3	4	5
Sales	4.5					
R&D	4.1					
Customers	4.0					
Production	3.9					
Marketing research	3.7					
Advertising	3.5					
Product service	3.4					
Distribution	3.1					
Finance	3.0					
Ad agencies	2.6					

(R&D), and customers. The mean, or average, responses for each area are shown in the middle column of Figure 2.2.

Depending on the company and situation, product managers play various roles in terms of cross-functional interactions. With regard to field sales, they answer questions from the field, assist on sales calls as needed, provide product information to simplify the sales process, suggest various incentives for new products, and/or develop literature and other customer pieces to help further the sales effort. They might also work with distributors or agents, suggest alternative channels, and/or expedite shipments. Figure 2.3 shows some of the groups with which product managers frequently interact. Those in shaded circles generally have the highest interaction. However, people fulfilling all these functions may turn to the product manager as the "answer person," which requires the product managers to allocate their time carefully. Following

FIGURE 2.3 ➤ Product management: primary role influences

are descriptions that might help product managers in generating their own "mutual expectations" table.

Sales

Product managers play a major role in helping salespeople accomplish the objectives of the company (not to mention the objectives of the salespeople themselves). The nature of the relationship varies according to the culture of the organization and the perception of product management. Some product managers are perceived as sales support, some as product developers who are out of touch with the market, and others as product experts. Regardless of the perception, product managers should resist the temptation to use home-office authority to "force" sales cooperation; this can severely damage the trust and respect required for a cooperative effort.

Development of sales forecasts is generally the domain of product managers, but they frequently cannot be created without sales input. Ask salespeople to estimate sales in their territories in total (or by customer and/or product). If the information is broken down by account, try to include an estimate of the probability of attaining the sales. Forecasts will generally be given to the regional or national sales manager and then collated and forwarded to the marketing department. Product managers should work in concert with these groups to arrive at a realistic forecast for the product line.

Communicating with Salespeople

On a day-to-day basis, product managers spend quite a bit of time communicating with salespeople and sales prospects. Sometimes the contacts are requests for price adjustments or special deals that require product management approval or authorization. Other times the contacts will be questions about product attributes. The more itemized a product fact book is (as described in the planning chapter), the more efficient a product manager will be in providing the answers. Even if salespeople have received the information previously, it is often quicker and more efficient for them if the product manager provides the information on the spot.

This does not absolve the product manager from also providing the sales force with written information. Salespeople should be informed of any product or marketing change that affects their relationships or nego-tiations with customers *before* the information reaches their customers!

Many companies require product managers to spend a certain amount of time (e.g., 25–30 percent of their working hours) meeting with customers, some of which is through calls with salespeople. These sales calls provide an opportunity for the product manager to learn more about the customer, or on some occasions to help close a sale. However, *prior to the call* everyone should be clear on the specific role the product manager is expected to play.

Most of these day-to-day activities will not appear on the product and marketing plans, although they might be part of annual perfor-mance objectives (e.g., percentage of time spent in the field). What should be included in the product manager's plans are budgets for travel expenses, any special incentive programs (for spurring sales of products that aren't achieving objectives or for introducing new products), or any activities undertaken as part of territory redesign or sales force changes.

Sales Training
Sales training can cover a variety of issues: sales skills, company data, product knowledge, and market and competitive intelligence. Training effectiveness can be a significant factor in making a new product launch successful. Although teaching sales skills per se will not typically be part of a product manager's responsibilities, any product training that is conducted should fit within the framework of the firm's approach to the selling process.

First, think about what information salespeople require for plan-ning sales calls. They need to know who is *most likely* to buy the prod-uct. Instead of describing the primary and secondary target markets, product managers should profile the *most likely* account, suggesting specific customers, if possible and appropriate. If noncustomers need to be cultivated, salespeople need to know the types of uses, applications, and functions of the product. For example, a company selling flat-panel display screens might direct salespeople to engineers in specific indus-tries who require a monitor with exceptional graphics clarity.

Both product managers and salespeople should understand the differences between key accounts, target accounts, and maintenance accounts (as well as, of course, "why bother?" accounts). *Key accounts* consist of the 20 or so percent of customers who make up the bulk of gross profitability. *Target accounts* are those customers who may be the competitors' key accounts or who are significant prospects for a new product or service. *Maintenance accounts* may include existing small customers and possibly future strategic accounts.

Next, product managers need to define what information salespeople must obtain from customers in order for them to qualify needs. What does the salesperson need to know about the prospect to determine the appropriateness of the sale? Customer satisfaction results from the best match between product benefits and customer needs. If the salespeople "successfully" sell to the wrong people or for the wrong applications, the revenue will be temporary. Therefore, product managers must provide customer-friendly questions that will enable salespeople to assess the fit before closing the sale.

Product managers should raise questions about how prospects perform the function(s) provided by the product, what tolerances are required, what applications they would have for it now and in the future, and so on. The questions should not simply push the prospect toward a sale, but rather indicate whether the prospect has a true need for the product (thereby screening out inappropriate prospects). For example, a college textbook product manager responsible for a line of products to be sold to university professors will need to provide questions that assess teaching philosophy, level of rigor, and content preferences of the faculty, while the product manager selling flat-panel display screens may need to determine whether the screen is used in bright sunlight or office light, whether the primary usage is text or graphics, and whether simple or complex software is involved.

Finally, the product manager needs to determine what support and materials will help salespeople be more successful. Product managers should work closely with the sales force to ensure that marketing messages are relevant to the key audiences being called on.

Operations and Research and Development (R&D)

Product managers of both service products and manufactured products are dependent on operations to create the right product at the right price and deliver it at the right time for customers. Whether "operations" refers to underwriting, loan management, manufacturing, or logistics, a close working relationship between operations and product management is critical for both new product development and strategic decisions.

New Product Development
Perhaps the most visible interaction a product manager will have with operations is during new product development. The research and development department will need to assess technical feasibility; manufacturing will need to evaluate future efficiency and productivity; procurement might need to be involved with make-versus-buy decisions; and overall capacity considerations will need to be taken into account. The role of the product manager is to represent the voice of the customer, balancing corporate return on investment (ROI), customer satisfaction, and manufacturing cost. Mutually acceptable standards for quality and customer service will need to be established so that manufacturing and marketing strategies are complementary rather than conflicting.

Strategic Interactions
The product manager may also be involved in strategy sessions with the operations function, beyond specific new product projects. During these sessions, the product manager will present marketplace problems and/or competitive moves that might trigger ideas for new products and focus the discussion on future capacity needs. This is also the time when product managers learn of technology looking for a market and are encouraged to think of ways to incorporate new technology into existing or planned products in a way that is acceptable to the market. For example, when Ford first developed front-disc brakes, there was concern about how to introduce them into cars given the inevitable price impact. Ford decided to introduce them as an upscale option on expensive cars until the price could be driven low enough through mass production to be appropriate for any vehicle.

   The product manager must work continuously with operations to improve and enhance the product line. This requires that product managers have at least a basic understanding (if in a manufacturing environment) of material scrapped because of worker error, the time it takes to set up a production line, and other operations performance measures. In insurance, product managers may need to understand basic underwriting guidelines. In financial services, product managers may need knowledge of the secondary market for loans and various financial ratios.

Product managers are frequently involved with operations on cost-reduction projects. Because product managers are expected to provide market insights, they have to focus on ways of reducing costs that will not compromise the perceived value of a product. Cost reduction should not be fleeting. That is, care must be taken that cost savings not be temporary, with the inevitable result of costs going up in the future.

Other operations-related activities a product manager might undertake include the following:

- Leading synergy sessions to ensure that all functions are moving in the same direction.
- Encouraging discussion of technological advancements that could affect future new products.
- Establishing task forces to conduct value analysis on existing products.
- Monitoring productivity improvements.
- Fostering teamwork to enhance productivity on an ongoing basis.

Customer and Product Support Services

Customer service as a function can exist in marketing, warehousing, sales, or some other department, depending on the organizational structure of the firm. Product managers should both gather information from customer service representatives (CSRs) on product performance, and supply information to them to increase customer satisfaction with the product line. Part of the added value for many products is the service provided by the company. Product managers have to ensure that service standards are established, understood, and attainable by the service staff.

For service standards to be attainable, CSRs require training. Product managers might request support from the company's human resources function, include CSRs in the product training done for the sales force, and/or develop specific training for them. The more important service is as part of the product's competitive differentiation, the more important it is for product managers to take an active role in making sure the training takes place.

The handling of warranties, for example, will require clarity among product support staff. If the warranty specifies thirty days and a complaint is received on the thirty-first day, what leeway does the support staff have in deciding how to handle the issue? What leeway should the staff have?

Finance

Product managers must work with finance to achieve a balance between the way products are costed and the market price desired. Customers don't care what internal cost allocation mechanism a company uses to set a floor for pricing. Their concern is simply whether a product has sufficient value given the competitive alternatives available. Although all costs must be covered for a company to remain profitable in the long term, contribution pricing in concert with market segmentation or product life-cycle decisions can be valuable. For example, pharmaceutical companies use contribution pricing to determine how long to sell an old product once a new one has been introduced:

> *Often new drugs are introduced that are more effective or have fewer side effects than older drugs, but the older drug still may be marketed. Then its price would fall. The company would discontinue the product when it no longer makes a contribution. It may discontinue the drug sooner if it can use existing capacity to produce products with a higher contribution.*[1]

Product managers must also rely on finance to provide line-item information for the budget, pro forma income statements, and/or product balance sheets. By negotiating what information is critical for decision making, both functions can operate more effectively. The relevance of specific costs varies by situation and depends on the decision to be made. Product managers who can work with finance to ferret out the appropriate costs will be in a better position to make the right decisions.

Marketing Communications

Whether dealing with an internal advertising department or an external ad agency, a product manager needs a general understanding of promotional alternatives to be able to evaluate copy and media recommendations effectively. Typically, product managers will determine what positioning they want for their products, but the communication of that positioning will be left to the functional specialists. Product managers need to describe the target market they are trying to reach as precisely as possible so that the advertising groups can use that information to select the appropriate communication tools.

If there are several product managers working for a company, they must consider the relative merits of advertising the company as a whole versus positioning the various products independently of the company. A number of companies are moving to an umbrella approach to branding, in which the company name, reputation, and position are being emphasized as much as or more than the individual brand. Product managers and advertising specialists can discuss the relative merits of each option and come to an agreement prior to investing heavily in promotion.

If a product manager can choose between an in-house and an external agency, which one should be selected? Obviously there are several factors to consider. An external agency can be preferable for the product manager who needs an outside viewpoint, faces internal resource constraints that make it difficult to meet deadlines, and/or wants to take advantage of an agency's potential for sharing costs. On the other hand, an internal department might be the right way to go if the product manager needs to capitalize on the expertise that results from knowledge of a very specialized market, has the necessary skill in-house, and wants more control over the total process.

There are several questions that should be asked in agency selection:

1. *What types of promotion, in addition to advertising, might need to be done?* Many companies, particularly in business-to-business situations, need direct mail, lead-generation programs, trade show coverage, e-commerce Web sites, or special sales promotion techniques.

2. *Does the agency understand the target and have the appropriate talent to speak the right language?* This does not mean that a technical message needs to be written by a technical person. In fact, a technical slant may be completely wrong in cases where the focus should be on customer goals rather than on product features. However, the copywriter needs to understand how to translate features into appropriate benefits for the customer.

3. *Should a large or small agency be hired?* Typically, the most effective arrangement is for the client size to match the agency size, and it may be better to be the big fish in a small pond than the reverse. However, there may be exceptions, particularly when innovative new products are concerned.

4. *Will the agency be expected to help with general marketing, Internet marketing, research, and/or strategic planning?* If so, this might narrow the pool of appropriate agencies.

Marketing Research

Although product managers must necessarily have good information about the market and the competition, they are not usually experts in data collection and analysis. That's why some customer research is farmed out to either internal research departments or external research agencies. Product managers can also take advantage of the marketing research supplied by many advertising agencies or trade associations.

Customers

Customer contact is expected for virtually all product managers. Consumer-goods brand managers usually reach customers through focus groups, Facebook, and other techniques. Business-to-business product managers are more likely to contact customers while they're on calls with salespeople and through customer visit programs. The critical point in meeting with customers is to be open to both long-term future needs and shortfalls in existing products. As difficult as it is, product managers must visualize innovations that anticipate and satisfy undefined and unarticulated needs.

INFLUENCING THE STAKEHOLDERS

In the corporate theater, product managers are both actor and director, staging a series of events for the benefit of the market—the final customers. Unless something happens, all the planning is for naught. Therefore, they must interact directly with all the functions discussed earlier as well as with top management. The extent of interaction will vary by company and the experience level of the product manager. Business Brief 2.1 describes product manager interactions in the electronics marketplace.

Business Brief 2.1

PRODUCT MANAGER INTERACTIONS IN THE ELECTRONICS MARKETPLACE

The electronics field is known for short product life cycles and fragmented customer segments. Competition and price pressure are intense. Facing these challenges, the product manager must be able to work with and through a variety of individuals.

The product manager's position will, of course, vary by company, as Bill Meserve points out in his *Electronic Business* article, "The Changing Role of Product Management":

At one components division of General Instrument Corp., product managers function mostly as coordinators between engineering product development and marketing, and between marketing and sales. They have direct responsibility for product line advertising and promotion budgets, but only provide marketing input to product development projects, which are initiated and managed by engineering. Hewlett-Packard Co. product managers, in contrast, are frequently the focal point for new product development. They prepare the product development plan, authorize its implementation and monitor its progress.

Regardless of the role given a product manager by a company, the product manager must develop management skills to be able to lead teams in product development and product marketing. This involves a number of things. First, the product manager shouldn't be afraid to admit ignorance. Even though most technical product managers do have significant backgrounds in their fields, chances are they don't have the technical skills or knowledge of the engineers on the team. Second, it's important to know when to intervene. Although it's essential that the team members learn to work together, especially in the new product endeavors, the product manager still has ultimate responsibility for the success of the product line.

These technical skills are built over time. According to Bill Meserve:

> *Beginning product managers with focused responsibilities need specific knowledge about the company's product and competitive offerings. As job experience and responsibility increase, the focus of skills building shifts to functional areas like financial analysis, promotion, pricing design, new product development and strategic selling. And when professional responsibilities progress to even higher levels, management skills become central. Product managers learn to build a team, achieve consensus, negotiate agreements, measure performance and handle personal relationships. Companies such as Allen-Bradley Co., 3M Co. and E.I. du Pont de Nemours & Co. supplement education with direct customer interaction, mentor relationships and cross-functional training to enhance product management skills.*

Source: Adapted from Bill Meserve, "The Changing Role of Product Management," *Electronic Business*, 9 (January 1989), pp. 143–146.

Communicate the Product Vision

Product managers realize that they must get buy-in for their strategies, but they often don't know *how* to accomplish that. While facts and statistics are critical, they must be woven into a story (or scenario) that moves people into action. The most carefully researched insights are greeted with cynicism when the message is lost in PowerPoint slides and dry hyperbole.[2]

Storytelling is one of the most powerful inspirational tools available and has been used throughout history. Product managers who can in a sense tell a story and paint a vivid picture of the future may transform a colleague's point of view and motivate the desired action. The product vision has to be something people can commit to, not just numbers to pursue:

> *Long-renowned for its story-intensive culture, 3M cultivates tales of past successes. Stories about winning innovations help inspire employees to keep new ideas coming. Sales reps are trained to use narratives to explain the advantages of using their products to customers. Recently, 3M leaders began to use stories for strategic planning, having found that this generates more excitement and commitment.[3]*

Build a Track Record

An early challenge for product managers is to build—and build *on*—a successful track record. While humility is important, product managers cannot assume that everyone in the organization has knowledge of their expertise. Sometimes telling a short anecdote about how a recommended approach worked in a prior position in another company not only provides some credibility for the *idea* but also for the *individual*.[4] Position yourself as an expert in that area—but don't stretch your expertise to include everything.

The task is a bit more difficult if you are still trying to *establish* a track record. In that case it becomes important to work with allies in the organization who can support your product vision and jumpstart implementation throughout the company. Select allies who have already gained respect in the firm.

Establish Trust

Trust flourishes in a climate characterized by several components. The first is honesty—no lies and no exaggeration. Do everything in your power to present information in a fair, objective manner. Second, maintain a willingness to share ideas openly. While some people hoard information in an attempt to increase their power, it is generally a bad policy in the long run. Third, demonstrate consistent and predictable behavior. While the element of surprise is useful in a competitive strategy, it should not be part of organizational behavior. And finally, accept and respect the individual differences and perspectives of the multitude of people you deal with as a product manager.

Keep Learning

Past successes can translate into future failure—and vice versa. Challenge yourself to gain new insights about the market and to be proactive in trend-watching. Interact with people who are different from you. Learn new hobbies. Get involved with futuristic organizations. Read voraciously. Learn to laugh at your mistakes and learn from them rather than be depressed by them. Listen—really listen—to people who have different perspectives, without automatically discounting what they say. However you accomplish it, just keep learning.

CHAPTER CHALLENGE

Develop a self-growth plan to expand your leadership, decision-making, and management skills. Include the steps you will take to establish trust with stakeholders, build a track record, and improve your decision making.

INTERVIEW WITH SCOTT DAVIS: PRODUCT MANAGERS CAN BE GROWTH LEADERS

Scott M. Davis, Chief Growth Officer, Prophet, www.prophet.com., sdavis@ prophet.com. (He can be found on Twitter as well: scottdavisshift.)

Scott, describe your role as chief growth officer for Prophet, including your decision to write The Shift: The Transformation of Today's Marketers into Tomorrow's Growth Leaders.

As a starting point I'd like to mention that Prophet is a global consultancy focused on a blend of strategy, analytics, creativity, and implementation. Over the past years we determined that many companies were woefully unprepared for the downturn, and many were even less prepared for a growth-driven recovery. So I took on the role of chief growth officer to help clients drive growth in new, dramatic, and unexpected ways.

This is all about why I wrote *The Shift*: A couple of years ago, I went back to a book that I wrote nine years ago (*Building the Brand-Driven Business*) to grab a quote from one of the people I interviewed. I discovered that not one of the interviewees was with the same company they were with at the time I wrote the book. I had similar experiences when I went to reunions at Kellogg School of Management and at Procter & Gamble. There was a ridiculous amount of turnover. Marketers often started jobs without a strong strategic perspective and left by year two. That gave me an epiphany.

Can you cite a couple of practical case examples of companies that have gone through the type of transformations you described?

Sean Burke was CMO at GE Healthcare (about a $10 billion business) at the time I was writing *The Shift*. He strategically led a team to complete a massive segmentation project—figuring out a different way to organize the marketplace—that resulted in a reconfiguration of the commercial organization. He wanted to figure out where the money was and how GE could win—and he succeeded wildly. This required several things: a P&L [profit and loss] orientation; bringing the right people in early as part of the process and solution; and being customer-led, strategy-led, and data-led.

Another example is Steven Quinn, the first CMO at Walmart. When he started, he was primarily expected to handle marketing communications. But he worked at night and on weekends to build an economically driven segmentation strategy. He started by anchoring on the most loyal customers and increasing share-of-wallet with them. Then he moved onto attracting new customers. His transformation resulted from taking a different way of looking at customers and the in-store experience.

It seems that growth is on just about every firm's agenda these days, and CMOs must take steps to fulfill that agenda. But what about product managers? What specific steps can product managers take to shift not just to being marketers but to being growth leaders?

Some of the great CEOs ran product lines with P&L responsibilities early in their careers. Too many marketers don't know how their companies make money—where value is being created and where value is being lost. Beth Comstock, GE Healthcare's current CMO, once said to me that marketers should be best friends with the CFO. They will help you sell ideas more effectively than you could ever do on your own.

So in terms of steps product managers can take toward becoming growth leaders, I would recommend several things. First, negotiate upfront to spend time in the field dealing with customer issues and sales calls. You need to be on the front line to understand customer issues, questions, and needs. Second, identify your friends and foes early. Find those one or two salespeople you can bring into your inner sanctum as a sounding board and surrogate voice-of-customer. And as mentioned earlier, become best friends with the CFO. Finally, work to better understand how your company works and makes decisions. If you don't have your internal influencers nailed down early, it will be difficult to have strategic growth.

I truly believe that product line and brand managers— especially those with the skills I just discussed—will be the CMOs and CEOs of the future.

Prior to writing The Shift, *you authored* Building the Brand-Driven Business. *In your opinion, what is the relationship between growth and brands?*

The two have never been more important. As I think about what most companies have in their growth agendas, it's some combination of product, customer, geographic, and brand arenas. They integrate those four important areas in their growth agenda. Those with well-defined brands (and by that I mean value propositions with a set of guiding principles behind them) generally have a growth agenda. A corporate mindset and nomencla-ture around the brand are important. In a brutal economy with almost overwhelming communication clutter, brands can help simplify the customer decision process, thereby contributing to a company's growth.

Given everything you've just discussed, what is the best advice you can give to product and brand managers?

CMOs and senior executives are clamoring for strategic growth plans that go beyond the budgetary considerations of dollars and cents. McDonald's growth plan, for example, has four or five growth imperatives—McCafe being one of them—designed to help the company win in the marketplace. Product and brand managers need to think in that same way. What are the five major imperatives you need to tackle to actually achieve your growth goals? What are the growth levers—the drivers that are going to take your company forward? If you can answer those questions, you will be in a leadership position to tackle your firm's growth agenda.

CHAPTER 3

Business Competencies

TRUE OR FALSE: Successful product managers work to increase product unit sales.

FALSE. This statement as worded is false, because one of the quickest ways to increase product sales is to essentially give items away. Product managers should understand contribution margins and use the information to increase *profitable* business. This might include increasing unit sales, but it might also include encouraging higher-margin sales to increase profitability, or managing pricing on a product-line basis to optimize sales of core products plus future consumables and accessories.

As mentioned earlier, I encourage product managers to think of themselves as entrepreneurs running a virtual business. This means being cognizant of the impact their product decisions have on asset utilization, cash flow, inventory, supply chain relations, and other aspects of running a business. Product development has clear cost implications that should be spelled out in the business case, but there are other situations where the important costs are less obvious. Pricing decisions, for example, have both customer value (marketing) and cost (finance) components. Product managers need to continue updating their knowledge of both. For new products, it's useful to prepare an economic value spreadsheet that estimates the monetary value of customer benefits (or loss of benefits) compared to competing products. For existing products, product managers should be able to acknowledge (and perhaps justify) both planned and ad hoc discounts that are part of the waterfall between list and actual prices.

BASIC FINANCIAL CONCEPTS

Consequently, product managers need to establish a framework of financial plans, budgets, and controls related to their products, services, and customers in order to be able to make sound decisions. The starting point is a foundation of financial and managerial accounting which makes it possible for product managers to better understand the profit contribution of their offerings so that decisions on product rationalization, pricing, and product-line management can be made intelligently. From a broader financial perspective, product managers should understand key ratios and concepts that are drawn from an understanding of financial statements. And finally, they should understand finance as it relates to pricing decisions. While product managers do not need to be experts in finance, they need a grasp of the basics as indicated in the CMO advice column—Financial Advice for Product Managers from a Chief Marketing Officer (CMO).

CMO ADVICE COLUMN: FINANCIAL ADVICE FOR PRODUCT MANAGERS FROM A CMO

Mark A. Phillips, Chief Marketing Officer, GE Healthcare Asia-Pacific

Good product managers do not need a finance degree or to be experts in finance. However, they should have financial skills sufficient enough to do two things: (1) determine the best pricing strategies, and (2) make solid business cases to justify a new product and/or additional distribution and marketing resources for their products.

The above two items require the individual to be proficient with spreadsheets, have a basic understanding of an income statement

(P&L), and be familiar with the basic concepts of breakeven analysis and price waterfalls. There are other more sophisticated tools out there, and other financial concepts that would be icing on the cake, but these are the necessary basics. In today's world, at a minimum, if you are a product manager, you better be familiar with this basic set.

Determine the Best Pricing Strategies

When determining the optimal price, most pricing tools require the ability to put together a basic spreadsheet and understand the finance (or in some cases just basic algebra) behind the tool. One example is an economic value estimator (EVE). An EVE helps you calculate the economic value a customer will derive from your product versus alternative products or not buying any products at all. These are great because they enable you to walk into a CFO's office (B2B example) and show how your product will either take out cost or help drive extra revenues. To create a viable EVE, you need to understand your customers' processes and the financials around them such as labor rates, volumes, or their pricing if your product will be a value-added component. So you need to be able to build a model in a spreadsheet with variables you can plug in based on the customer's input to drive the model. This is not financial rocket science, but it takes a basic understanding of a spreadsheet model, how your customers use your product, and the financial impact of their using your product.

Another example is breakeven or price-volume analysis. The ultimate goal here is to understand your price/volume elasticity and be able to find the "sweet spot" for your product's price. In this case, again, you need to be able to work a spreadsheet so you can estimate demand at different price points, overlay profitability for each price and volume point, and determine the price at which you maximize profit.

Consider the causes of price changes over time and under different circumstances: items like deal-sized mix, subproduct mix (if you are looking at a product line), segment mix, currency fluctuation, and similar items. Knowing the elements that drive price fluctuation and the math behind them will arm the product manager to artfully challenge sales teams and others on what is happening in the field.

Many product managers may only be measured by or concern themselves with price to gross margin (GM). However, this is very limiting, and I encourage product managers to go beyond GM all the way to contribution margin (CM). In addition, I encourage product managers to go beyond invoice price to pocket price. The ability to do both of these requires some spreadsheet skill and knowledge of the financials involved.

Price to CM requires an understanding of the variable cost components involved with selling, delivering, and installing a product at a customer's location. Knowing those items and what drives them can help product managers drive more profitability from their products for the company. This enables going beyond the usual three levers of volume, price, and cost of goods sold.

In some cases when looking at price erosion, product managers will only look at the invoice price or price on which sales commission is earned. However, this is not always the true price or pocket price that a company nets. Understanding the financial elements involved that can erode price from invoice price to pocket price can be the extra edge a product manager needs to succeed. Elements that come into play may be volume discounts awarded at year end, discounts for early payment, emergency shipping, and other less visible items. By understanding these other elements and how they are impacting your products' profitability could make a big difference in how much value your company is deriving from your product. You may have to go to the finance department to get them to run the report on these elements for you; that is okay—it's their job. Your job as a product manager is to know enough about the elements driving your product performance so you know what to ask them for and where to dig for change.

Building Solid Business Cases

When I was a product manager, and now as a CMO, I spend a great deal of time working on business cases for everything from new products to new sales teams and, of course, marketing dollars! The finance involved is not sophisticated; however, you do need to understand how your company looks at a P&L and the key elements that drive it. No need to get into taxes, interest, and other corporate assessments. Just be able to walk from sales revenue to gross margin to contribution margin to operating profit. And of course, a great product manager will know how much a salesperson can drive the ultimate sales of their products, how much a salesperson will cost, how much marketing dollars you will need to be successful.

Lastly, always befriend your finance team. A positive relationship with them can take you a long way.

General Cost Classifications

In manufactured product environments, there are two major cost classifications—manufacturing and nonmanufacturing—each of which has subclassifications. *Manufacturing costs* include all costs related to the transformation of raw materials into final products, including direct materials, direct labor, and manufacturing overhead. For example,

- *Direct materials*, such as wood in tables and steel in cars, become an integral part of the finished product and can be considered direct costs. Other materials, such as glue, may be more difficult to link to individual units of production and may be classified as indirect materials which should be included in overhead.
- *Direct labor* includes the labor costs directly traceable to the creation of products. Research and development, support staff time, and other labor not directly related to manufacturing are included in *indirect* labor.
- *Manufacturing overhead* includes all costs of manufacturing, excluding the direct material and direct labor costs described above. Included in this category are items such as indirect material, indirect labor, heat, light, and depreciation.

Nonmanufacturing costs include the marketing, sales, administrative, and support costs not directly related to the production of products. These are typically included on the SG&A (selling, general, and administrative) expenses line of an income statement. Historically, the nonmanufacturing costs have been less significant than the manufacturing costs for most products. However, the growth of services and the emergence of various technologies have reversed the relative weight of these costs in most companies. Among nonmanufacturing costs are:

- *Marketing and selling* costs include advertising, shipping, sales commission, and salaries.
- *Administrative expenses* include executive, organizational, and clerical salaries.

Both manufacturing and nonmanufacturing costs result from the normal operation of a business. In addition, there may be other expenses, such as the purchase of an asset, that are charged to the income statement for the period, even though they are not operating expenses. The cost of goods sold includes the direct material and labor as well as manufacturing overhead. The data are frequently derived from standard costs and are a combination of fixed and variable expenses. (*Standard costs* are predetermined amounts that represent what something's cost *should* be under the most efficient methods of operation; in other words, they are benchmarks for measuring performance.) Similarly, the overhead expenses (composed of the nonmanufacturing, or SG&A, expenses) may be a combination of fixed and variable costs. Figure 3.1 shows a basic, simplified income statment.

FIGURE 3.1 ➤ Basic, simplified income statement

Sales
−Cost of goods sold

Gross profit
−Operating expenses

Net income from operations
+Other income
−Other expenses

Net income before taxes
−Income taxes

Net income

Put in simplified terms, you derive net income from an income statement by doing the following:

- Subtract cost of goods sold from sales.
- Subtract operating expenses from gross profit.
- Add other income to and subtract other expenses from net income from operations.
- Subtract income taxes from net income before taxes.

The income statement resulting from the above process provides a historical review of the results of operations. It does not necessarily provide the information a product manager needs for planning and improving the decision-making process of product management. To provide this type of information, it is necessary to distinguish between the variable and incremental costs associated with products so that the product manager can better understand their contributions to overhead and profit.

Concepts of Segmented Reporting

Variable costs are those that vary in direct relation to the level of activity related to those costs. If activity level doubles, total variable costs double as well. This is true because the cost per unit stays approximately constant over a relevant range of activity. Direct materials and direct labor are variable production costs, and sales commissions represent a variable sales expense. In addition, there may be step-variable (similar to incremental or semifixed) costs. Setup time, seasonal labor, and similar activities related to a specific amount of business can be considered variable with respect to that piece of business. *Fixed costs,* on the other hand, do not change regardless of changes in the level of activity; they exist whether or not the product is even produced. Since fixed costs remain constant in total, the amount of cost per unit goes down as the number of units increases. It is sometimes said that variable costs are the costs of *doing* business, whereas fixed costs are the costs of *being in* business.

Once costs have been separated into fixed and variable elements, it is easier for product managers to determine the contribution of different products or customer segments. It is also easier for companies to evaluate the performance of product managers. A comparison of a

Table 3.1

Traditional Income Statement Versus Contribution
Income Statement

Traditional			Contribution		
Sales		$17,000	Sales		$17,000
less cost of goods sold		11,000	less variable expenses		
			variable production	5,000	
			variable administrative	2,200	
			variable selling	500	7,700
Gross margin		$ 6,000	Contribution margin		$ 9,300
less operating expenses			less fixed expenses		
administrative	2,000		fixed production	$4,000	
selling	3,000	5,000	fixed administrative	1,500	
			fixed selling	2,800	8,300
Net income before taxes		$ 1,000	Net income before taxes		$ 1,000

traditional income statement (using historical cost information) and a contribution income statement (separating fixed and variable costs) is shown in Table 3.1.

Note that in Table 3.1 the top line (Sales) and the bottom line (Net income before taxes) are the same using both approaches. However, by using the contribution margin approach, it becomes clear that these particular sales contribute $9,300 to fixed costs (prior to breakeven) and then profit (after breakeven is achieved). This concept of contribution reporting can be applied to business units, departments, product managers, product lines, customers, or similar units of analysis. When applied to these segments, direct costs and common costs must be understood.

Direct costs are costs that can be identified directly with a particular unit of analysis (i.e., product manager, product, customer, etc.) and that arise either because of the unit or because of the activity within it. *Common costs* are those that cannot be identified directly with any particular unit, but rather are identified in common with all units. The common costs (most likely fixed costs) cannot be allocated except through arbitrary means. An example of contribution reporting is shown in Table 3.2.

Table 3.2

Contribution Reporting

	Units of contribution analysis		
	Total Company	Product Manager 1	Product Manager 2
Sales	$900,000	$500,000	$400,000
Less variable expenses			
Cost of goods sold	400,000	270,000	130,000
Other variable expenses	100,000	70,000	30,000
Total variable expenses	500,000	340,000	160,000
Contribution margin	400,000	160,000	240,000
Less direct fixed expenses	150,000	80,000	70,000
Product manager margins	250,000	$80,000	$170,000
Less common fixed expenses	160,000		
Net income	$ 90,000		

	Product Manager 2	Standard Model	Custom Model
Sales	$400,000	$150,000	$250,000
Less variable expenses			
Cost of goods sold	130,000	50,000	80,000
Other variable expenses	30,000	20,000	10,000
Total variable expenses	160,000	70,000	90,000
Contribution margin	240,000	80,000	160,000
Less direct fixed expenses	30,000	10,000	20,000
Product margins	210,000	$70,000	$140,000
Less common fixed expenses	40,000		
Net income	$170,000		

	Custom Model	Contractors	Residential
Sales	$250,000	$180,000	$ 70,000
Less variable expenses			
Cost of goods sold	80,000	60,000	20,000
Other variable expenses	10,000	3,000	7,000
Total variable expenses	90,000	63,000	27,000
Contribution margin	160,000	117,000	43,000
Less direct fixed expenses	10,000	7,000	3,000
Customer segment margins	150,000	110,000	$ 40,000
Less common fixed expenses	10,000		
Net income	$140,000		

Note that the example shown in Table 3.2 presents an income statement constructed for product managers as if they were businesses. In the figure, company revenues are $900,000, of which $500,000 comes from Product Manager 1 and $400,000 comes from Product Manager 2. They contribute $80,000 and $170,000, respectively, with $160,000 in overhead not allocated to either. The $400,000 revenue of Product Manager 2 comes from a standard model ($150,000) and a custom model ($250,000) contributing $70,000 and $140,000, respectively. Product Manager 2 has $40,000 of fixed expenses not related directly to either product. The custom model receives $180,000 from contractors and $70,000 from residential customers to generate its $250,000 in revenue. The segment contributions are shown without an arbitrary allocation of the $10,000 of fixed costs for the custom model which aren't directly related to either customer group.

Cost Drivers

Before product managers can price a product or evaluate a product line, they must understand what the cost drivers are for the various products and customers. Some customers require additional expediting charges, others require special shipping and handling, while still others expect free services. Each of these costs should be allocated to the particular product or customer to determine the true financial contribution.

FINANCIAL STATEMENT ANALYSIS

As suggested earlier, financial statements are historical documents indicating what happened during a particular period of time. The perspective they provide helps a product manager judge past performance through the use of ratios. In addition, by comparing changes in the statements over time, it is possible to identify performance trends and use the information for making subsequent decisions.

Directly or indirectly, product managers may be involved in capital budgeting decisions in the preparation of investment proposals for new products, new markets, or new business ventures. The most common methods of evaluating different proposals are average rate of return, payback period, present value, and internal rate of return.

The *average rate of return* is the ratio of the average annual profits to the investment in the project. Using this method, the product manager prepares a forecast of the improvement in profit from a given investment over a number of years. The total profit is divided by the number of years to give an average annual profit, and this is then expressed either as a percentage of the original investment or as a percentage of the average investment per year. Assume the following stream of profits from, for example, a new product:

Year 1: $100,000
Year 2: $200,000
Year 3: $300,000
Year 4: $250,000
Year 5: $350,000
Total: $1,200,000
Ave.: $240,000 ($1,200,000 ÷ 5 years)

If the initial investment had been $1 million, the average annual profit would be the $240,000 as a percent of $1 million, or 24 percent. Alternatively, the $240,000 could be expressed as a percentage of the average investment for each of the five years. In either case, the rate would be compared to hurdles used by the company or to industry norms.

The *payback period* is calculated by determining the length of time (number of years) it takes to recover an initial investment. In the above example, the investment of $1 million is recovered during the fifth year. After four years, the cumulative profits are $850,000, with the remaining $150,000 being earned some time during the final year. Here again, the payback as an absolute value is less important than the relative values of different projects.

The *present value* (or net present value) refers to the value of future cash inflows compared to the current outflow of the initial investment.

The *internal rate of return* is the interest rate that makes the present value of all projected future cash flows equal to the initial outlay for the investment. In other words, it is the rate that makes the net present value (NPV) equal to zero. The calculation is somewhat complex mathematically. That's why it's so important to make finance a business partner as discussed in the end-of-chapter interview with Doug Vaughan, the vice president of finance for Ingersoll Rand.

GAUGE *RELEVANT* COSTS FOR PRICING DECISIONS

Evaluating the costs related to the pricing decision is often more difficult than it seems. Companies use different approaches for allocating costs, so the variable and fixed costs can become blurred. Nevertheless, definitions of these common pricing terms are relevant.

As mentioned earlier, *variable costs* are those that vary (in total) with production of the product or service. This could include costs for direct materials and labor. For a given production level, these are constant per unit and provide the floor for pricing decisions. In the long run, *all* costs must be covered. All costs should be considered when determining the long-term pricing of products. However, in the short term, any price obtained that exceeds variable costs can at least contribute to fixed overhead and (potentially) profit.

The cost of goods sold (COGS) line item on financial statements is perhaps your best approximation of variable costs (even though it traditionally includes some standard allocations) and therefore might provide the only incremental costs relevant to a pricing decision. There are exceptions when fixed costs are incurred in a bid situation, for example, that are incremental to that decision. In that case, the incremental fixed costs must be added to the variable costs to determine the floor for a pricing decision.

The following breakeven formula can be used as a starting point for evaluating a price. The standard breakeven formula shows the number of units that must be sold at a given price in order for all costs to be covered. The formula is shown in Figure 3.2.

Suppose a product manager of a consulting service handling ten projects for $10,000 each has direct costs of $4,000 per project and overall overhead costs of $42,000. Based on those data, it would be necessary to generate sales of seven units to break even. By experimenting

FIGURE 3.2 ➤ Standard breakeven formula for a price change

$$\text{Break-even units} = \frac{\text{Fixed cost}}{(\text{Price} - \text{Variable cost per unit})}$$

with different price levels and matching them with expected demand, the product manager can begin the pricing analysis. In addition, a target return (profit) can be included in the numerator (along with fixed costs) to assess the unit sales necessary to generate a specified profit. For example, if a required profit of $12,000 were added to the fixed costs in the numerator, it would be necessary to generate sales of nine units to break even.

Building on this example, we can look at contribution margins and evaluate different decisions. Each project contributes $6,000—the difference between the current price and the variable costs—to overhead and profits. The operating profit would be $18,000, as shown in column 1 of Table 3.3.

If the product manager drops the price to $9,000 per project, each project would contribute only $5,000 to overhead and profit. Assuming no other changes, the new revenue would be $90,000, and the new bottom-line profit would be $8,000. The 10 percent drop in price (from $10,000 to $9,000) would result in a 55 percent drop (from $18,000 to $8,000) in operating profit (see column 2 in Table 3.3).

To keep its profit at $18,000, the firm would need to land two more jobs. Because we assume that operating expenses—fixed costs—don't change with an increase in unit sales, the objective is to provide

Table 3.3

Price/Profit Comparison

	(1)	(2)	(3)
Revenue			
(10 @ $10,000)	$100,000		
(10 @ $9,000)		$90,000	
(12 @ $9,000)			$108,000
Cost of sales			
(10 @ $4,000)	40,000	40,000	
(12 @ $4,000)			48,000
Contribution margin	60,000	50,000	60,000
Operating expenses	42,000	42,000	42,000
Net operating income	$ 18,000	$ 8,000	$ 18,000

a contribution margin of at least $60,000. Hence, the firm would need to handle 12 projects rather than 10 ($60,000 divided by the new per-project contribution of $5,000), as shown in column 3 of Table 3.3. The two additional jobs represent a 20 percent increase in sales to compensate for the 10 percent drop in price.

By adapting the breakeven formula presented earlier, it is possible to quickly look at the impact of a price change. The modified formula is shown in Figure 3.3. CM stands for contribution margin (the difference between price and variable cost, or $10,000 − $4,000 = $6,000, in this example). The %CM refers to the contribution margin per unit expressed as a percentage of the price ($6,000 divided by $10,000 or 60%). The result is the percentage change in unit sales necessary to contribute the same profit return as now. In other words, with a 60% contribution margin, it would require a 20% increase in sales to have the same bottom line impact after the 10% price cut.

This formula can be used in a spreadsheet to display the impact of price changes. Putting relevant contribution margins in the columns, potential price changes in the rows, and the formula in the cells yields a spreadsheet similar to the one shown in Table 3.4. Note the solid lines (1) connecting the 60 percent contribution margin and the 10% price with the cell yielding the 20% increase in sales.

What would have been the necessary change if the variable costs were lower (e.g., $3,500) so that the contribution margin was 65 percent, with everything else being equal? (See the dotted lines under 2.) In this case, it would have been necessary to increase sales by only 18 percent to break even. What if variable costs were significantly higher

FIGURE 3.3 ➤ Modified breakeven formula for a price change

$$\% \text{ break-even sales change} = \frac{-(\% \text{ price change})}{(\% \text{ CM} + \% \text{ price change})}$$

$$\% \text{ break-even sales change} = \frac{-(-.10)}{.60 + (-.10)} = \frac{.10}{.50} = .20$$

Table 3.4

Spreadsheet Example of Break-Even Analysis of
Price Changes

Price Change (%)	0.65	0.60	Contribution Margin						
			0.55	0.50	0.45	0.40	0.35	0.30	0.25
0.10	−0.13	−0.14	−0.15	−0.17	−0.18	−0.20	−0.22	−0.25	−0.29
0.09	−0.12	−0.13	−0.14	−0.15	−0.17	−0.18	−0.20	−0.23	−0.26
0.08	−0.11	−0.12	−0.13	−0.14	−0.15	−0.17	−0.19	−0.21	−0.24
0.07	−0.10	−0.10	−0.11	−0.12	−0.13	−0.15	−0.17	−0.19	−0.22
0.06	−0.08	−0.09	−0.10	−0.11	−0.12	−0.13	−0.15	−0.17	−0.20
0.05	−0.07	−0.08	−0.08	−0.09	−0.10	−0.11	−0.13	−0.14	−0.17
0.04	−0.06	−0.06	−0.07	−0.07	−0.08	−0.09	−0.10	−0.12	−0.14
0.03	−0.04	−0.05	−0.05	−0.06	−0.06	−0.07	−0.08	−0.09	−0.11
0.02	−0.03	−0.03	−0.04	−0.04	−0.04	−0.05	−0.05	−0.06	−0.07
0.01	−0.02	−0.02	−0.02	−0.02	−0.02	−0.02	−0.03	−0.03	−0.04
−0.01	0.02	0.02	0.02	0.02	0.02	0.03	0.03	0.03	0.04
−0.02	0.03	0.03	0.04	0.04	0.05	0.05	0.06	0.07	0.09
−0.03	0.05	0.05	0.06	0.06	0.07	0.08	0.09	0.11	0.14
−0.04	0.07	0.07	0.08	0.09	0.10	0.11	0.13	0.15	0.19
−0.05	0.08	0.09	0.10	0.11	0.13	0.14	0.17	0.20	0.25
−0.06	0.10	0.11	0.12	0.14	0.15	0.18	0.21	0.25	0.32
−0.07	0.12	0.13	0.15	0.16	0.18	0.21	0.25	0.30	0.39
−0.08	0.14	0.15	0.17	0.19	0.22	0.25	0.30	0.36	0.47
−0.09	0.16	0.18	0.20	0.22	0.25	0.29	0.35	0.43	0.56
−0.10	0.18	0.20	0.22	0.25	0.29	0.33	0.40	0.50	0.67

(e.g., $7,000) so that the contribution margin was only 30 percent? Again, with everything else the same, what sales change would be necessary to break even? Now the answer is 50 percent, which translates to five additional projects. Price increases can also be evaluated by using the modified breakeven formula contained in Figure 3.3. However, if a price increase is being considered, it can be useful to time the increase with a product change or additional service that adds value.

So in looking at price changes, it is necessary to understand what impact those changes have on required volume to break even. Then you need to ask a couple of questions: How much leverage do competitors have? If their variable costs on this product are lower than yours, they would be able to withstand a price cut longer. How likely is it that they would want to cut price and sustain it? Also, how sensitive are customers to price changes? Is it possible to sell the required volume change? Remember that the information in the spreadsheet doesn't give you "the answer." It simply provides one data point to help you make a better decision.

Estimated Economic Value Modeling

Pricing strategy is based on a blending of both objective and subjective data and can be particularly challenging for new products. For capital expenditures such as equipment, product managers may be tasked with trying to monetize the value of product benefits compared with competing products. Look at the estimated economic value model in Figure 3.4. (Note that this is a variation of the Economic Value Estimation (EVE) approach developed by Tom Nagle in his book, *The Strategy and Tactics of Pricing*.)

FIGURE 3.4 ➤ Estimated economic value model

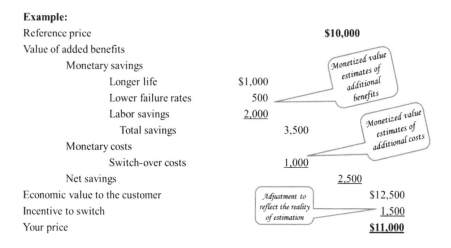

In this example, the reference price would be whatever the customer uses as the starting point in examining a product. It could be the price of a competing product, the price of the company's prior product that is now being replaced, or the cost of the functionality provided by the customer. Once that point is determined, the product manager works with knowledgeable and cooperative customers to estimate the monetary value of benefits and costs of the new product compared with the reference alternative. The estimates for standard products would be based on the input of several somewhat representative customers, whereas the estimates for a custom product would be based on the specific customer's operations. So if the average perceived cost savings of the new product's anticipated longer life is $1,000, that would be used in the value model. However, these are indeed estimates based on several assumptions. Therefore, it will almost always be necessary to allow for some flexibility (adjustment) in determining the final price.

The Pocket Price Waterfall

The last financial area that should concern most product managers is an understanding of potential price erosion between the invoice price and the street (or pocket) price, known as the pocket price waterfall. (See Figure 3.5.) Price erosion (or leakage) can come from a variety of discounts and incentives provided to customers in an effort to close the sale. Different departments may offer different discounts to customers

FIGURE 3.5 ➤ Pocket price waterfall

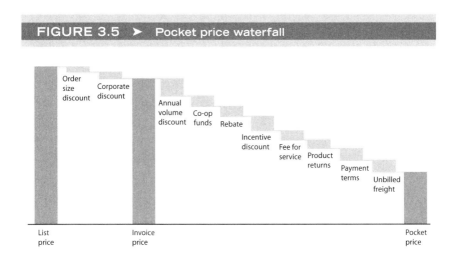

for a variety of reasons. When establishing pricing strategies, deciding on whether to authorize price exceptions, or analyzing a product's true value, product managers need to uncover the "real" price customers are paying for their products.

CHAPTER CHALLENGE

Learn basic financial concepts that relate to the pricing and profitability of your products. Find a financial ally in your organization to help you accomplish that goal.

INTERVIEW WITH DOUG VAUGHAN: BECOME A BUSINESS PARTNER WITH FINANCE

Doug Vaughan, Vice President, Finance, Ingersoll-Rand, vaughan36@aol.com. (He can also be found on LinkedIn.)

Doug, you have worked as finance executive or CFO for a number of companies. While much of your work deals with internal controls and treasury management, you and your staff are also responsible for providing input into decisions on product development and ongoing operations. Can you talk a bit about your role(s) in working with product managers regarding product development and maintenance?

Successful product managers have to understand the economics of the products they are managing. What is the profitability of the product? What is the total cost of the product—cost to manufacture, distribute, sell? What are the margin trends for the product—what is happening to pricing and to costs? What is the impact of product mix? Finance's role with product management is to make sure we provide accurate, understandable, economic analysis of the product line and help product managers understand and draw insights from that economic analysis.

Another area where good finance support is important is in the area of investments. For example, when a product manager is considering an investment in a new product, finance can help develop a sound business case financial analysis to aid in the decision about whether to make the investment or not. And beyond the basic go or no-go decision, a good finance person can help make that investment a success. For example, what is the key to making the investment pay off? Is it hitting a cost target? Is it gaining market share? By helping identify the key success factors and helping to prioritize resources and efforts toward them, the finance person can help make the project a success.

Product managers are usually encouraged to "run their products as a business." This would require that product management and finance be strategic partners. In your opinion, what does it take (on both sides) to have a strong relationship between these two groups?

It starts with finance providing good financial data to product managers to enable them to manage their products. In the most successful situations, it goes well beyond that, though. Finance needs to be a business partner. This means that the finance individual has the business acumen, communication, and relationship skills to be a member of the product management team. Finance people work closely with the product manager, have a deep understanding of the business, and apply their financial and business skills to help product managers make the right decisions and drive the right actions.

So that's the positive side of the relationship between finance and product management. What do you think are areas where improvements can be made?

There are a number of areas in the typical organization where improvements need to be made. Accounting systems or financial systems are often not structured to provide the right kind of data. So work needs to be done to organize the information in a way that is useful to product management. Another area is the finance organization itself—both in terms of structure and capability. The best case is where there is a clear organizational alignment between product management and finance. In other words, each product manager has a finance person assigned to work with him or her. That finance person has to have the skills to be effective in the role. The attitude of the finance person is critical. He or she has to have the attitude of being a part of the team and of striving to make the product manager successful. A finance person who uses information to blindside a business partner will quickly be ostracized from the team and cannot be effective.

In terms of financial literacy (from developing new product business cases to refining prices for existing products), what are the three to four most important skills you feel every product manager should have?

Clearly understand the income statement for their product. Understand revenue and any deductions from revenue. Deeply understand the product's cost structure and all the other costs (such as sales, engineering, bad debt) associated with bringing the product to market.

Understand the concept of return on invested capital and how that applies to managing the product on an ongoing basis ("What is the trade-off between inventory and service levels?"), as well as how that applies to investment decisions ("What is discounted cash flow?").

Pricing: Be able to understand a price waterfall as well as how to map features and benefits versus price for the product and versus competitive products.

Forecasting: Understand how to use the firm's financial forecasting process to spot trends in product-line profitability and then take the appropriate actions based on the data.

Are there any other "words of wisdom" you can provide to product managers?

If you have a good finance partner, make that person a part of your team and involve him or her in everything you do. If you don't have a good finance partner, demand one.

CHAPTER 4

Intelligence Gathering

TRUE OR FALSE: The customer is always right.

Ah, an interesting—yet incomplete—statement. The customer is always right if it is the right customer. Without this qualifying phrase, product managers can be led in the wrong direction. In the process of researching customers, product managers must be vigilant to maintain a focus on the customers that are their future (and not just their past). They shouldn't assume that all customers are right all the time.

Successful product managers gather intelligence about numerous facts from numerous sources. External information on market conditions is critical. This includes market segment sizes and growth rates; customer-specific expectations; competitive products and strategies; regulatory requirements and restrictions; economic and political factors; as well as trends or shifts in any of these. Internal information is also important. This includes knowledge of broad company competencies; costs and financials surrounding the product manager's products; process flows; and internal politics. In this chapter we cover both types of intelligence, starting with the external kind.

Product managers are always pressed for time and working against the clock. So they should start thinking with the TIME clock. (See Figure 4.1.) Notice the categories related to this acronym: technology, industry, market, and events. The clock symbolizes the fact that none of the information is static, and the dynamism of the changes and trends requires an ongoing intelligence in order to build a base of knowledge.

FIGURE 4.1 ➤ Intelligence-gathering TIME categories

FIGURE 4.1 ➤ Intelligence-gathering TIME categories

We examine each of these as part of the external intelligence-gathering process below.

TECHNOLOGY

Product managers should think about technology on two levels: new technology that can *be* the product (or a component thereof), or technology that can be an external variable (such as social networking) that becomes an enabler or plan-shifter. For example, several years ago Hewlett-Packard discovered a cross-current of trends affecting its printer business. Most existing PC owners already had printers, so the market for new sales was expected to be virtually flat. Competitors had become more aggressive, causing HP's market share to drop. Meanwhile, a new industry of cartridge refillers emerged, hurting HP's ink sales. While HP's printer division was still significant (accounting for 73 percent of its earnings in 2004), this mix of trends could not be ignored and required efforts in new product development.[1]

Technology trends provide both opportunities and threats. Nanotechnology, while still in the fuzzy front end of innovation, has the potential to affect a multitude of industries.[2] The Web provides an overwhelming amount of data, but it can also provide opportunities. As more and more hospitals curtailed visits by pharmaceutical sales reps, product managers turned to the Web for possible solutions. Online detailing, product Web sites, and e-mail marketing are expected to receive increased spending.[3]

INDUSTRY

Industry knowledge includes a broad understanding of the "rules" of an industry as well as more detailed knowledge of specific competitors. Regarding broad industry knowledge, most leadership training incorporates Porter's five forces analysis (see Figure 4.2) to evaluate

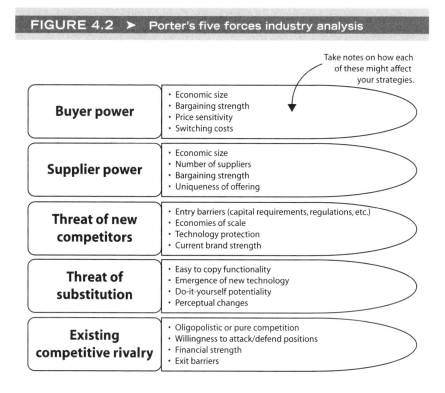

FIGURE 4.2 ➤ Porter's five forces industry analysis

Take notes on how each of these might affect your strategies.

Buyer power
- Economic size
- Bargaining strength
- Price sensitivity
- Switching costs

Supplier power
- Economic size
- Number of suppliers
- Bargaining strength
- Uniqueness of offering

Threat of new competitors
- Entry barriers (capital requirements, regulations, etc.)
- Economies of scale
- Technology protection
- Current brand strength

Threat of substitution
- Easy to copy functionality
- Emergence of new technology
- Do-it-yourself potentiality
- Perceptual changes

Existing competitive rivalry
- Oligopolistic or pure competition
- Willingness to attack/defend positions
- Financial strength
- Exit barriers

the "attractiveness" of a particular industry. These forces include: (1) the power of buyers; (2) the power of suppliers; (3) the threat of new competitors; (4) the threat of substitutes; and (5) the intensity of competitive pressures.

The power of buyers and suppliers depends on their economic size and impact relative to a manufacturer. Buying from Intel or selling to Walmart, for example, might reduce the negotiating ability of a product manager. This should be taken into account in the planning of supply chains and market strategies. See Business Brief 4.1, "The Man Who Said No to Walmart."

Business Brief 4.1

THE MAN WHO SAID NO TO WALMART

Consumer product managers often want to sell through big box retailers like Walmart, Home Depot, or Staples in an effort to get huge volume. These can be very powerful buyers in an industry, changing the dynamics of your strategy and exerting pressure on pricing. Consequently, it's important to remember that it is a business decision, not a foregone conclusion. Stihl Inc., for example, sells handheld outdoor power equipment such as trimmers, brush cutters, and blowers through servicing power equipment retailers—not mass merchants. For years the company has run ads of specific products with headlines such as, "What makes this trimmer too powerful to be sold at Lowe's or the Home Depot?"

Another example, covered several years ago in *Fast Company*, is Simplicity lawn equipment. According to the article, company management decided that selling Snapper lawn mowers at Walmart was not compatible with its brand and strategy:

Tens of thousands of executives make the pilgrimage to northwest Arkansas every year to woo Walmart by marshaling whatever arguments, data, samples, and pure persuasive power they have in the hope of an order for their products or an increase in their current order. Almost no matter what you're selling, the gravitational force of Walmart's 3,811 U.S. "doorways" is irresistible. Very few people fly into Northwest Arkansas Regional Airport thinking about telling Walmart no, or no more.

In 2002, Jim Wier's company, Simplicity, was buying Snapper, a complementary company with a 50-year heritage of making high-quality residential and commercial lawn equipment. Wier had studied his new acquisition enough to conclude that continuing to sell Snapper mowers through Walmart stores was, as he put it, "Incompatible with our strategy. And I felt I owed them a visit to tell them why we weren't going to continue to sell to them."

Selling Snapper lawn mowers at Walmart wasn't just incompatible with Snapper's future—Wier thought it was hazardous to Snapper's health. Snapper is known in the outdoor equipment business not for huge volume but for quality, reliability, and durability. A well-maintained Snapper lawn mower will last decades; many customers buy the mowers as adults because their fathers used them when they were kids. But Snapper lawn mowers are not cheap, any more than a Viking range is cheap. The value isn't in the price; it's in the performance and the longevity.

While the Porter analysis might indicate that the presence of powerful buyers makes an industry less attractive, the analysis or intelligence is not the end. Product managers must then decide whether there are sufficient benefits to overcome the inherent risks. Or they must decide on alternative strategies (such as with Stihl and Snapper) that change some of the rules in the industry.

Adapted from Charles Fishman, "The Man Who Said No to Wal-Mart," *Fast Company* (Jan.–Feb. 2006): 66+.

The threat of new competitors depends partly on the entry barriers in an industry. If there are no restrictions in terms of brand equity, capital expenditures, or regulatory compliance, product managers can expect the individual competitor set to fluctuate on an ongoing basis. Consequently they will need to broaden their competitive comparisons. If changes in technology or perceptions on different ways to provide a given functionality suggest new substitutes, product managers will need to build that into their plans. For example, if consumers can use products like Dryel in place of out-of-home dry cleaning, this can have an impact on the revenue stream for that industry, even though it is not a direct competitor.

And finally all these factors, along with exit barriers, can affect the intensity of rivalry. How aggressively will industry players compete to keep their factories running? By considering these various industry factors, product managers can attempt to "change the rules" to create more favorable circumstances for their product strategies. If any of your product strategies take you into a new industry, it may be useful to evaluate the impact of these forces.

So far we've taken a macro look at competition. Now let's shift the process of competitive intelligence and take a more micro look.

COMPETITIVE ANALYSIS

A critical aspect of a product manager's job is to objectively define the product's strengths and weaknesses in relation to the competition *as perceived by the market*, and to use that knowledge to implement competitive strategies successfully. To be able to implement competitive strategies on an ongoing basis, you must have access to an ongoing stream of information about the competitive environment for your product and the impact it has on your ability to compete. The process of collecting and analyzing this information is called competitive intelligence (CI).

The *competitive analysis* is a summary of information compiled from electronic, published, and human sources. Annual reports, newspaper articles, trade shows, salespeople, government and trade association reports, and informal conversations with customers can provide much of the necessary information. This type of competitive intelligence is an important part of a product manager's job and provides some of the foundation concepts for developing competitive strategy and product positioning. Here are a few questions to consider as part of the analysis:

1. To which competitors have you lost business, and from which have you gained business? (This is an indication of the competition from the customer's perspective.)

2. Where (in what regions, applications, industries, etc.) is competition the strongest? Why?

3. What are the corporate competencies of the companies that own competing products? What is the relationship between the competencies and the products?

4. What are the list prices of the competing products? The actual prices?

5. What is the market perception of the competing products? Awareness level? Customer loyalty?

6. Are there any specific product features that are "best in class" against which your product should be benchmarked?

7. Are competing products a small percentage of their company's business, or are they the main products of the company? How important are these sales to the competitors, and how much are they willing to invest to protect these sales?

Establishing a Competitive Intelligence Process

There are a number of reasons product managers should be aware of the competitive arena. It can help them anticipate marketplace shifts. It can help them anticipate actions or reactions of specific competitors, or identify new competition. It can help them learn from the successes and failures of others. It can help them learn about new technologies, processes, or events that could change their product strategies. It can help them craft tools and approaches to be used by the sales force or marketing communications people.

Let's say that a salesperson tells you that a competitor lowered the price of a product that competes directly with your highest gross margin item. Before lowering your price to match, ask yourself whether *this* competitor offering *this* price drop could affect your ability to compete. If the answer is yes, you should do a bit of "sleuthing" to answer the following questions. Is the price drop an apples-to-apples comparison, or have select features or services been modified? Is the price drop sufficient to overcome customer inertia to change? If so, does the competitor have the capacity to handle increased demand without damaging customer satisfaction? Is the price change restricted to one territory or account, or is it across the board?

You should consider analogous questions when *initiating* a product or marketing change and anticipate the potential competitive response to your actions. Failing to do so can put you at a competitive disadvantage. When Bristol-Myers launched Datril (emphasizing savings of a dollar compared with Tylenol), it seemingly did not anticipate the speed and strength of response from Johnson & Johnson. J&J used competitive intelligence to identify the projected entry strategy and was able to blunt its effectiveness through a media strategy of its own.[4] Similarly, when Corel purchased the WordPerfect suite in the mid–1990s, it attempted to use a low price to compete directly against the Microsoft Office Suite but did not have the ability to compete long term in a price war against Microsoft.

Who Are Your *Real* Competitors?

A starting point for developing a competitive intelligence process is to determine which competitors to study continuously and which to study episodically. It is impossible to gather all data about all competitors on an ongoing basis; it is important to prioritize. You might miss some information by restricting your focus, but the greater manageability will provide more actionable data.

Start with a deceptively simple question: Who is your competition? Many of you will answer the question with, "It depends." This is a valid answer. That's why it may be useful to look at competition from a variety of perspectives. The key competitors are most often (but not always) the direct competitors offering a similar type of product or service—competing packages of toothpaste (e.g., Crest vs. Colgate) or equipment (e.g., Caterpillar vs. Komatsu). To compete at this level, you must articulate specific feature advantages over the main competing products.

Another level of competition is category competition. While there may be a few identified competitors under *direct competition*, with category competition you might be competing against dozens of companies that comprise your category or industry. For example, manufacturers of component parts for industrial equipment might compete with a number of local, privately owned shops. Here product managers are challenged to position their products as best in the *category*.

A third level is substitute competition where the customer obtains functionality without using the product of *any* company in the category. Some companies may choose to manufacture the product or perform the service themselves. For example, a bank might choose to self-insure rather than use the products of a private mortgage insurance company. Several industries are jumping on the do-it-yourself bandwagon. (See Business Brief 4.2, "Do-It-Yourself Competition.") Or a new industry (such as satellite TV) may try to displace an existing industry (like cable TV). In these situations, product managers must demonstrate to customers the risk of staying with their current approach to addressing their needs, or prove their products are superior to the current approach.

Business Brief 4.2

DO-IT-YOURSELF COMPETITION

Given the weak financial status of the airline industry, many airline companies are making parts for themselves rather than purchasing them from suppliers—especially parts that are replaced repeatedly. Continental Airlines made tray tables and window shades in its Houston facility, saving $2 million annually. It also molded its own plastic toilet seats for $88 compared to a $719 original equipment manufacturer (OEM) price, and made bathroom mirrors for $460 rather than the $3,000 it was quoted. American Airlines makes an aluminum part, which it had previously purchased, for $5.24, saving the company $170,000 per year.

Rising health-care costs are also resulting in some do-it-yourself (DIY) efforts in corporations. Since 1990, Quad Graphics has increasingly handled its own primary care. It employs its own internists, pediatricians, and family practitioners—26 in all. It owns a laboratory, pharmacy, and rehabilitation unit, and it contracts with local hospitals for advanced care. Quad Graphics spent $6,000 per employee on medical costs in 2004—20 percent less than the average competitors in its home state of Wisconsin. Perdue Farms,

Sprint Corporation, and Pitney Bowes run their own medical centers. Toyota Motor Company, Kohler Plumbing, and Miller Brewing are considering this approach as well.

While many companies are increasing their outsourcing of many tasks in an effort to save money, others are taking the opposite approach as discussed here. Any changes such as these could affect your approach to competitive intelligence.

Source: Melanie Trottman, "Nuts-and-Bolts Savings," *Wall Street Journal* (May 3, 2005) pp. B1–B2. Vanessa Fuhrmann, "One Cure for High Health Costs: In-House Clinics at Companies," *Wall Street Journal* (February 11, 2005) pp. A1–A8.

Another example of substitute competition is caused by technology convergence and disruption. The Apple iPod, for example, sparked a minirevolution by allowing music to be purchased through Internet downloads rather than through retail CDs. But it is also now facing competition from wireless companies that are encouraging their customers to use their cell phones to download songs over the air.

A fourth type of competition is budget competition. This is perhaps the most challenging for product managers because it is the least tangible. A customer may choose to buy a new software system instead of investing the money in new office furniture. Similarly a homeowner may decide to buy hardwood floors rather than a hot tub. Although product managers cannot design a strategy to convince customers to buy their products before spending money on *anything* else, it's important to at least be aware of this level of competition and adjust sales forecasts accordingly.

The final type of competition is organizational competition. For many B2B products and for many services, customers make purchase decisions based not just on a product's features, but also based on the services and incentives they get from a specific company, a potential *bundle* of products they might have access to, or the relationship they have established with the firm. In these cases the product manager must work collaboratively with others in the organization to establish a sustainable advantage on a corporatewide basis. Each of these categories of competition is listed in Table 4.1

Note that different markets may view the set of competitive suppliers differently, and the product manager will need to decide how to best position products based on the importance of the market/competitor combination. Sometimes separate strategies will need to be developed. For example, a consumer packaged goods product manager may need to have a marketing strategy aimed at competing against other directly competing products at the consumer level, while simultaneously competing against other organizations (with different value propositions) at the channel level.

Table 4.1

Types of Competition

Type of competition	Identify who they are	Future impacts	Implications
Directly competing products	List competitors and specific product features	What percent of the competition does this represent both today and in the future? For which customers?	How can you establish a differential advantage over these products?
Category	Describe the category of competition and the companies and products within the category	What percent of the competition does this represent both today and in the future? For which customers?	How can you position your offering as best in category?
Substitutes	Describe the actual "need" the products and services fulfill with their functionality	What percent of the competition does this represent both today and in the future? For which customers?	How can you influence the perceived risk of customers shifting to substitutes?
Budget	Highlight the potential resistance of customers to spending money on your type of product or need	What percent of the competition does this represent both today and in the future? For which customers?	How can you encourage shifting of budgetary expenditures to your product?
Organizational	Explain the "augmented" product provided by competing companies	What percent of the competition does this represent both today and in the future? For which customers?	How can you develop collaborative efforts to better position your company over competing companies?

Remember that customers consciously or subconsciously make purchase decisions by comparing what *they* perceive to be competitors. Determining whom your customers perceive as your competitors provides a clue to their price sensitivity. These key competitors should be regularly tracked to enable you to identify strategy shifts that might require a change in your pricing or marketing strategy. Several methods may be used to identify whom customers perceive as your competitors. For consumer products, purchased data from syndicated sources such as Nielsen can be used to determine brand-switching behavior. This helps identify whom you have lost business to or gained business from—a behavioral indicator of perceived competition. Another approach (that can be used for services and business products in addition to consumer products) is similarity assessments. With this approach, customers are given either the products or product *cues* (such as literature or product names on three-by-five cards) and asked to divide them into groups based on similarity.

On the other hand, the competitive set in which the customer places you may not fit your *desired* position. You might want to be perceived as a higher or lower price-point competitor, or as a niche player. In this case, you would need to examine the companies in the *desired* competitive set and decide whether you can reposition what your customers believe, or whether you should add a new brand. There is an example of each approach from the California wine industry. Glen Ellen and Gallo decided to move from the low-end ("popular") price category of wines to the faster-growing premium segment. Gallo made the transition by creating a new brand, Turning Leaf, and pricing this new brand at the premium-category price point. Glen Ellen attempted to make the transition *without* a new brand by focusing on its brand heritage, wax seal, and upgraded product quality.[5] In both cases, the higher price points positioned the wines against new competitors.

Regardless of your situation, reduce the number of competitors you *continually* obtain information about to a manageable few. (The manageable few may vary as competitors enter and exit a market, so don't be afraid to change as conditions dictate.) Competitors not included in the manageable few should be studied periodically or on an as-needed basis.

What Do You Need to Know?

Not all snippets of information are equally valuable. What is your competitive edge? What knowledge about the competition might help you protect your edge? If your competitive edge is superior delivery, stay abreast of competitive delivery standards that could threaten this advantage. If your differentiation is superior technological support, monitor competitive support activities that could have a negative impact on your position. Your goal is to avoid surprises that might force you into price competition. That being said, most product managers are understandably concerned about obtaining competitive price and cost information. (Just remember that if the only competitive data you gather are prices, you may be forced to compete solely on price.)

Many competitive prices are available in the public domain. Except in closed bid situations, most companies are able to get competitive price lists from trade shows, the sales force, common customers, or the Internet. Although these may not be the "actual" prices that customers pay, you may still be able to glean information by tracking the price list over time and looking for changes. A *change* in the published prices should trigger some additional evaluations on your part. Is the price change related to other factors such as an organizational restructuring or a change in capabilities? These factors are frequently part of a shift in strategy.

Several factors could signal a potential shift in strategy: a change in management, a change in capabilities, or a change in mission statement. Let's examine each of these three factors, starting with a change in management. If a competitor has a new management team, it may signal a new direction (especially if the old management team was ousted by the board of directors). The new management team may have been hired to repeat accomplishments achieved for a prior employer. By studying the strategic direction the new managers took at their previous organizations, you can get an idea of the possible similar strategy they might apply in their new company.

A change in capabilities could arise from a new location, additional investment in R&D, or increased staffing. By piecing together this information from industry journals, trade associations, help-wanted ads, and personal sources, you can estimate what effect this could have on your competitor's *future* strategy. Help-wanted ads not only alert you to what your competitor's strategy requires in terms of future staffing (e.g., competence in a particular scientific field or increased emphasis on customer service), but they may also provide important knowledge about the company since it is trying to "sell" itself to prospective employees.

Finally, a change in mission statement can also suggest a new direction. For example, the revised wording of a firm's mission statement from, "To be the premier customer-driven real estate company in the U.S.," to, "To be the premier customer-driven real estate *services* company in the U.S.," highlights the increased importance of services in its new strategy.

Monitor account-specific activity. Competitors may be offering special incentives to major accounts. Promotional blitzes may indicate a renewed emphasis on certain products or market segments, or they may be a direct attempt to get a key account away from you.

Perhaps the most significant source of information on an ongoing basis is the sales force. Salespeople have the most direct contact with customers and consequently have customer feedback on the competition that is both real and perceptual. However, since their primary job is to sell, it's important to be meticulous about their involvement in competitive intelligence activities.

To be successful in collecting information from the sales force, you must prove to both the sales reps and their managers that the process has value to them. That means that a certain amount of homework is necessary. Find out what information is already available internally from sales. Call reports, won-lost reports, and sales records can be analyzed for red flags and trends. A competitive move in one territory may seem insignificant until it is added to information from other territories, or when it is examined as part of a larger global rollout strategy. Then by augmenting these findings with public data (from published sources and industry analysts), you may be able to offer the sales force tips on competing more successfully.

After completing this homework, it's time for face-to-face contact with the sales force. (No amount of corporate posturing, e-mails, or dictates will replace it.) Take the time to introduce yourself to salespeople and learn about their customers. Demonstrate your commitment to sharing vital information that will help them close sales. Learn about their world. By initiating the information-sharing process, you will encourage reciprocity on the part of sales by demonstrating "what's in it for them." Be prepared to work through sales administration, marketing, or other departments as necessary to coordinate your efforts.

Once salespeople trust that sharing information with you will indeed help them be more successful on the job, you have to decide on the best way to handle the data collection and dissemination. Ask sales to forward to you any price lists, customer input, or competitive data as they relate to your products.

Salespeople and other employees can gather good competitive intelligence at trade shows if they are asked to do so and if they are provided with specific goals. Develop a checklist of issues you would like explored at a trade show and provide "assignments" to the booth staff. For example, you might want to learn about an announced price cut by Competitor A, a proposed product launch by Competitor B, and a change in promotional positioning by Competitor C. Assign each of these issues to an individual to explore both while staffing the booth and while walking the floor. Check back with these people at the end of the day or at the end of the show.

New product sales training can be another subtle forum for planting the seed of information gathering. A portion of the training might include a motivational explanation of the need for and use of market intelligence by product managers and how providing this information can help the salespeople. A standard intelligence report form can be built into a call report, designed into the menu system on an intranet, or included as part of the expense form. Because this information typically comes into sales management or sales administration, a process would need to be established to send a copy of relevant product-related data to the appropriate product manager. The type of information useful for submission might include the following:

- New-product announcements by competitors.
- Effective and ineffective approaches to selling a product.
- Changes in competitive strategies.
- Unusual product applications by customers, especially if they indicate a trend.
- Perspectives on market trends that might affect company strategy.

How Do You Put the Pieces Together?

It's useful to break the competitive intelligence-gathering process into three categories: continuous, periodic, and project-based. *Continuous* competitive intelligence (CI) focuses on the most direct competitors (or industries, technologies, etc.) that you want to monitor on an ongoing basis. These should include the aspects of the external environment that might have the biggest potential impact on your ability to compete in the marketplace. Having a stream of information from the sales force (as mentioned earlier) is part of continuous data collection, but it doesn't need to stop there. After defining the type of information that you need, and the periodicals, journals, newspapers, and Web sites that you want to monitor, set up an automated CI alert program. Many proprietary services such as Factiva, Dialog, and Lexis/Nexis offer electronic alerts, but if your company does not subscribe to these services, you can set up more basic alerts with Google.

While you cannot monitor everything all the time, you should conduct periodic CI on the less direct competitors or trends to determine whether anything has changed. *Periodic* CI can be conducted monthly, quarterly, or annually, depending on the rate of change in your industry. The value of a periodic search of information is that it may highlight unexpected changes that could shift the priorities for your continuous data collection process.

Project-based CI, as the term implies, is conducted on an *as-needed* basis, similar to a marketing research project. When continuous or periodic data collection uncovers some unexpected findings or you are ready to launch a new product or you need specific insights for a new strategy, it may be necessary to launch a specific in-depth analysis of the issue. One technique that could be used in this category is the use of war games. (See www.fuld.com for some brief video examples of war games.) To structure this approach, you may need help from sales, marketing, or other employees in the company. Select the top two to four competitors and assign each one to a team of three to six people. Each team "becomes" the assigned competitor and gathers data in an effort to think like the competitor. Then the teams meet to share the insights they've gained.

One of the main goals of all these CI efforts is to forecast what competing companies are likely to do in the future. If you are competing in an oligopolistic industry, your concerns may be with the actions of individual competitors. How will they respond to the request for proposal (RFP) you are bidding on? When will they launch a superior product? On the other hand, if you are competing against numerous competitors in more of a "pure competition" environment, you may be more concerned with the macro movements in the industry.

Competitive intelligence requires a balance between competitor data and customer data. It's risky to be too focused on one, especially it if causes the neglect of the other. Information on both is necessary to be truly market-oriented. But just gathering market-oriented data is not enough. Product managers must use the information they gather to improve their competitive strategies. Otherwise, says Rebecca Wettemann, vice president of research at Nucleus Research in Wellesley, Massachusetts, "It's like having a bank account with millions of dollars in it but no ATM card. If you can't get it out and can't make it work for you, then it is not really useful."[6]

At the most basic level, comparing the relative strengths and weaknesses of product features can help a product manager establish positioning strategies, marketing communications, and sales support materials. As mentioned earlier, the Apple iPod is facing competition from the wireless networks. Although they are not direct competitors in the "purest" sense, they pose a potential threat to the iPod's future ability to compete. Technological advances in storage, compression, and battery life have made it easier to receive and store music by phone and other mobile devices.

Pharmaceutical companies are faced with competitive challenges as they try to anticipate the emergence of generics after the expiration of product patents. Product managers need to monitor competitive intelligence on the manufacturers of generic products. They can then create models (perhaps as Excel spreadsheets) to estimate the impact of sales or market share loss to the competition under varying scenarios. They can also estimate the likelihood of these scenarios actually taking place.

MARKET AND CUSTOMER INTELLIGENCE

Now we shift to what is perhaps the most important category of intelligence gathering: information about market segments and customers.

The ability to segment and target customers has grown increasingly more sophisticated with the growth of technology. So product managers have to stop thinking that their job is to sell products. Rather, their job is to help customers *buy* products. Since different customers have different needs and expectations, product managers must clarify what these differences are, as well as the significance of these differences in their plans.

The cornerstone of an effective business strategy is the ability to attract and retain high-profit customers. There should be more focus on growing customers than on just growing product sales. Product managers must have a clear-cut understanding and appreciation of the market(s) for their products. These markets could include existing customers as well as potential customers, singular clients as well as groups or market segments, and individuals using the product as well as those influencing its purchase. This section focuses on the issues involved in analyzing markets and developing plans to maximize their profitability.

PRELIMINARY CUSTOMER SEGMENTATION QUESTIONS

Market analysis refers to studying current and potential customers for a product or product line. Start by asking yourself some basic questions about existing customers:

1. Is there a group of heavy users of the product(s)? What percentage of the purchasers are in this group?
2. Is the primary target market growing, stable, or declining?
3. Under what circumstances do customers purchase the product(s)?
4. How and why is geographical coverage limited?
5. What percentage of customers are national accounts? International?
6. Are most customers new or repeat buyers?
7. Are the customers the end users? If not, what information is available about the end user?
8. Are your customers progressive? Traditional? Passive?

9. How sensitive have customers been to past price changes?
10. Does the customer base consist of a few large customers or many small buyers?

Then, if you haven't already done so, put current and potential customers into categories or segments. The segments are groups of customers with common demographics, common needs, common psychographics, and/or common uses/applications for the product. The process of segmenting allows the marketer to get closer to the customer by focusing on the requirements of smaller groups. Although Web communications strive to get closer to one-to-one marketing, most product development efforts require a minimum market size beyond one (as defined by segmentation parameters) to be profitable.

It's important to break a total market into submarkets for a variety of reasons. First, it helps provide a better understanding of the aggregate market, including how and why customers buy. Second, it ensures better allocation of resources because the benefits that specific groups are looking for are better understood. This should make it possible to build competitive features or services into the product offering. And finally, segmentation enables the company to exploit opportunities by uncovering hidden niches.

To begin the segmentation process, use criteria most appropriate for your industry, as shown in Table 4.2. Consumer product companies use demographic variables such as age and family status or psychographic variables such as attitudes and lifestyles. The objective of classifying customers into groups is to find similarities in the way they might respond to your product strategies. And of course, one needs to remember not to overstate the dissimilarities, as Liz Torless notes:

Understanding what connects people to each other in the category decisions they make and the brands they choose is far more revealing than determining how they differ. And usually, what connects them is their mood and frame of mind, not their demo- or psychographics. A 19-year-old female bicycle courier from Toronto and a 58-year-old male farmer from Saskatchewan have nothing in common: different demographics, completely different lifestyle, and likely different values. But they both love Kraft Dinner, vote NDP [New Democratic Party], shop at discount stores, get their news on the Internet, and go to Vegas.[7]

Table 4.2

Segmentation Criteria

Type of Factor	Product and Market	
	Consumer	Business-to-Business
Demographic	Age, sex, race Income Family size Family life cycle stage Location	Industry (NAICS) Geographic location Company size Functional decision maker Profitability
Psychographic	Lifestyle Attitudes	Risk categories Psychology of decision maker
Application/Use of Product	Frequency of purchase Size of purchase How product is used	Application Importance of purchase Volume, frequency
Benefits (Possibly Beyond the Product)	Emotional satisfaction	Support requirements Service requirements Relationships

Industrial product companies use the North American Industry Classification System (NAICS),[8] company size, or functional titles. Many companies use end use of the product as a segmentation variable. For example, a product manager for nylon might break segments into end-use groups such as menswear, tires, and upholstery. Most B2B segmentation is multilevel. For example, a supplier of products to hospitals might first look at different company types, such as teaching hospitals, community hospitals, owned specialty practices, home health businesses, outpatient clinic, foundation, or company-sponsored facility. At a second level, there are segments or business units within hospitals, such as oncology, pediatrics, telemetry, cardiac services, behavioral lifestyle, general surgery, obstetrics, case management, rehabilitation, and emergency. And finally, specific functional titles could represent different needs, such as physician, nurse manager, nurse, and so forth. It's worth noting that the different personalities and interests of people within the same function may suggest a different level of interest in your products and services.

Service companies use intensity of need, risk categories, or distance from the company. There may also be lifestyle differences that could be the basis for segmentation. Aramark, in studying customer segments for its hospital food service, identified five categories of health-care workers based on individual insights. Banks build models of propensity to buy among customers. (See Business Brief 4.3, "Market Segmentation for Service Operations.")

After identifying segments that have different needs, examine the product's performance in each segment. What is the average

Business Brief 4.3

MARKET SEGMENTATION FOR SERVICE OPERATIONS

Aramark spent several months researching customers in an effort to improve its retail food service operations for hospitals. The research consisted of focus groups, interviews with 700+ health-care employees, and 40,000 "customer insight surveys." Based on the research, Aramark identified five categories of health-care workers: healthies, loyals, bringers, refuelers, and skippers:

Healthies: Health is a deciding factor in what they eat
Loyals: Satisfied with hospital dining
Bringers: Brown-bag lunch crowd
Refuelers: Eat on the go
Skippers: Avoid hospital food because of their negative opinion of it

As part of the research, Aramark estimated the percentage of customers falling into each segment, a ranking of targets, and the best way to develop a strategy to reach them. This psychographic segmentation approach used criteria more relevant to making improvements in product development and marketing communications than could be obtained with standard demographic variables.

More and more community banks are also segmenting customers based on a variety of criteria beyond traditional demographic variables. These banks typically analyze the profitable customers in their own databases and match the information with data from the outside to develop models of potential:

About five years ago Commercial Federal began using predictive modeling, scoring customers on their propensity to buy certain products. Now its monthly mailings (about 33 a month, promoting everything from checking accounts to home equity loans) are triggered by propensity scores based on factors like a maturing loan or a customer's anniversary with the thrift. Segmentation marketing works by analyzing the characteristics of customers who have bought certain types of products. To determine likely prospects for a home equity line of credit, for example, a program would examine the thousands of such customers in a bank's database. It would then apply standard methods to develop a model for identifying prospects with the same characteristics.

Similarly, Tri-Tech Corporation, an electrical components distributor, decided to segment its customers according to how they wanted to buy from Tri-Tech. "Now, field reps call on the customers who want an in-person sales process, and the telesales-people handle customers who want to order products via the phone or Internet." This type of segmentation process is particularly suited to the needs of a distributor.

Source: "Aramark HMS: Hospital Foodservice Customers Ready for Their Close-Ups," *Nation's Restaurant News* (April 4, 2005), p. 16. Chris Costanzo, "Finer Customer Segmentation Paying Off," *American Banker* (December 14, 2004), p. 6A. Andy Cohen, "Addressing Their Needs," *Sales and Marketing Management* (July 2004), p. 18.

order size, the share of segment sales, and/or the revenue generated? The example in Table 4.3 shows four identifiable market segments.

Table 4.3

Segmentation by Key Buying Factors

Common purchase-decision criteria (buying factors)	Negotiator segment	Big-lot segment	Solutions segment	Custom segment
	• Technical self-service	• Large customers	• Solution-seekers	• Nonstandard motors
	• Standard products	• Very price sensitive	• Modified-standard products	• Special features
	• Large purchases	• Standard products	• Medium-sized lots	• Small lots
	• Strong price negotiators	• Large purchases	• Moderate price sensitivity	• Price often secondary
Price	2	3	4	5
Quality/features	5	4	3	2
Delivery	3	4	4	3
Installation	5	5	3	2
Marketing/engineering support	5	4	3	1
Sales coverage	4	4	3	1
Size and share	$89 million	$113.4 million	$69.3 million	$66.6 million
	13%	31%	30%	25%
Average order size	$1,500	$6,998	$2,345	$923
	Industry: $15,000	Industry: $5,000	Industry: $2,000	Industry: $3,000

Key to importance of buying factors: Low 5 4 3 2 1 High

The *negotiator segment* consists of the largest companies with special demands and the market power to negotiate for those demands. In rating the importance of six purchase criteria on a scale of 1 to 5 with 1 being "essential" and 5 being "low importance," price has an importance level of 2; quality/features is rated 5; delivery, 3; installation, 5; manufacturing/engineering support, 5; and sales coverage, 4. Based on industry data, the company estimates that the overall sales in the segment are $89 million with an industry-average order size of $15,000. Its share of this market is 13 percent, with an average order size of $1,500. By studying all the information, it appears that the company is most successful with the *big-lot* and *solutions* segments. In both situations, there is a significant market share, and the order size is greater than the industry average.

After listing potential ways of segmenting the market, including both old and new market segments, the next step is to reduce the number of categories into a manageable number (three to seven). Eliminate any segments that the firm *cannot* serve, for whatever reason. Then examine the remaining segments in terms of fit with company resources, long-term strategy, cost to reach, and risk to serve. Rank these segments so that the greatest proportion of resources will be devoted to the most important segments.

One way product managers approach this is to simultaneously evaluate the attractiveness of different markets and determine their firm's ability to satisfy the needs of those markets. All customers are not created equal, and trying to build loyalty among all customers can be detrimental to the health of a firm. Product managers must determine *which* customers offer the best future return on investment. For mass-market products (e.g., fast-moving consumer goods), profiling heavy users and developing a plan to appeal to them is common. The profile might include standard demographic variables such as age, sex, income, geographic location, marital status, and family size, as well as psychographic characteristics such as perceptions of oneself and desired personality characteristics. For industrial products (e.g., capital equipment), customers requiring specific applications or uses may be more profitable than others and therefore considered the "best" customers.

MARKET AND CUSTOMER ANALYSIS PROCESS

Let's use an example of a hypothetical food service company called Progressive Foodservice, Inc., which sells food items to two major market categories: food service distributors and operators, each of which may be further segmented. The food service distributors consist of full-line distributors, specialty distributors, and buying groups. The food service operators consist of commercial operators (lodging, fast food, restaurants, cafeterias, caterers, and retail hosts) and noncommercial operators (health care, educational institutions, airlines, and vending companies). Starting at the highest level of segmentation, the first step is to determine which needs are distinctly different among the segments. Assume that the full-service distributors and distributor buying groups are interested in centralized purchasing, volume buying to get a discounted price, and specialized distribution specifications. The specialty distributors, who carry a specific line of products or target a specific type of account, are interested in unique products and possible merchandising support to reach their customers.

For those sales directly related to food service operators rather than through distributors, end customers also have varying needs. Within the commercial group, fast-food restaurants demand just-in-time shipments of food products at the lowest possible price. The remaining commercial operators (to varying degrees) desire menu support and presentation ideas. The noncommercial operators are interested in consistent inventory replenishment and long shelf-life products. After studying these needs, Progressive's product manager recombined the markets into five broad need segments and then looked at two things: (1) how attractive the segments are as a whole and (2) whether the firm had any competitive advantages in addressing the segment needs.

To determine market attractiveness, the product manager examined market size (the total number of customers in each segment), the growth rate, the strength of the competition, the price sensitivity of the customers, the revenue and profitability of existing customers in these segments, and similar variables. Then the PM rated each segment on a 1–5 scale with 1 being "unattractive" and 5 being "highly attractive." General distributors (segment A) were rated 3, specialty distributors (segment B) were rated 4, fast-food chains (segment C) were rated 2, commercial operators (segment D) were rated 3, and noncommercial operators (segment E) were rated 1. Note that there is some blurring of customers and noncustomers at this time, since we don't want to limit the analysis to what is happening now but keep in mind the potential for growth. Compare the size, purchase volumes, and growth rate for each segment in the entire market with the size, purchase volumes, and growth rate for the respective segment of existing customers. Ask questions during this analysis. What is the demand in each segment for the product? What is the product's penetration? How many prospects are there in segments that purchase only competitive products? Why do they purchase only those products? Are you gaining or losing share? Do you participate in the most profitable segments in the industry? Summarize the information in a table similar to Table 4.4.

Table 4.4

Attractiveness Ratings of Market Segments for Progressive Foodservice, Inc.

Market Segment	Percentage of Company Sales	Percentage of Industry Sales	Characteristics of Market Attractiveness (size, growth rate, purchase volume, etc.)	Rating (1–5)
General Distributors	39%	27%	Top five play a pivotal role in the industry. Price is a driving factor.	3
Specialty Distributors	14%	13%	Showing growth due to special food-service demands of aging population.	4
Fast-Food Chains	16%	22%	Approaching saturation of our type of product. Heavy competition and price pressure.	2
Commercial Operators	22%	30%	Pockets of rapid growth (e.g., retail delis) due to dual-income families. Strong potential for our type of product.	3
Noncommercial Operators	9%	8%	Static or declining potential.	1

To determine whether Progressive had any competitive advantages in addressing the segment-specific needs, the product manager honestly appraised the company's competencies and rated its ability to satisfy the needs of the segments. Again using a 1–5 scale, the PM rated Progressive 1 if there were strong competitors with significant abilities to satisfy the specific needs, 3 if it was at the same level as the competition, and 5 if it was significantly superior to the competition. Progressive's competitive ability-to-serve ratings are shown in Table 4.5. The "requirements to satisfy needs" column highlights improvements or changes Progressive would need to make to address the needs of each of the five identified segments. The ratings identify how well Progressive can meet the needs compared to its competitors.

Combining the information on market-attractiveness and ability to serve yields the matrix shown in Figure 4.3. For example, the general distributors segment has a 3 for market attractiveness and a 3 for ability to satisfy needs, placing it right in the center.

Table 4.5

Ability-to-Serve Ratings for Progressive Foodservice, Inc.

Market Segment	Needs	Requirements to Satisfy Needs (Product, Skill Set, Locations, Costs)	Rating (1–5)
General Distributors	Centralized purchasing: volume buying at discounted price; specialized distribution specifications	Improved carrier terms, established BI function	3
Specialty Distributors	Unique products; merchandising support	Commitment to R&D and new product development	4
Fast-Food Chains	Just-in-time shipments at lowest price	Shared-cost shipping services	2
Commercial Operators	Menu support; presentation suggestions	Consulting chef de cuisine on call; test kitchens; online educational programs	4
Noncommercial Operators	Consistent inventory replenishment; long shelf life	Product development efforts on extending shelf life	1

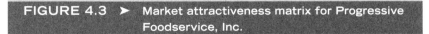

FIGURE 4.3 ➤ Market attractiveness matrix for Progressive Foodservice, Inc.

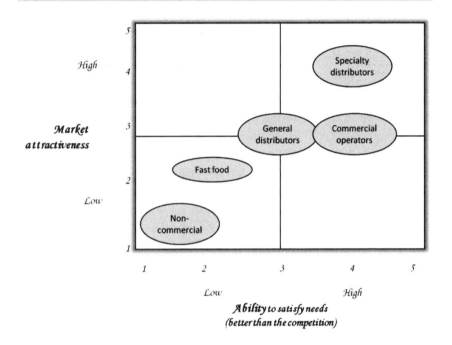

All else being equal, the best target market(s) would be in the upper right-hand quadrant where a company has determined it has a highly attractive customer segment and a high competitive advantage in serving the segment. As expected, there are other considerations. First, there may be no segment that falls solidly in this quadrant. In that case, a firm might target the most attractive segment that exists and determine what products and skills it would be necessary to develop to shift the segment to the right. Second, there may be a segment in the upper right quadrant having relatively little future profit potential compared with other segments. To help visualize this, the circles can be adjusted in size to represent the potential opportunity in that segment. Third, a segment in the upper right quadrant could already be dominated by the company, with little to be gained by increased resources. In that case, allocating sufficient marketing dollars to customer retention may be appropriate, with more resources being diverted to other promising segments. To help visualize this in the matrix, it is useful to draw the circles as pie charts with a distinction between attained market and future potential. Finally, some segments that appear to be less attractive on an absolute basis might indeed turn out to be quite attractive if they are underserved by the competition.

To compile this information, you need to refer to both internal and secondary (published) sources. From an internal perspective, sales records should be correlated with demographic characteristics to determine which variables relate most closely to profitability. Does company size, geographic location, type of application, or any other variable help "predict" sales? Once these variables are identified, you can extrapolate them to noncustomers to estimate market and growth potentials. The "deliverable" from this step of the analysis is a "knowledge chapter" in your product fact book (as described in the planning chapter) summarizing the drivers of loyalty and defining profitable customer segments.

It's worth noting that as companies design and implement new services to satisfy customer expectations, their processes usually become more complex and costs usually increase. Conventional cost accounting methods do not properly identify differences in cost to serve. They fail to identify some of the postproduction costs that are caused by responding to segment-specific needs. It's important to recognize that costs are not just uncontrollable occurrences, but rather are caused by measurable factors that can be managed. Therefore, an understanding of segment reporting and possibly activity-based costing needs to be part of the product manager's repertoire of skills.

Once this information is compiled, the product manager can create the visual matrix described earlier for Progressive Foodservice, Inc. The information can then be used to identify primary and secondary target markets, the needs of those markets, and the issues a firm must address to satisfy those needs. Note that the prior example blurred the distinction between a channel customer and an end customer. Although not a "pure" or "ideal" instance, this is a real situation. Some product managers (especially consumer brand managers) will refer to the channel as their customer and the end user as a consumer. In many circumstances, understanding the needs and expectations of the channel customer is critical for survival. P&G, for example, relies heavily on its relationship with Walmart (contributing 17 percent of sales or $8.7 billion in 2005).

The companies share data and plans, and they link their computer systems for efficiency.

BALANCING CUSTOMER RETENTION AND CUSTOMER ACQUISITION

Once the profiling of the target market is completed, the next concern is how to grow customer equity. (See Figure 4.4.) This could involve one or a combination of (1) increasing the profitability of existing customers, (2) attracting new customers with the potential for future high-value business, or (3) "firing" low-potential customers. To increase existing profitability, invest in the highest-value customers first. How can add-on sales and cross-selling (of even other product managers' products!) increase customer equity? (Don't let a product or brand management focus hurt this effort. Remember that brands don't create wealth; customers do.)[9] What behaviors should you try to change in the market to increase profitability? What behaviors do you need to change in your own company to increase profitability?

Database programs can help product managers understand the specific needs of market segments and subsegments. Product managers

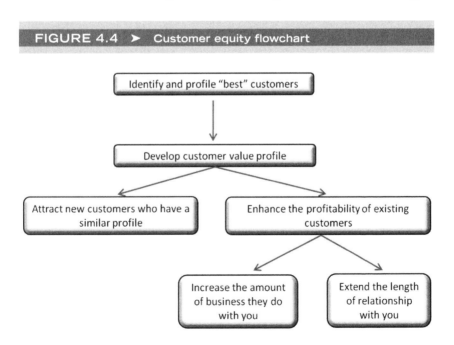

FIGURE 4.4 ➤ Customer equity flowchart

should try to determine the necessary actions to get existing customers to increase the amount of business they do with the firm, to get "good" customers to become more loyal, and to get secondary customers converted into primary customers. Then, by taking advantage of flexible manufacturing and delivery, the product managers can provide cost-effective offerings tailored to each group—offerings such as product features, price discounts, service arrangements, and purchase warranties. This approach has been used by industrial firms, by service-sector companies, and by resellers such as wholesalers and retailers. A Canadian grocery store chain, for example, analyzed a "typical" store which served around 15,000 households, with annual revenues of $25 million, and with an operating margin of 2 percent. It uncovered the following information:

First, the company segmented the customer base surrounding the store into three categories: primary shoppers (those who give the store 80 percent or more of their grocery business), secondary shoppers (those who spend more than 10 percent but less than 50 percent of their grocery budget at the store), and nonshoppers.

Second, the company calculated the impact on the store's profitability of small improvements in the behavior profiles of existing customers. Given the fixed cost structure of a grocery store, the contribution margin from each additional dollar spent by a customer can earn ten times the store's net profit margin. Thus, the company found that even small improvements in one of many customer behaviors led to very significant profitability gains. Expanding the customer base by 2 percent with primary shoppers, for example, would increase the store's profitability by more than 45 percent. Converting just two hundred secondary customers into primary customers would increase profitability by more than 20 percent. Selling one more produce item to every customer would increase profitability by more than 40 percent. Persuading every customer to substitute two store-brand items for two national-brand items each time they visited the store would increase profitability by 55 percent.

Rather than focusing directly on these opportunities, though, the company, like most other organizations, had been paying attention to more traditional objectives, such as productivity, market share, and quality. As a result, it had overlooked the possibility of closing this full-potential gap by optimizing customer value exchanges.[10]

FIRING YOUR CUSTOMERS

A particular challenge many product managers face is saying no to an unprofitable customer (or even an unprofitable segment). All companies have customers who demand special services (with no additional revenue generated), who demand rock-bottom prices for everything, or who require changing the basic product or service to fit their unique needs. When any of these situations arise, there are only a few options available: raise the price, reduce the cost of servicing the customer, or discontinue doing business with the customer.

Raising the price to compensate for the value being supplied is the most obvious solution. However, this may be difficult to pull off. Customers must perceive and believe in the competitive value, and if a particular customer is not part of the target market, there might not be a good fit between that customer's needs and your firm's capabilities. This leads to the second option: reducing the cost to serve. It's crucial for the product manager to clearly understand the total costs "caused by" the customer. Table 4.6 provides an example format for including both direct and indirect revenues and costs by customer. Only by understanding the true costs can an effort be made to reduce them.

Discontinuing business with a customer may be a last but necessary resort. Typically it happens indirectly through the changing of policies

Table 4.6

Customer Profitability Analysis

Customer: Atkins, Inc.
Industry: Semiconductor machinery manufacturing

Product	Product Revenue	Product Cost	Contribution
Total			
Other customer revenue +			
Other customer expenses −			
Total contribution =			

or raising of prices. However, before this happens, ask a few questions. Does this customer bring in business simply by being a customer? Will this customer grow into a strategic customer in the future? Does the customer absorb overhead that would need to be allocated elsewhere if the business relationship is ended? Provide an honest appraisal of the situation, and be prepared to say no if necessary.

EVENTS AND TRENDS

There are numerous externalities and trends that may require a product manager's attention. Social trends and changing mores, political upheavals, macroeconomic influences, environmental events or changes, regulatory compliance issues, and a host of other trends can affect product success. Product managers, whether they are involved in brainstorming new product ideas or crafting innovative go-to-market strategies for existing products, must be adept at spotting and capitalizing on trends (or minimizing any negative consequences).

It is far too easy to get caught up in the business of day-to-day fire-fighting and lose sight of what's happening all round us. Trend-spotting can be a full-time job. Therefore, you should determine which trends you will *actively* seek out, and which you will *opportunistically* evaluate. Create folders (virtual or actual) with labels of the key trends you want to follow. For example, a technology product manager may follow virtualization, cloud computing, and business analytics. A foods product manager may follow obesity, labeling, and regulatory trends. Sometimes it is helpful to ask colleagues to help with this. Establish a trend analysis group (TAG team) and have each colleague agree to feed you information on a particular trend. In any case, create these folder labels as well as a folder labeled *opportunistic* for random thoughts and insights. File articles, customer data, channel and sales insights, various downloads, and random ideas in these folders. Then develop the discipline to review the information on a regular basis.

Monitoring demographic trends and shifts can also highlight the need for new products, language modifications, and/or marketing strategy changes. While it is considered the norm to focus on youth for most new consumer products, many companies have started to reach out to older adults. Proctor & Gamble identified about 30 products that it can market directly to people 50 and older, and Sony has increased advertising to make its high-end gadgets more appealing to the 50–64 age group.[11] The aging of the global population also results in physical challenges to traditional car design, and the Japanese have been incorporating features to address these challenges. (See Business Brief 4.4, "Japanese Car Options for the Elderly.")

Business Brief 4.4

JAPANESE CAR OPTIONS FOR THE ELDERLY

With the dramatic increase in the percentage of elderly in the populations of virtually all developed countries, there will be a growing demand for products and services that are designed to serve the needs or wants of the elderly. Japan has noted that about one-fourth of its population is over 65 years of age, and it has begun to address the issue. At the 31st International Home Care and Rehabilitation Exhibition in Tokyo, "elder car" options were displayed next to booths showcasing adult diapers and home elevators.

A subsidiary of Nissan Motors offers wheelchair ramps for vans, as well as products for smaller cars including swivel seats and a motorized crane to lift a wheelchair into and out of a trunk. Toyota is exploring "barrier-free cars," and has developed a car seat that doubles as a wheelchair. Even Ford Motor Company has developed a full-body jumpsuit that restricts movement to help designers understand the limitations of old age. The jumpsuit comes with glasses to simulate weaker eyesight.

The current market for these types of vehicles is less than 1 percent of all automobiles sold. Many are adaptations of vehicles designed for the handicapped. Most car companies are taking a cautious, wait-and-see approach to the issue because of concerns such as product liability. However, the demographic trend is real and could have a significant impact on future product demands.

Source: Adapted from Jathon Sapsford, "Japan's Auto Makers Ply the Aged with 'Elder Car' Options," *Wall Street Journal* (November 5, 2004), pp. B1–B3.

It is absolutely critical that you stay on top of trends that could affect your markets, your product, your competitors, and your technologies. As always, some prioritization is helpful. Categorize the trends in terms of probability and significance. (See Figure 4.5.) *Probability* refers to the likelihood the trends will happen within your current planning cycle. *Significance* refers to the positive or negative impact the trend could have on your product strategy. Focus first on trends that have the highest probabilities and significance factors.

RESEARCH PROJECTS

Gathering customer information is generally the responsibility of marketing research, so this is simply a primer to provide definitions and jargon. I start by differentiating primary, syndicated, and secondary research. *Primary research* refers to surveys, focus groups, observation, and other methods designed to gather information for a stated purpose. A sample is selected and a questionnaire is designed specifically for this purpose. *Syndicated research* often refers to a "shared cost" study in which a firm may insert a question or two in a generic study.

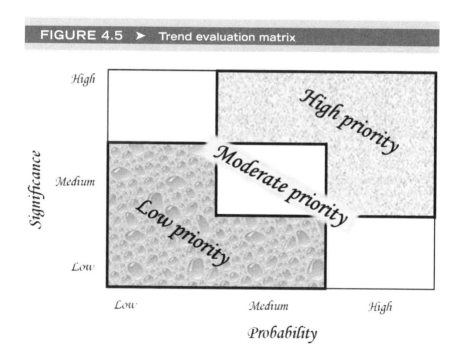

FIGURE 4.5 ➤ Trend evaluation matrix

The sample and questionnaire are not specifically focused on your firm's goals but are used when the sample is deemed "close enough." Syndicated research also includes warehouse and retail sales data compiled by companies such as A. C. Nielsen. *Secondary research* refers to an analysis of census data, trade association statistics, and other previously compiled and published data.

Research can also be categorized as qualitative, quantitative, or experimental. *Qualitative* research, such as focus groups, ethnographies, and case studies, attempts to provide richer, deeper answers and insights than is available through standard questionnaires. Gerry Katz, executive vice president of Applied Marketing Science, Inc., has an interesting four-minute YouTube video describing the use of ethnography or observational research. In this primer he describes how observing nurses using dialysis machines uncovered an unarticulated need that was converted into a highly successful product feature.

On the other hand, the advantages of qualitative research are obtained at the expense of it being representative—the results cannot be statistically projected to the overall customer base. Since the sample size is necessarily small, it might not be representative of the population; also, the fluidity of the questions challenges a statistical analysis of results.

Quantitative research is essentially at the opposite end of the continuum from qualitative research. It requires a questionnaire with carefully worded, closed-ended questions and a true probability sample. Both of these requirements are necessary to project the results from the sample to the population (from which the sample was drawn), with any statistical confidence. In reality, most customer research incorporates some aspects of both qualitative and quantitative research. And it's worth remembering that there is no such thing as a perfect questionnaire, so even with probability research, there are no guarantees of the total "truth."

Experiments are used less frequently than qualitative or quantitative research when customer information is compiled. Consumer product managers may use market tests or in-store tests to determine which package design or advertising message "pulls" better than another. In setting up a market experiment, the researcher strives to select similar groups of customers (controlling for as many extraneous variables as possible), and then gives each group a different package design (or price or ad message or other variable). Split-testing of messages is easier with the Web, since the different treatments can be randomized. The comparative reactions to the variations of this one factor are measured and used as a basis for decision making.

The Web has really exploded as a research tool for accessing the "wisdom of crowds." Opinions on existing products, suggestions for improvements, ideas for new products, and insights on attitudes can trigger possible opportunities to increase customer satisfaction and/or the firm's profitability.

If you do not have the skills, access, or funds for a comprehensive customer research project, there are a few alternative approaches. (1) Split the research into several small projects that focus on the most critical questions but that are more affordable. (2) Share the cost with another product manager who needs information from the same set of customers. (3) Find a college marketing research class that will take it on as a semester project. (4) Hire an intern with the right skill set to conduct the research. (5) Determine if a secondary research project (perhaps conducted by consultants in your industry) provides information that can sufficiently augment what you already know.

Product managers can also obtain much information using informal techniques. Customer visits, trade show conversations, suggestions and comments made to customer service reps, user group input, complaint letters, product repair records, blogs, dealer/distributor/rep advisory councils, and other person-to-person sources yield potential areas for product improvements.

INTERNAL INTELLIGENCE

The last category of intelligence comes from internal data. Knowledge of product successes and failures, results of marketing efforts, financial reports on products and customers, awareness of necessary refinements in internal processes, and other data contribute to product improvements. Take a look at Business Brief 4.5, "Leaning Product Management," to learn about lean marketing efforts at Springs Window Fashions in which streamlined processes are being used to improve product management functions.

Business Brief 4.5

LEANING PRODUCT MANAGEMENT

Gloria Green, senior manager for lean marketing at Springs Window Fashions, possesses over 30 years' experience helping companies capitalize on synergies by linking marketing and operations. She has created and implemented successful marketing plans while developing improvement programs to facilitate better practices. With experience in a variety of industries, she has expertise in strategic planning, marketing, product management, lean marketing, and project management: from defining goals and deliverables to using evaluations and surveys to ensure satisfactory completion.

In the assemble-to-order world of window treatments—with hundreds of collections and color combinations in numerous brands—tracking what is available where and getting that information to those who need it consumes an inordinate amount of a product manager's time. Multiply that by 10 different product lines and Springs Window Fashions' product managers spend thousands of hours each year just managing data. And this is just getting data together so it can accurately be: programmed into our order entry system; configured for online order entry; pre-configured for customers' order entry systems; added to our virtual decorator and online swatching; added to our price lists; and used to ensure our sample books contain the correct collections and colors.

Springs Window Fashions, a manufacturer of innovative blinds, shades, and drapery hardware under the brand names of Bali and Graber, tackled this challenge with a new lean process for product management. It started by mapping the information flow for updating product lines, as shown in the following product information map [Figure 4.6].

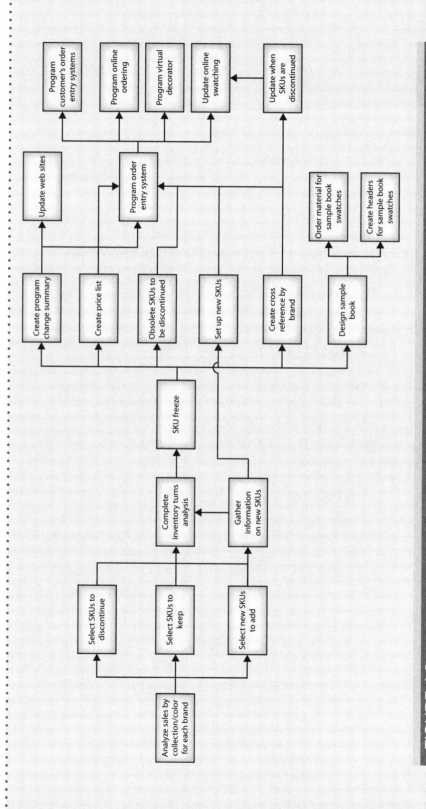

FIGURE 4.6 ▶ Product information map

During the process of mapping the information we determined *how* product managers got, used, and shared data (primarily through Excel), thereby identifying several areas of *muda,* or waste. [*Muda* is a Japanese word meaning "waste."]

Underutilized Resources
Product managers spend thousands of hours manipulating data in spreadsheets instead of adding value by analyzing the data.

Over Processing
While using VLOOKUP and the Pivot Tables in Excel has reduced the workload, there are still many limitations. Every member of a cross-functional product team needs different information. In an effort to eliminate *multiple* spreadsheets (that don't always get updated with the latest changes), we created *massive* spreadsheets. Team members, whose Excel skills vary widely, need to spend time manipulating the spreadsheet to access the specific data they need.

Motion
It only takes *one* person to sort the information incorrectly (or break a link) to make *all* of the data inaccurate. As that is often not discovered right away, the data can't just be retrieved, but often have to be re-created.

Overproduction
All product managers create spreadsheets for their product lines in their own way. Then team members have to figure out how to work with the data on every project. Features, functions, and options get named differently on different product lines. This translates into using different terminology in our sampling and merchandising material.

Defects
Reviewing the accuracy of data in a spreadsheet with 300 rows and 50 columns is an impossible task. Team members often decide to save off the information they need in a separate spreadsheet; consequently, updates and changes get lost.

In an effort to *lean* our marketing efforts, Springs Window Fashions is creating a Product Information database using SharePoint.

Team members will save time by entering data into forms designed to show *only* the information needed. Drop-down lists will be used to standardize terminology for every product line. Workflow will be streamlined since team members will know when the prior task is complete and the database is ready for them to take the next step. Standardized reports will be created so team members can download the data to create product development documents for new SKUs, program change summaries (showing what's new, what is being kept and what will be obsolete), price list information, list of materials to order for swatches in sample books, headers for swatches in sample books, and collection information charts.

Am Curet, Manager-Integrated Marketing, is looking forward to getting the entire lean process into place. "Our creative services department spends a significant amount of time verifying the accuracy and consistency of the information and data that we use in the marketing materials we create. This will allow our graphic and Web designers to focus their efforts on art direction to increase the impact of our work."

The database is being designed to offer additional benefits as well. It will enhance the ability of product managers to:

- Monitor SKU productivity (pulling sales volume by brand/collection/color and thereby freeing up the product manager to analyze the data)
- Gain instant access to the information needed by our customer service and sales teams
- Notify customer service and sales on SKU discontinuation
- Notify our e-business team on changes in collections/colors for Web site swatching and our virtual decorator

While the Product Information database has not yet been implemented, product manager Jennifer Ismail says: "The time savings and efficiencies to be gained will allow for a major reduction in hours spent managing data on a daily basis, freeing up time for the analysis needed to fully strategize for the future of the product line."

CHAPTER CHALLENGE

Determine what information you need continuously, what you need periodically, and what you can obtain on an as-needed (project) basis that will help you make better decisions. Consider both the external TIME factors as well as internal data. Then structure a system that works for you. Remember, without data you are just another person with an opinion!

INTERVIEW WITH PAULA GRAY: CAPTURE MARKET KNOWLEDGE THROUGH ANTHROPOLOGY

Paula Gray, Anthropologist-in-Residence, Association of Product Marketing and Management (AIPMM), paula.gray@aipmm.com.

Paula, not many people have the title anthropologist-in-residence. What's the story behind that?

Well, I am an applied cultural anthropologist. I don't study indigenous tribes in jungles though. I study human behavior in the cultural context: that can be within a corporation (Microsoft), a community (in person or virtual), a geographic region (Los Angeles), a group sharing beliefs and behaviors (like drug users, or engineers, or snowboarders), or a company's existing or potential customers. Then I use the information I learn to answer questions and help solve problems.

My focus with the AIPMM is twofold: I study the worldwide population of product managers and offer my insight to the AIPMM to help them support their members, and I also collaborate on a curriculum to teach product managers some of the skills of anthropology that are particularly relevant to their work.

I am intrigued by how product managers manage to gain support while wielding little to no official power and how they navigate a fairly complex social system where they are often held accountable for processes and tasks they don't control. I think they are a pretty impressive group as a whole.

The "in-residence" part of my title means that I am also free to pursue additional independent research interests and projects.

Product managers are constantly looking for better ways to obtain customer insights and voice of the customer (VOC). First of all, can you differentiate between ethnography and anthropology, and then explain how they can contribute to product development and marketing?

Anthropology is a social science discipline that is concerned with the study of human behavior and interaction in the cultural context. Anthropologists conduct ethnographies. An *ethnography* is a research method and tool unlike other methods of gathering behavioral data because it investigates not just what people say, but also what they do. We long ago recognized that people speak of the ideal but behave differently, even if they are not aware of the inconsistency.

Participant observation is a key component in an ethnography—think of it as meeting people where the behavior *happens* rather than pulling people out of their daily patterns and *forcing* a behavior in a lab or controlled situation. There is certainly value in surveys, interviews, focus groups, and other methods, but they do not hold a complete picture; they are only pieces. That's what makes an ethnography so valuable. It is a complete picture containing all of those components; it is comprehensive and rich in detail.

After we gather the data, we then use the tools of anthropological culture theory to analyze it. An ethnography, as a heavily *qualitative* data-driven project, needs the tools of culture theory to help make sense out of it all. Anthropologists are uniquely skilled in this domain because we are trained to look for patterns of behavior, speech, belief systems, symbols, and social networks among other components that are part of the integrated system of culture.

In *product development*, the insight gained from an ethnography can reveal where a product is situated in the life of the consumer and in the sociocultural context. Often a product can hold symbolic meaning that extends far beyond its functionality. Consumers may use a product differently than its intended use because it serves a different need for them. Ethnographies also reveal underlying beliefs, values, and unarticulated needs that shape what features may be needed to meet the needs of those consumers. These insights are then translated into products and/ or features that have a higher likelihood of engaging the consumer.

In *marketing*, the ethnographic insight into the deeper meaning and context of product usage can be used to design messaging that supports and draws upon those meanings. Insight into the wider cultural context allows marketers to understand how their product is situated differently within different cultural environments and can adjust their targeting accordingly. Ethnographies are especially useful in providing understanding of the diverse global cultural context of the market and competitive environment.

Can you share a couple of specific case examples of using these tools?

Many companies with their own anthropologists and those who work with outside firms are reluctant to share the results of these ethnographies since they offer a competitive advantage only if they are kept secret. However, there are a few well-known cases.

Christina Wasson, professor of anthropology at the University of North Texas, has conducted significant research in anthropology and design. She mentions Steelcase, a manufacturer of office furniture and components that create cubicles and work spaces out of large rooms, worked with the firm E-Lab (now part of Sapient) to conduct an ethnography to gain some insight into how their products were put to use in offices. Steelcase's design team envisioned how companies would construct these work spaces and designed the products accordingly. They believed that individual work spaces would be used when people were working alone and group areas would be used for group interaction. They did not realize that the way the office systems were actually being put to use by their customers' employees did not necessarily match the designed function. The ethnography revealed that impromptu meetings and interactions were occurring in hallways and other undefined spaces, turning them into significant work areas. Based on the insight, they began to focus on products that would support the use of these spaces—thus having significant implications in future product design.

Paco Underhill, retail anthropologist and principal of Envirosell, a consulting company, worked with a consumer product manufacturing company to study shopping and buying behaviors in supermarkets over the course of two years. The ethnography revealed the extent to which children selected their own products, who shops for each product type, and what the overall brand predisposition was. The company was then able to change the product display areas based on the insight, allowing them to more accurately target the product's core purchaser.

How might a product manager use these tools differently for consumer products versus nonconsumer products versus services?

As far as the product manager is concerned, ethnography as a tool is equally relevant in the three areas. The anthropologists will know how to modify the data collection based on the research question for each of the goods or services. B2B products tend to have more levels of customers to study so the team will need to go deeper to gain that picture of context. For example, there is the initial purchaser or customer who may use it as a component of a larger product, which then has its own customer. An ethnography, therefore, needs to include the study of each level of customer—all the way down to the end user—in order to gain that complete picture.

In addition to the information you have already shared, what advice might you give to product managers to add to their repertoire of customer-focused tools?

As so many companies design and market their products in a global cross-cultural environment, it's important for product managers to learn about those geographic regions and their cultural characteristics. Without specific training and education in anthropology, a product manager can still find out some key factors that affect and shape the lives of those customers, such as some commonly held beliefs, values, customs, major taboos, and the region's predominant religion. Though this isn't a deep study, the knowledge will help product managers gain a more complete understanding of some of the findings of an ethnography, and it will allow them to better represent the voice of those customers' needs.

I think it is also important for product managers to conduct their own informal observations of customers whenever possible. They need to get face time with these customers in order to gain an understanding of the complexity of these individuals. This informal observation can add insight and a layer of firsthand knowledge to augment the product managers' own perspective.

CHAPTER 5

Planning Frameworks

TRUE OR FALSE: Fill-in-the-blank templates for product managers increase the likelihood of a plan's success.

MAYBE. Maybe not. Good templates can highlight important topics to evaluate as part of a planning process—and this *might* reduce the probability of a product manager overlooking a critical fact. Unfortunately, templates can also become an end in themselves, causing product managers to "go through the motions" without giving sufficient thought to their answers. The result is a "rinse 'n repeat" plan which short-circuits the planning process. Be careful about this.

Planning at the most fundamental level is an attempt to close the gap between where you are and where you want to be. If you are an average golfer and want to improve a couple of notches, you can plan to close the gap with training and practice. If you weigh yourself and decide that there's a gap between your current weight and your desired weight, you can develop a plan to close the gap. The philosophy for business plans is similar.

I resist using the term "best practices," since vastly different approaches to planning may be "best" under different circumstances. Managers look for experts' best practices as a short-cut to excellence. But often there is no short-cut, just the real work of creating your own best practices by thoroughly understanding the context that frames your decisions. This chapter presents the contextual issues that product managers should consider as they assess their planning processes and frameworks.

A PLANNING FRAMEWORK

There is no shortage of perspectives on planning approaches and frameworks. That's probably good since product managers from different companies benefit from different "realities" in how they strategize. Business-to-business product managers need a strong understanding of how to help salespeople and distributors sell to commercial customers. Consumer product managers not only require a clear "brand manager" perspective of household buyers, but they must also have the ability to motivate trade partners. Global product managers have different responsibilities depending on whether they design products for foreign purchasers, or accept existing products from their headquarters in another country to "glocalize" within their domestic borders. Many planning principles are common across all these situations, although the implementation of the principles might vary.

There are distinctly different upstream and downstream planning frameworks. On the strategic, upstream side, product managers may need to prepare long-term road maps, innovation charters, and new product development (NPD) supporting documents such as business cases and launch plans. On the downstream side, emphasis shifts to life-cycle plans reinforcing core products, renewing those that have plateaued, resurrecting prior concepts/brands that were "before their time," and retiring end-of-life products. Parts of these plans may need to fit into annual marketing and business plans. While there are many types of plans, documents, reports, and recommendations for which product managers may be responsible, some must necessarily bridge upstream and downstream efforts.

The annual product business plan is the current year's tactics to execute your product life-cycle strategies. But the process of planning is in reality a check and balance. It starts with an examination of data (past and present) as well as future projections so that your plan is built on fact rather than fad. The planning process should be more than merely filling out forms or number crunching. And the plan should provide the basis on which product managers can justify resource utilization, as well as provide continuity in the event of management or staff turnover. Financials are an important component in gaining approval of the plan.

The planning generally addresses five fundamental questions that link long-term and short-term thinking. (See Figure 5.1.)

1. Where are you now (your background analysis and intelligence)?
2. Where do you want to go long term (your strategic product and portfolio vision and strategies)?
3. What are you going to do this year to come closer to your long-term vision (objectives)?
4. What actions will help you accomplish your objectives (tactics or action plan)?
5. How will you implement, track, and evaluate results (metrics and measurements)?

The process is not necessarily linear; some companies may start with the long-term vision (step 2) and move on to data gathering (step 1) or go back and forth between steps as new information emerges or as a result of negotiation with senior management. However, all steps are generally covered in some manner.

FIGURE 5.1 ➤ Planning process

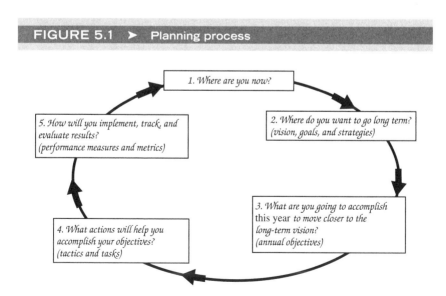

WHERE ARE YOU NOW?

Earlier in this book we addressed several of the categories of external information that related to the question, "Where are you now?" You should summarize the most significant data from the TIME analysis, including technology issues, industry conditions, market segmentation, and relevant externalities and events. Then add internal data about the performance history of products and marketing activities.

The performance history looks at how well various products performed over time and relative to what was planned. It focuses attention on the market share and financial and other numeric or statistical indicators of performance. In addition, answers to product mix questions like the ones listed below provide qualitative data that could highlight problems and opportunities to be addressed in the plan.

Your Products

Your accounting department most likely provides routine data on the sales and profitability of the product(s), but the analysis should go beyond quantitative statistics to include qualitative variables, such as:

- In what stage of the product life cycle are the products? Which are in the beginning phases, which are in growth, which are mature, and which are candidates for elimination? Do the answers to these questions confirm your prior thinking about reinforcement, renewal, and retirement?
- What does the name of the product imply? Can it be branded?
- Which features or products are distinguishable by the customer?
- For each feature, ask "So what?" to identify the benefits from the customers' point of view.
- Are the products supplied through intermediaries (e.g., dealers)? If so, the analysis of features, benefits, and values should be handled in two steps.
- If a numeric rating were given to product quality (with 1 being low and 7 being high), what would that rating be? Would the rating be the same for all customer segments? For all products?
- What does each item in the product line contribute to sales and profits? To customer satisfaction? Can some of the products be pruned?

- How does the product line rate of return compare with the company's overall rate of return?
- Are the product designs conducive to an efficient manufacturing process?
- What are the engineering costs for product development, product engineering, and manufacturing engineering?
- What are the unit breakeven sales volumes for the products?
- Are product guarantees competitive?
- What would happen if the products were more standardized? More customized?
- What is the company's attitude toward private labeling?

The Sales Force

Even though product managers typically have no authority over the salespeople, an examination of sales force effectiveness can highlight potential opportunities or problems that need to be addressed by product managers in the product plan(s). Product managers should ask the following questions:

- Is the current sales force structure appropriate for achieving the product objective?
- Are the target customers being reached in the most effective and efficient manner?
- How effective have the product and sales training been?
- What sales tools do the salespeople actually use to sell the product?
- Has the sales force been taught how to help customers visualize the benefits of the product?

Pricing

The right price covers all relevant costs, is positioned appropriately given the competitive value of the products, and takes into account customer perceptions. The product manager should assess whether company policies enable these things to happen by asking:

- Has a significant amount of business been lost because of product prices?
- Are errors frequently made in pricing?

- What is the perceived cost of buying the product or service?
- Is the company a price leader or a price follower?
- What is the pricing policy of the company?
- What types of discounts are offered? How do they compare with those of the competition?

Promotional Campaigns

Promotional campaigns should be part of an integrated marketing communications effort, with the product manager pushing for a consistent message being sent to customers. Product managers should pay attention to changing approaches to customer communications including product placements, e-mail campaigns, test drives, "advergaming," social networking, mobile apps, search engine optimization (SEO), and other techniques. They should ask these questions:

- What is the current image customers have of the product? Is it consistent with the advertising?
- Did prior advertising strategies work? Why or why not?
- What nonadvertising promotion has been tried? How well did it work?
- What has been the effectiveness of trade shows?
- Are the product-specific Web pages (landing pages) adequate, up to date, and appropriate for search engine optimization?

The Distribution Strategy

The sales force and distributors may be the most important face-to-face contacts with customers. The effectiveness of these contacts cannot be left to chance and should be built into the plan. Ask these questions:

- What are the channels of distribution? What percentage of product sales result from each type of intermediary?
- What is the company's relationship with intermediaries (e.g., distributors, agents, retailers)?
- What are distribution costs as a percentage of sales?
- How does the company's policy for distributor or retailer margins compare with those of the competition?

■ What has been the recent history of stock-outs, substitutes, and back orders?

Support Services

To complete the full cycle of customer value, installation and repair services may need to be considered in the product's marketing plan. For example, has the value of repair services changed (because of cost increases, repair person efficiency, or any other reason)?

Trend and Event Dynamics

Think about the trends you summarized earlier. What impact do they have on your product line's success? Consider these issues:

■ What technological changes are likely? How might they affect product sales within the next several years?
■ Describe industry trends in the following areas:
  • Product changes
  • Price levels/policies
  • Distribution changes
  • Power shifts in the channel
■ What leading indicators correspond with product sales?
■ What are the basic trends and changes in the economy?
■ Are there regulatory or political forces that could affect product sales? What are their trends?
■ What is the probability of the above trends occurring?
■ What impact do these trends have on the product(s)?

Product Fact Book

All this information, along with the resulting plans and metrics, should be part of a product fact book. (See Figure 5.2.) This fact book helps a product manager become the answer person at meetings and helps organize thinking about strategy. It can come in many formats and sizes, so don't look for a one-size-fits-all approach. A classic description of such a compilation is presented in Business Brief 5.1, "Colgate-Palmolive's Bundle Book."

FIGURE 5.2 ➤ Product fact book

Fact Book on Product Intelligence

Compile and organize external data and trends
- Technology inputs and processes
- Industry structure and key performance issues
- Competitive profiles and strategies (including possible substitutes)
- Segment size, growth rates, psychographics, and demographics
- Trends, events, and externalities affecting the product line

Evaluate past product performance against goal
- Financial metrics (sales, profits)
- Customer metrics (satisfaction, repeat purchase, referrals, brand equity)
- Product-line metrics (complementary value, life cycle, depth and breadth, relevance to future goals, 4R status)
- Marketing metrics (awareness, plan effectiveness)

Update goals, portfolios, road maps, strategies

Business Brief 5.1

COLGATE-PALMOLIVE'S BUNDLE BOOK

Colgate-Palmolive historically used what it called a bundle book—a three-ring binder containing everything the company knew about a product or category—to create global brands. The bundle book was distributed to Colgate subsidiaries to provide consistency and uniformity in rolling out brands to different regions. While digitization has changed the format of the book, the concepts are still valid.

According to Sharen Kindel in her article "Selling by the Book," Colgate's bundle books provide descriptive plans for a product rollout:

Bundle books contain such information as: a product overview, a definition of the marketing opportunity, the product's uniqueness, a vision statement, the product family, a digest of consumer research, packaging, graphics, and pricing strategy. Also included are the advertising plan, support materials, a professional relations program, information pertaining to advertising claim substantiation, and even specific advertising executions. The book will answer questions regarding such technical issues as the formula, additives, fragrance, color and stability and provide a list of key contacts to check information or answer questions. Says John Steele [head of global business development], "We send the subsidiaries the kind of advertising we want. They're tested ads that are already working in some markets." Detailed country profiles provide specifics on the rollout plan and how the brand has performed to date. Information on competitive brands and their advertising support is also included.

The printed bundle books can be 150 to 200 pages in length and in some situations may exceed one volume. When Colgate launched its Colgate Total toothpaste in 1993, the launch was preceded by 18 months of research, resulting in a two-volume book. One volume contained the results of test marketing in six countries which were carefully selected to provide a representative range that provided different marketing opportunities and constraints. The second volume covered public relations and advertising claim substantiation. Advertising, packaging, pricing, and positioning were consistent among all subsidiaries. Using the bundle book, Colgate's subsidiaries were able to launch Total in 66 countries within 2 years, the fastest global launch in Colgate's history at that time.

The material in Colgate's bundle book provides the essence of the intelligence analysis for product planning as well as details about the action program. Although Colgate emphasized the book's use for global new-product rollouts, the basic concepts are appropriate for annual planning and domestic strategies as well.

The *internal assessment* coincides with the general culture of the company and its impact on the plan. In Colgate's case, the books were in line with the company's centralized marketing philosophy. Colgate preferred to give direction to its subsidiaries, whereas one of its major competitors, Unilever, allowed its subsidiaries more freedom in the use of specific marketing tactics.

The *market analysis* focused on selecting the appropriate customers for allocation of resources. For Colgate, the bundle books provided a consistent way of looking at the market—even small, fragmented markets. They provided input on the demographic and psychographic profiles of the consumers most likely to use the products. This helped subsidiaries uncover new market segments that were highly profitable or were underserved by the competition.

The *competitive strategy* varied depending on Colgate's relative position within a category. Since toothpaste was a core product for Colgate, the launch of Total required global speed so that the company could preempt competitors from bringing out competing products and limiting its effectiveness at the time of launch. In the bleach category, a different approach was necessary. Colgate had only recently entered this business through acquisitions. Therefore, the competitive portion of the bundle book contained new information to educate employees. The competitive portion identified competitors' general strategies, product differentiation, future moves, and consumer perceptions.

The *performance history*, since Colgate's bundle books focused on new products, contained test market results. Colgate tested Total in Australia, Colombia, Greece, the Philippines, Portugal, and the United Kingdom. The information gathered on sampling, the use of television, and other variables was incorporated into the bundle book. For these books to be used for annual planning, it would be necessary to compare planned versus actual sales figures, along with the related analysis of why differences occurred.

Trends also played a role in Colgate's strategy. In the past, when there were few global brands and limited international technology, there was little need for a standardized approach to megabrands. Now, with instantaneous global communication available through the Internet, providing a common brand strategy using a bundle book becomes valuable.

Adapted from Sharen Kindel, "Selling by the Book," *Sales & Marketing Management* (October 1994), pp. 101–107.

WHERE DO YOU WANT TO GO, LONG TERM?

Generating a "vision" of what the product portfolio should be like in the future is critical. First, determine the vision and strategy of the overall company. The vision is the mental picture of what the company will be in the future—the products it will offer and the markets it will serve. The corporate and divisional strategies are the general plans to move toward the vision. The product plans and marketing tactics should be consistent with the vision and strategies and move the company closer to superior customer satisfaction. The vision and corporate strategies are broad, with a focus on developing and leveraging core competencies. The product-specific strategies and tactics focus on customer-specific needs.

The vision should highlight the core capabilities the company has or is willing to develop. For example, Komatsu, a Japanese manufacturer of earth-moving equipment, had a vision as early as the 1960s of beating Caterpillar (the construction and mining equipment manufacturer). The strategies specified the skills it needed to acquire and the products it needed to develop to move toward that vision. (See Business Brief 5.2, Komatsu's Long-Term Marketing Challenge.)

Business Brief 5.2

KOMATSU'S LONG-TERM MARKETING CHALLENGE

Komatsu, a Japanese manufacturer of bulldozers, developed a strategic vision of being a global player in earthmoving equipment—in essence a vision of beating Caterpillar. This required a series of short-term plans that focused on the immediate problems and opportunities Komatsu had to respond to in the process of achieving its long-term goal. (See Table 5.1.)

In the 1960s, Komatsu was about a third the size of Caterpillar, limited to one product line (small bulldozers), and was scarcely represented outside of Japan. When Caterpillar threatened Komatsu in Japan, Komatsu's short-term objective was to protect its home market. The strategies used to accomplish this were product improvements,

Table 5.1

Kotmatsu's Long-term Vision: Beat Caterpillar

Date	Corporate challenge	Activities
Early 1960s	• Protect Komatsu's home market against Caterpillar	• Licensing deals with Cummins Engine, International Harvester, and Bucyrus-Eric
Mid–1960s	• Begin quality improvement efforts	• Several quality and cost-reduction programs
1960s to early 1970s	• Build export markets	• Komatsu Europe established • Service departments to assist newly industrializing countries
Late 1970s	• Create new products and markets	• Future and Frontiers program to identify new businesses based on society's needs and company's know-how • Enters U.S. market

cost reductions, and new-product development through licensing agreements. In the early 1970s, Komatsu's challenge was to develop export markets. Since it was not yet strong enough to compete head to head with Caterpillar, it chose markets where Caterpillar was weak. Then, in the late 1970s, Komatsu felt prepared to compete against Caterpillar in the U.S. market.

Note how the company stated a long-term vision or direction (become a more dominant global player than Caterpillar). Then, on a shorter-term basis it focused on the current problems and opportunities that might affect its ability to move toward its vision. The corporate challenges represented the shorter-term objectives of the planning process. In other words, the company focused on the steps that needed to be taken at the current time in order to enable it to move closer to its future picture of itself. Finally, the activities column lists a brief summary of the action program or the tactics used to address the corporate challenges.

Source: Adapted from Gary Hamel and C. K. Prahalad, "Strategic Intent," *Harvard Business Review* (May–June 1989), pp. 63–76.

Understanding the Strategic Direction of the Company

The corporate assessment also looks at the general culture of the company, the strengths that provide the core competence, the weaknesses that must be minimized, and the role a product line plays in accomplishing the corporate strategy. The culture refers to the way a company operates: its philosophies, management style, and structure. A product manager cannot change the culture over the short term but rather must understand and attempt to work within the culture. Example cultures include *the innovative, fast-paced organization* on one hand or *the conservative, "blue-chip" organization* on the other. The management style could be autocratic or democratic, with a resulting impact on a product manager's effectiveness.

Product managers are often uncertain as to how their products contribute to the attainment of corporate goals (beyond revenue). To be sure, it's not an easy question to answer. But it needs to be considered. If the company is changing its position from economy products to more quality products, this will affect the strategies of its product managers. Hyundai, for example, declared in 2004 that it would be the industry's top-quality producer, displacing Toyota, by 2008. While it has not yet attained that vision, it remains a performance motivator. In 2004 it tied with Honda on J.D. Power & Associates Initial Quality Survey—jumping from tenth to second place.[1] From a strategic perspective, product managers must consider these linkages.

There are several questions to ask as part of this assessment to help you identify key strengths and weaknesses of management, core competencies, the planning process, and other functional areas.

Management

1. Who are the actual movers and shakers of the company? Which ones should be part of a new-product venture?
2. Who is responsible for the budgeting process?
3. Does the company have any unusual business practices that are different from those of the competition?

Distinctive Competencies

1. What capabilities form the *core* of the firm's reason for being?
2. Are the various products leveraging these competencies effectively? How can product managers leverage the capabilities of other parts of the company?

The Planning Process

1. What is the basic approach to tactical and strategic planning?
2. Is it more likely that the company will grow by acquisition, penetration of new markets, or increased market share?
3. To what extent are documented objectives used in planning?
4. Where is the emphasis placed for the development of new products (e.g., product-line extensions, new applications, new-product ventures)?
5. What are the plans for global or international growth?
6. What significant new products are under development?

Other Functional Areas

1. What is the background of the research and development manager?
2. What is the overall caliber of the research staff?
3. What is the company's technical position?
4. Does the company have idle plants and excess capacity?
5. What is the major research and development thrust?
6. How is R&D organized?

Your Strategic Product Vision

Earlier, in the Komatsu example, we looked at a long-term vision statement for a company and saw how it related to short- and medium-term strategies. Product managers should have similar vision statements (or goals) for their areas of responsibility, tied to the corporate vision. Samsung's vision to move from laggard to leader in consumer electronics had a significant impact on the firm's products. (See Business Brief 5.3,

"Samsung's Vision.") What would you like your product offering to "look like" three or five years into the future? What new products, services, or technologies do you expect will exist? Will you be serving the same customers, or will you have added new market segments? How large will your product offering be (in terms of market share, volume, or product categories)?

Business Brief 5.3

SAMSUNG'S VISION

The Korean company, Samsung Electronics, began to reinvent itself several years ago from a me-too producer of electronics to a designer of "cool gadgets." Yun Jong-Yong, Samsung's chief executive, had a vision "to be the Mercedes of home electronics." To accomplish this, Samsung focused on keeping its product designs at the leading edge without losing relevance to its users.

Designers worked in three- to five-person teams from various specialties; this was a departure from its historical top-down tradition. Many of the new designs came from outside the company and were built on a commitment to customer research and testing. In 2004, Samsung won 5 citations in the Industrial Design Excellence Awards (IDEA)—more than any American or European rival—and 33 total awards in top design contests in the United States, Europe, and Asia. The designs increased Samsung's brand value and market share.

While some analysts question whether Samsung has the breadth and depth to achieve its vision, there's no question that it has made progress toward it. The future will depend on its ability to continue to anticipate customer demands and maintain an advantage over the competition.

Source: David Rocks and Moon Ihlwan, "Samsung Design," *BusinessWeek* (December 6, 2004) pp. 88–96.

Sometimes it's useful to think in terms of writing a future (and a somewhat hypothetical) annual report just for your area of responsibility. If you are responsible for new product development, envision the new products that will be part of your portfolio. If you are not responsible for new products (e.g., your job is a "downstream" position focused on supporting the sales effort), envision the competitive position your product will have in the future. Commit this vision to paper. As you work through your analyses, the vision may need to be tweaked or adapted—but that shouldn't be a major stumbling block for an entrepreneurial product manager.

A common challenge of managers of multiple products is balancing the demands of the complete portfolio with individual products and new with existing products. If the number of products is small, set an objective for each one. If the number of products is too large for that to be practical, there are at least three possible approaches. One is to identify the key products (similar to identifying the key accounts in your customer base), or categorizing them into reinforce, renew, relaunch, and retire groupings (as explained in Chapter 10). Then develop individual goals for those products and a broad, overall objective for the remaining products. A second approach is to group products by customer segment or application (if relevant), and establish goals on that basis. The third approach is a combination of product and market goals.

In any event, be prepared to make changes in emphasis dictated by changes in the marketplace. PepsiCo, for example, decided to shift its flagship brand to Diet Pepsi rather than regular Pepsi because obesity concerns and aging baby boomers affected sales. While the company isn't about to drastically cut marketing expenditures for the main product, it has increased its marketing spending on Diet Pepsi.[2]

As part of the goal-setting and visioning process, product managers sometimes have to think in terms of a portfolio or portfolios. Product managers often balance three different types of portfolios consisting of R&D concepts, work-in-process new products, and existing products. (See Figure 5.3.) The first portfolio contains potential product ideas for the future. Some items may be simply ideas in a database, whereas others are being researched, but they are not yet at a point to be entered into the new product pipeline. These are ideas truly at the "fuzzy front end"

FIGURE 5.3 ➤ Product portfolios

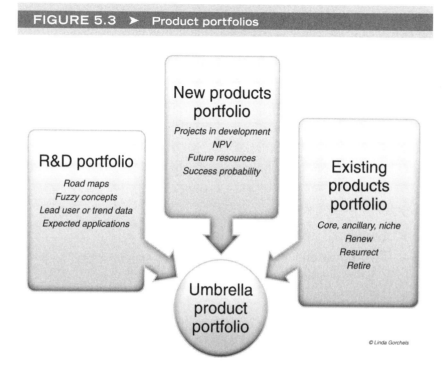

New products
portfolio

Projects in development
NPV
Future resources
Success probability

R&D portfolio

Road maps
Fuzzy concepts
Lead user or trend data
Expected applications

Existing
products
portfolio

Core, ancillary, niche
Renew
Resurrect
Retire

Umbrella
product
portfolio

© Linda Gorchels

of development. The second portfolio consists of product concepts somewhere in the development process. Product managers enter ideas into the new product pipeline and guide them through development. The final portfolio contains assets that generate current cash flow for the organization. As stewards of this portfolio, product managers determine the best approaches to profitable life-cycle management. The first two portfolios are part of upstream activities, and the final one is the world of downstream product management.

The total portfolio plan should specify the mix of new and existing products. A product portfolio—similar to a stock portfolio—is a group of investments. This group of investments should increase long-term profitability by balancing risk. Since forecasting sales and profitability is at best an inexact science, product managers strive to have some products that are low risk and some that are high risk (assuming an expected high return). DuPont, for example, determined that it was diverting too many resources—two-thirds of its R&D budget—to making improvements on existing products rather than investing in new ones. In 2003 the split was 50–50, with a goal of increasing to 65 percent the spending of the R&D budget on new products.[3]

Going back to the concept of portfolios, let's cover some basic definitions and move into more detail on each. A *portfolio* is a set of products (i.e., existing assets and/or planned investments) that provides an appropriate level of diversification to minimize random risk. Financial planners stress the importance of diversification. Since the duration, intensity, and frequency of market changes are hard to predict, a mix of funds helps manage risk. These tips apply to product portfolios as well.

In *The Secret Code of the Superior Investor* (Three Rivers Press, 2002), James Glassman suggests that superior investors:

- Are not outsmarters but are partakers
- Own a portfolio that looks like the U.S. economy might look 10 years from now
- Know the kinds of investments they should (and should not) be making
- Understand when to start selling, thereby rebalancing portfolios on a regular basis

Each of these four financial points has a product corollary. Successful portfolio managers don't try to outsmart the market. They realize that they will never have perfect information. Even though they may strive to select the best stocks, they participate broadly so shocks in one sector can be softened by successes in another. Companies beyond the start-up phase are well advised to look for a mix of new products that have varying risk/return profiles, have short- and long-term cash generation, and are planned to avoid being at the same point in the development cycle at the same time. It's worth noting that first-mover advantages are often illusory, and unless the market is truly ready for a new product, the first to market may fail.

Portfolio managers who invest for the long haul invest in a portfolio that looks like the future. For product managers, products that are part of the R&D portfolio or in the new products portfolio should fit the future marketplace of customers and competitors rather than today's marketplace. Product managers should focus on future scenarios and conduct solution brainstorming to be sure there will be complete solutions for customers when the products are launched.

Financial portfolio managers not only look at what they *should* invest in, but also consider what does not fit. Product managers should be sure new and existing products are aligned with business strategies, brand architecture, and external factors.

Finally, portfolio managers are prepared to sell as necessary. They recommend rebalancing a portfolio on a regular basis as priorities change. The corollary for product managers is that they must be prepared to expose products and projects to "kill" criteria—and follow through as necessary. As projects are evaluated, some shift in their overall importance to the firm and may require a reprioritization of time and resources. This final step might affect pipeline management—the spacing of new product projects throughout the stage-gate (new product development) process.

Compare where you are *now* with where you *want to go* long term. Product managers may need to devise separate plans (or separate sections of an overall plan) to address the requirements of different products or product categories. The gap between where you are and where you want to go will likely require more than one year's effort. Therefore, you must decide what you will do *this* year to move one step closer to where you want to be.

WHAT ARE YOU GOING TO ACCOMPLISH DURING THIS PLANNING CYCLE?

The next step—defining what you will accomplish this year—actually has several components, including an objective, a target market definition, and a positioning statement. It starts with the identification of problems and opportunities that need to be addressed in the annual plan. Then it moves to the forecast of sales volume, the marketing objectives that specify the market segments from which the volume will be generated, and the positioning of the product in the customers' minds.

Problems and Opportunities

After examining the market, the competition, the historical performance, and any significant trends, you need to synthesize that information to look for problems or opportunities and decide where to go from there. Problems or opportunities are the conclusions drawn from any part of the background analysis. For example, the analysis might uncover new niches that previously had been overlooked, a declining market share that was camouflaged by a growing market segment, or an inconsistent product image. In any case, focus on problems to correct or opportunities to leverage in the plan. Without this step of drawing conclusions, the data collection process is often perceived as a waste of time and not relevant.

Forecasts should be linked to both problems/opportunities and to the annual objectives. Frequently a product manager is given a financial sales goal, and his or her job is to design a program to make it happen. In other cases, the product manager must present the sales forecast to management with a justification or rationale. Typically, there is some combination of the two approaches.

Sales Forecasting

The product manager is responsible for forecasting product sales or, at a minimum, understanding the forecasts received. There are three categories of forecasting techniques that might be used:

1. *Time series forecasts* are based on historical data about past product sales. This is appropriate for short-term sales figures.
2. *Compiled forecasts*, as the term implies, are compilations of data from qualitative and quantitative research.
3. *Causal forecasts* are derived from relating sales to the factors that cause the sales to happen.

Time Series Forecasts

A logical place to start forecasting future sales is to look at historical sales patterns. Time series analyses look at changes in sales over time. Plotting a product's sales over time gives the product manager a picture of the product's sales trends. Trend-fitting, or regression, plots the sales over time and uses a statistical formula to fit a line through the data points and then project that line into the future. It can be accurate in the short term if there are no external factors that make the future sales environment significantly different from the past sales environment.

There are several averages that are based on time series. A moving average forecasts sales using a given number of time periods from the past (e.g., the average of the past 12 months' data). Each data point has the same weight unless seasonal indexes or other weights are built in. As the average moves into the future, it drops off the oldest data point from the calculations. Exponential smoothing is a form of moving average that provides heavier weights to the most recent data. This is done when it is assumed that recent data are more valuable in predicting future sales than are older data.

Time series techniques are appropriate when the sales environment does not change and when the effectiveness of a plan has no impact on sales. Generally, neither of these is true. As a result, it may be necessary to add other approaches.

Compiled Forecasts

Forecasts can result from compiling secondary and primary data, as well as qualitative and quantitative data. Some of the secondary data can be pulled from your product fact book. For example, look at average market share over time. Multiply this average by the projected industry sales for the next fiscal year to get an approximate sales forecast based on the industry projection. Adjust this forecast using qualitative information on trends or other elements that could influence product sales.

Salespeople often provide estimated sales by account or territory, and regional managers provide estimates by distributor or channel type. An example sales force customer analysis form is shown in Table 5.2. In the example, the salespeople are asked to estimate sales for each major account for selected products, with their best estimate of the probability of closing the sale during the upcoming quarter. The form can be adapted to include volume rather than dollar revenue, annual rather than quarterly estimates, or other industry-specific variables. The product manager can calculate the expected values by multiplying the sales estimates for each product by the relevant probabilities. In the example, the expected sales of Product A for this particular salesperson would be $3,150 (the sum of the sales times the probability for each account). Customers can also be surveyed directly to assess their probable purchases by product or for the entire line.

Table 5.2

Sales Force Customer Analysis Form

Account	Product A		Product B		Product C	
	Sales	Probability	Sales	Probability	Sales	Probability
Vaporware	$1,000	0.60	$600	0.60	$400	0.60
Tunnel Vision	2,000	0.50	700	0.80	700	0.60
Virus-Aid	1,500	0.70	900	0.75	300	0.90
Data Notes	1,000	0.50	600	0.85	500	0.80

Qualitative forecasting techniques are also useful, particularly for new products. Concept testing, in conjunction with intent-to-buy surveys, can yield a rough estimate. Another tool is the Delphi technique. This involves gathering independent forecasts from select experts, sharing the rationale for the forecasts without identifying which expert gave which rationale, and continuing until the forecasts converge. The process eliminates the peer pressure that exists with committee or group forecasts since the input is "blind."

Causal or Correlation-Based Forecasts

Causal techniques attempt to find relationships between sales and other variables. For example, tire sales are related to vehicular sales, and sales of many household products are related to housing starts. If there are leading indicators (such as vehicle sales or housing starts) that can be used to better understand the sales environment for a product, they should be used in the forecasting process. Sales can also be affected by advertising expenditures, number of salespeople, price changes, or other marketing variables. If a causal relationship between a change in marketing expenditures and a change in sales can be demonstrated, that information can be used not only in forecasting, but also as justification for spending a given amount in the marketing plan.

The forecasted sales figures used in a marketing plan should be based on a variety of inputs. Do not rely exclusively on trend projections, and do not accept upper management's sales forecasts without question. Try to reconcile the unit and dollar amounts based on the background analysis and the anticipated marketing plan/budget.

Setting Objectives

Objectives answer the question, "What are you going to do this year to move a step closer from where you are now to where you want to be?" They also answer the question, "What do you need to do to reach the sales forecast?" Let's say that you have categorized your products into reinforce, renew, and retire (as described in Chapter 10), with ten, three, and two products, respectively. You decide that the 10 maintenance (protect) products will require *no* changes in marketing, so that leaves five products to focus on. Define what results you want to obtain by year end for each product (i.e., the objectives), and state it in terms that are SMART:

*S*pecific
*M*easurable
*A*ttainable
*R*esults-oriented
*T*ime-bound

Specific objectives are quantitative, such as a given percentage of increase in market share, unit growth in volume, or a specified number of product trials. *Measurable* refers to the ability to track results. Having a goal of, say, reaching 32 percent of scientists with artificial limbs is specific but would be very difficult to measure. Being *attainable* is subjective. Goals, by their very nature, require a change in the status quo, but if they are impossible to attain, they are really dreams. The *results-oriented* criterion is perhaps the most important. If the objectives specify the results (rather than the activities) you strive to achieve, they accomplish two things. They provide direction for the plan, and they become a metric against which to compare actual performance. *When* to compare these results metrics against actual performance is bound by the final criterion, *time*.

Objectives can be stated in terms of units or dollars (revenue and/or margin), market share, consumer satisfaction level, and so on. Emphasis should be given to the specific target customers you will focus on and may include customer acquisition and retention goals.

Typically the objective starts with a verb (increase, maintain, solidify, etc.) acting on a specific goal (repeat purchases, new trial,

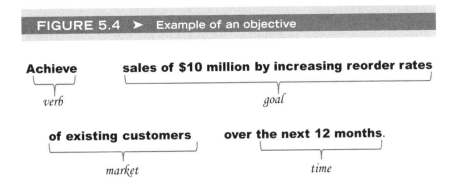

FIGURE 5.4 ➤ Example of an objective

Achieve **sales of $10 million by increasing reorder rates**

verb *goal*

of existing customers **over the next 12 months**.

market *time*

sales volume/revenue, etc.) for a stated market (profiled market segment or account) within a specified time period (typically a year). An example objective is shown in Figure 5.4.

Target Market

What type of customer or group of customers is the most likely to buy your product? Resist the temptation to put every possible prospect into the description. You want to focus on the "ideal" customer—the one who has the greatest need for your product, who perceives value from it, and who is likely to respond to your marketing efforts. Describe the person (and company) in archetypal terms, using both demographic and psychographic variables. The profile not only clarifies whom you are trying to reach with your marketing, but also implies whom you are not going after. The needs of this target customer drive your product design efforts, your pricing, your channel decisions, and your marketing communications. (If people who are not in your target market want to buy your product, that's fine, as long as it doesn't require a change in the factors just listed.) No product can successfully be all things to all people. Trying to make it so results in a diluted product and/or marketing position.

Sometimes to be effective in accomplishing the stated objectives, it may be necessary to go beyond the target market of users and identify the influencers who require additional marketing communications. Or it may be necessary to pursue a secondary target market by using a slightly different marketing approach. Note that this is *not* the same thing as having a shotgun approach to the market, but rather you focus on a small number of targets. There will very likely be a primary target market as well as secondary targets. The segments the product manager elects to target determine the marketing strategy as well as the product positioning and communication approaches. Several years ago Marvin Windows isolated different needs among different segments of window buyers and advanced its position from eighth to third in the industry by stressing the most relevant benefits to each group. See Business Brief 5.4, "Segmentation at Marvin Windows."

Business Brief 5.4

SEGMENTATION AT MARVIN WINDOWS

Marvin, a family-owned and controlled window manufacturer in Warroad, Minnesota, discovered the value of market segmentation in reaching its customers more effectively. By studying buying processes, it identified builders, dealers, remodelers, and architects as influence groups and designed segment-specific advertising messages to reach them. For example, remodelers wanted windows that fit existing openings and didn't require "customizing" the wall to fit a standard window. For this group, Marvin positioned itself as the made-to-order window manufacturer. In reaching building supply dealers, Marvin focused on a lowered need for inventory, thereby increasing dealer profitability. For builders and architects, Marvin emphasized its ability to meet both aesthetic and budgetary constraints.

Source: Adapted from Kate Bertrand, "Divide and Conquer," *Business Marketing* 74 (October 1989), pp. 49–50.

The target market decision will also include the marshaling of resources to get the greatest impact for the marketing investment and to accomplish an objective such as being an industry leader. Industry leadership in the past meant being the biggest and having the most visible brands. Now, with markets fragmenting, leadership can be defined with a niche concept. By focusing a firm's resources on smaller segments, the firm becomes more visible and gains a perception of leadership in that segment:

> *The most important insight is the degree to which this whole concept validates the merits of a "niche" or "focus" strategy—seeking to become a large fish in a small pond. A brand of ice cream or beer carried in 500 retail outlets will benefit disproportionately if all those outlets are in Iowa, not spread over the Midwest, and even more if they are in Des Moines. A business-to-business marketer can achieve the same level of visibility and "leadership position" by focusing on one industry. Becoming the leading supplier of inventory software for meatpackers may be not only a feasible objective, but also one that confers all the "snowball" benefits of brand leadership within that industry.[4]*

Positioning Statement

With even the most careful targeting of customers, product managers will not escape competition and will need to develop a well-thought-out positioning statement. While the selection of a target market identifies *whom* you are going after, the selection of a positioning strategy identifies *what perception* these customers should have of your product compared with that of the competition. Different positioning alternatives are described in the branding chapter. Here it becomes necessary to convert the thinking into a statement that becomes the foundation for several subsequent marketing activities. Repositioning is occasionally necessary because of changing conditions, as Hewlett-Packard found out when it introduced inkjet printers as alternatives to dot matrix printers. (See Business Brief 5.5, "Repositioning the Deskjet.")

Business Brief 5.5

HEWLETT-PACKARD: REPOSITIONING THE DESKJET

Hewlett-Packard introduced the DeskJet in 1988. Sales came slowly. By 1989, the product wasn't meeting its sales goals even though there was an absence of strong competition. An analysis determined that the DeskJet was taking business away from HP's own laser printers rather than the competition. This resulted in a lower profit margin per sale.

After identifying the problem, HP decided to reposition the Desk-Jet as a competitor to dot-matrix printers rather than as a lower-cost alternative to laser printers. To attain this objective, HP started by thoroughly studying Epson, the leader in the industry. The company began to track Epson's market share. It evaluated Epson's marketing practices, profiled its top managers, and surveyed its customers. Engineers tore apart Epson printers to better understand the technology used. HP discovered that Epson printers were placed in prominent spots in stores, customers perceived the printers as reliable, and the products were designed for easy manufacture.

Armed with this information, Hewlett-Packard planned the actions that were necessary to reposition the DeskJet. First, the company convinced stores to place DeskJets next to the Epson dot-matrix printers to emphasize the competitive positioning. Second, HP extended its warranty to three years to assure buyers that the DeskJet was reliable. And finally, the inkjets were redesigned with manufacturability in mind.

Source: Adapted from Stephen Kreider Yoder, "How HP Used Tactics of the Japanese to Beat Them at Their Game," *Wall Street Journal* (September 8, 1994), pp. 1+.

Positioning refers to deciding how a product is to be perceived in the minds of the customer relative to the competition. Imagine talking to a customer who asks, "Why should I buy from you?" What should your answer be? What makes your product a better buy than competitive products? In this analysis, consider the customer's frame of reference (i.e., the products they would consider likely competitors). Different customers will have different frames of reference that could require different positioning. Therefore, the positioning statement should identify the relevant market segment, that segment's frame of reference, the product's point of differentiation, and an indication of

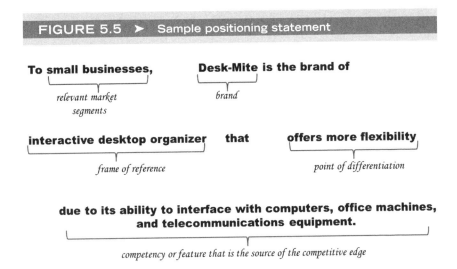

FIGURE 5.5 ➤ Sample positioning statement

To small businesses,   **Desk-Mite is the brand of**

relevant market segments   brand

interactive desktop organizer   **that**   **offers more flexibility**

frame of reference   point of differentiation

due to its ability to interface with computers, office machines, and telecommunications equipment.

competency or feature that is the source of the competitive edge

why a product provides that differentiation (i.e., the internal strength or competitive edge that makes a claim of differentiation credible). A sample positioning statement is shown in Figure 5.5.

Start by identifying the attributes customers are looking for when they buy from the product category, and find out how important each attribute is. Is delivery important? How about minimum tolerances? Next, have customers rate the product in question and all its important attributes compared to the competition. Try to isolate attributes for which customers already believe the product is competitively superior and that the company can protect using its core abilities, knowledge, or other strength. If this cannot be determined, the job of the product manager is to determine how to build it into the product.

Planning FACTS

To help you be more effective in step 3 ("What are you going to do this year to come closer to your long-term vision?") and step 4 ("What actions will help you accomplish the objective?"), I want to introduce you to my FACTS of planning. (See Figure 5.6.) FACTS is an acronym for some of the most common generic tools of planning and implementation: flowcharts, action maps, checklists, templates, and schedules:

■ *Flowcharts* are diagrammatic representations of operations, activities, and decisions, with symbols to indicate the various

FIGURE 5.6 ➤ Planning FACTS

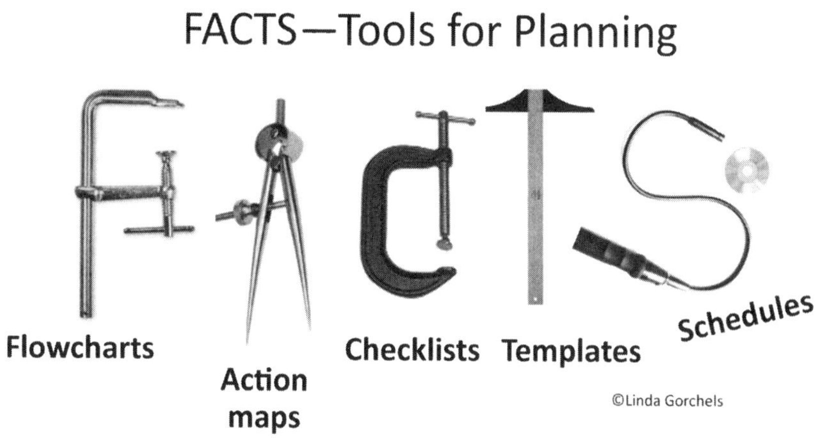

FACTS—Tools for Planning

Flowcharts   Checklists Templates Schedules

Action
maps   ©Linda Gorchels

phases of a process. Stage-gate processes, activity networks (such as critical path and PERT), and other step-by-step sequencing of phases are examples. (Some types of flowcharts, for example, are affinity diagrams, which capture information useful as an input into planning, so I include them as input rather than as part of the planning and implementation.)

■ *Action maps* are visual or textual representations of future direction. Longer-term maps, such as technology road maps, scenario plans, and portfolio strategies may or may not provide detailed activities and decisions. Shorter-term maps, such as verbal descriptions of activities, tactics, and financials provide more complex details for implementation.

■ *Checklists* are very basic listings of tasks but can be quite powerful because of their simplicity. Checklists of important standard tasks to be completed prior to a product launch or a gate review meeting can reduce the probability of a critical piece of a plan falling short.

■ *Templates* are generally simple fill-in-the-blank worksheets. Similar to checklists they help minimize the chance of a product manager overlooking an important element of a plan. However, as mentioned above, it's important that they not be used as a substitute for adequate examination of data during the planning process.

■ *Schedules*, the last item in the FACTS toolbox, are essentially annotated calendars with specific individuals assigned specific dates to complete required activities. As such they are necessary for assigning responsibility and deadlines for implementation of plans. While any of these could be used at any point in the planning process, flowcharts and action maps are most useful for analysis and process, whereas checklists, templates, and schedules are important tools for compliance (with internal requirements) and implementation.

Throughout this book I supply examples of each of the FACTS tools. There is an example process flowchart in Chapter 4, a description of road maps in Chapter 6, checklists provided for several activities, sample templates throughout the chapters, and a description of schedules in the new product development discussion. While all of these tools serve a purpose, they are worthless without the discipline to act on them.

HOW ARE YOU GOING TO ACCOMPLISH YOUR OBJECTIVES?

Step 4 of the process details the activities and tactics expected to accomplish the stated objectives. Product managers should keep in mind the role of objectives versus tactics. Since the objectives are the desired results of the plan, they are more "concrete," while the tactics should be more fluid and responsive to the environment. In most situations you should be more flexible in the tactics than in the objectives. The relative stability of objectives married with the flexibility of tactics yields a dynamically stable plan.

The purpose of a plan is to provide top management with a concise summary of objectives and strategies along with the requirements to achieve the objectives. There should be enough rationale to enable top managers to approve the necessary expenditures without the detail available in a product fact book. Keep the plan as brief as possible, perhaps no more than six to ten pages. Too much detail obscures the main issues. Product managers are not paid to make the inevitable happen, so it's not necessary to include the ordinary routines of your job in the plan. Focus on the surprises—the things you will change—and relegate the mundane to an appendix. (Typical contents of a product plan are described in Table 5.3.)

Table 5.3

Components of a Typical Product Plan

Category	Description
Vision statement	Concisely define the future directions of your product portfolio and how this particular plan fits in. Link your plan to corporate goals and visions as necessary.
Goals or objectives	State the long-term goals or short-term objectives in the SMART format. Add composite profit projections and augment them with target market profiles and positioning—unless they are addressed more specifically by product later in the plan.
Internal review	Summarize high-level product performance history, as well as product and company strengths and weaknesses relevant to this plan. If specific templates or checklists ensure compliance with company goals, include them here.
External review	Summarize high-level components of the TIME analysis relevant to this plan. Include your insights as to what these mean for your product portfolio.
Product innovation	Describe key product development activities, projects, and initiatives that fit within the planning cycle, including any launch initiatives. Highlight forecasts, market profiles, competitive benchmarks, and "reasons to believe."
Life-cycle management	Describe efforts for reinforcing, reviewing, relaunching, or retiring products during this planning cycle. Attach forecasts, market profiles, and positioning by product or product category as appropriate. Include rationales and assumptions.
Resource requirements	Explain what support (people, time, money, operations, competencies, etc.) will be required to realize this plan.
Stakeholder involvement	Specify the people whose functions will necessarily contribute to the execution of the plan and what their roles will be. This should include both internal partners (such as R&D and marketing) and external partners (channel, supply chain, lead users, and others).
Appendices	Include financials (P&L), supporting research, and continuation of ongoing activities from prior plans.

On the other hand, do not use the desire for brevity as an excuse for not collecting information. If some information needed to support a recommendation is not available, mention it in the plan (at least as a footnote) to demonstrate that critical data are not being ignored, but that there is sufficient confidence with the other information to justify taking the risk. Include other assumptions you've made that might have an impact on the validity of the plan.

If the product plan is to be presented orally as part of a meeting, be sure to come prepared to answer any questions that might arise. Nothing is more frustrating to top management than to reschedule a meeting or make it longer than necessary because of a product manager's lack of preparation.

Several objectives in the product plan may be necessary in order to reach a stated sales forecast. For example, a product objective could be to attain sales of $X for each of three major products. The supporting strategy would explain what modifications this would require in terms of quality improvements, "bundling," or new uses. The rationale would explain why this is possible given the background analysis.

Branding and packaging might or might not be a crucial part of the plan, but they should at least be considered. Be sure that customers' needs are addressed and explain why a specific product satisfies a particular need better than the competition does. Also mention the effect of other products on the product line and/or the effect of the line on the company product mix. If some maintenance products will be self-sustaining during the fiscal year, mention that fact and include the routine activities in an appendix.

You might want to keep plans for new products separate because they usually cover a different time period from the annual plan's time period. However, because they affect a product manager's bottom line, they should probably be summarized here. New product specifications, positioning, budget, and event schedules can be included.

The plan is an investment in the product's future equity and should have a positive impact on the current year's sales. Therefore, a profit and loss statement should be included either here or in the appendix.

WHAT ARE YOUR METRICS FOR TRACKING RESULTS?

The highest level metric for your plan is the attainment of the results you specified in your objectives. However, you probably don't want to wait until the end of the year (or whatever the planning cycle is) to measure progress. Rather, build into the plan checkpoints where you can determine if you are on track or whether corrective action should be taken. Beyond revenue, metrics could include customer responsiveness on sales calls, percent of distributors stocking the product, requests for demos, Internet buzz, or similar measures. The sooner you can adapt and flex your tactics, the higher the likelihood is that you will reach your goals.

CHAPTER CHALLENGE

Spend sufficient time on developing clear and correct objectives before *you decide on tactics and action items—and be sure the objectives guide you toward* results. *Then practice* dynamic stability *by flexing tactics as necessary to maintain progress toward these results.*

INTERVIEW WITH BRAD ROGERS: PLANNING WITH A GROWTH PLAYBOOK

Brad Rogers, Director of Enterprise Integration and Process Excellence, TIAA-CREF , BradRogers@tiaa-cref.org. (He can also be found on LinkedIn.)

Brad, you've been heavily involved in process excellence for several firms, from TIAA-CREF to Bank of America, to GE. Can you talk a bit about your most recent efforts to enhance the product management function at TIAA-CREF?

Sure. We are definitely focusing considerable effort on improving our product management function at TIAA-CREF, striving for a world-class capability. First, let me mention that we look at the product management function as one of four key capabilities in our *growth ecosystem*: product management, product development, innovation, and governance. Our goal is to enable growth and retention in all of our product sets by defining and then building a discipline and culture of product excellence and innovation. I am leading that effort.

Regarding our efforts in defining, building, and operationalizing an enhanced product and product portfolio management function, we have determined that there are several key elements that comprise the full capability, with each element being built out in a multigenerational fashion. I'll describe a couple of the elements. One of those elements of product management is *strategy and execution*, which emphasizes the annual product planning process containing key high-level stages with deliverables. A key output is a thoughtful document we call the product plan or sometimes *the growth playbook*. It contains the description of both the "thinking" part of the product management process (including value proposition, voice of customer, competitor information, and strategy maps), and also the "doing" part of the plan (the goals, three-year plan, and partnership agreements). I feel it is a critical discipline for driving growth and excellence in a product or portfolio, year after year.

A second critical element of the product management capability is *talent*, for which we developed a multiyear road map to world-class status. First let me say that our talent was already first rate. Nevertheless, we developed a training curriculum that included strategic agility, financial acumen, negotiation, go-to-market, design thinking (innovation), VOC (voice-of-customer) research, and more.

Tell me more about the "growth playbook" you mentioned earlier. What have you learned and what have been your successes using that as part of the process?

As I mentioned, the product management process follows an annual cadence that begins with an assessment of the current situation, then measurement and analysis of gaps and root causes, then identification of interventions and corrective action plans, and finally execution. This high-level annual process is actually modeled after best-practice continuous improvement methodologies. Key outputs are rigorous, fact-based, and vetted intervention decisions described in an integrated product plan document (that we call our growth playbook). Some key learnings and successes are:

- *Strategic planning:* This type of process and documentation drives bottom-up thinking and planning that is tightly integrated with the top-down corporate strategic planning process and the annual budgeting process. I like to say that it gets a company out of the business of "brainstorming for projects" every year. One learning is that everyone has his or her own vision of what a product plan ought to look like, so developing a template with the proper balance of prescription and flexibility to tell your own story is important.

- *Governance, resource allocation, and decision making:* Ideally, this is part of an annual process and a documented product plan facilitates the management of an entire portfolio and the choices and trade-offs between products. The product plan helps the governance team understand the rationale, potential, and trade-offs of executing the plan. A key success I've seen is when the product plan includes the specific commitments, objectives, and resource expectations for each key partner involved in developing and executing the plan. A key learning is having a governance team with representatives from the key units to facilitate capacity planning and sequencing across a portfolio. Another key learning is that governance teams have two primary goals: (1) make risk/reward decisions and (2) allocate resources. Product plan governance meetings should avoid being forums used for design sessions or for risk assessments; they need to be decision-oriented.

- *"Who's the boss?"* In large, matrixed organizations and a variety of budget/resource pools, it can be challenging to develop a cross-functional macro plan because of competing goals and priorities. A single plan involving multiple key players, such as product, marketing, distribution/sales, and IT begs the question, "Who's the boss?" A key success I've seen is when we behave as if the *plan* is the boss. And since we all created the plan, the turf issues subside. A key learning is that this thinking and behavior need to be reinforced through monthly governance routines. The skills of a world-class product organization make them a natural to be the leader of leaders in developing the plan.

I believe you mentioned that you won an award for your innovation program at Bank of America. Can you elaborate on what you did and on the result of your efforts?

While I was at Bank of America, I was part of a team that studied innovative companies to determine what it takes to grow organically. The team found that sustainable innovation requires much more than a flow of ideas. In fact there were several variables that showed strong correlation to growth through innovation, including; a "batting average" culture, protected funding, talent management, true growth aspirations with commitment from the top, and an innovation process that allowed for more than product innovation, but innovation in services, customer experience, processes, and business models.

It was very fun and exciting, as innovation was seen as a leadership trait and not an eye-roller. A steady stream of new ideas, customer insights, and new thinking was seen as necessary to enable differentiation and improve the attractiveness of the value proposition.

To recognize this commitment to innovation and the ability of these processes to consistently develop successful new products, the Product Development and Management Association (PDMA) awarded the bank the Outstanding Corporate Innovator award, the first time for a financial services company.

Congratulations on the award! Can we step back a few comments? What do you mean by "batting average" culture?

A "batting average" culture expects that a certain percentage of the new idea/new product portfolio will not pan out as expected.

Otherwise, counting on a 100 percent success rate for a pipeline of inherently risky endeavors will likely drive counterproductive behaviors that suppress the culture and benefits of innovation.

Your professional path has been quite varied. Give us a capsule overview of your career, and how you got from where you were to where you are.

Indeed my path has been varied, with a common thread of designing and building world-class capabilities, businesses, or products.

Over 20 years ago, I began my career as an aerodynamic/ thermodynamic engineer in a management training program alongside two senior executives at Parsons Brinkerhoff, the largest pure design firm in the United States. Engineering was a very influential experience as I learned how major, one-of-a-kind projects require innovative thinking up front and highly integrated blueprints from many disciplines. At one point I was project manager for the biggest full-scale primary research project on fires in tunnels to develop design standards for the "Big Dig" in Boston. Imagine over 90 tanker-scale fires in an abandoned auto tunnel in the mountains of West Virginia!

After getting my MBA at night, I was recruited by Arthur Andersen, a major management consulting firm, where I led several transformation and reengineering efforts at Fortune 500 companies, including Panasonic, Merrill Lynch, the *New York Times*, and several insurance companies. I went from an engineer to a reengineer! At one point, a colleague and I defined a new methodology to focus more on the "revenue enhancement" needs of companies, rather than cost-out. I was bitten by the growth bug. Major learnings and influences I got from consulting related to the critical importance of change management—the people side of transformation, and the skill and discipline of selling an idea or solution that will change the buyer's organization.

I was recruited by GE, where my business DNA was influenced forever by being immersed in a culture that relentlessly pursued being the absolute best in leadership, discipline, culture, and results—indeed in those days it was the most admired company in the world. I was trained and certified as a Six Sigma Master Black Belt and worked for some incredibly inspiring leaders. Going from engineer to consultant to MBB, I was sold on leveraging the tools, discipline, and philosophy of Six Sigma to drive growth. I applied them to the front end of three different GE businesses; two were completely redesigned (25 percent year-over-year growth and 70 percent core growth in two years) and one was a major start-up. I researched and visited best-of-breed product development companies and developed our own new product introduction process. My leadership roles spanned new product introduction, sales force effectiveness, fulfillment, and strategic marketing. My unit ended up getting sold, and I was asked by Bank of America to join a very special team to drive growth.

At Bank of America, as SVP-innovation and product excellence executive for Global Wealth and Investment Management, I led a team that developed a growth process and framework that included new product development, product management, and repeatable innovation capabilities. We trained the product managers and implemented the discipline for over 20 product portfolios. In those days, the corporate goal was to be the most admired financial institution in the world. I was very much influenced by seeing how a credible vision of customer-centric excellence and a commitment to a disciplined approach united and mobilized a huge workforce. I saw the culture change right before my own eyes, and it was impressive.

After that I was recruited by TIAA-CREF to help them drive growth and excellence, some of which I've described in your first question.

What major piece of advice would you share with product managers planning their careers?

In my mind, a key measure of the effectiveness of product managers is their ability to attract, mobilize, and motivate the resources to optimize their product. This requires an ability to (1) craft and sell compelling business cases; (2) negotiate, collaborate, and execute on plans; and (3) demonstrate leadership to gain followership.

Taking roles that build these experiences would help accumulate a strong, complementary product management skill set. I would add that the ability to sell is not about flash but about credibility, which can be built with aligned priorities, empathy for the customer and stakeholders, support of influencers, and confidence you can deliver.

PART II

UPSTREAM PRODUCT MANAGEMENT: STRATEGIC NEW PRODUCTS AND INITIATIVES

CHAPTER 6

Road Maps, Innovation, and the Fuzzy Front End

TRUE OR FALSE: Long-term planning is not useful since the future is unknowable.

Whether this statement is considered true or false may cause some argument. I believe it is false. Even though the future is unknowable and long-term *plans* may become obsolete, the process of *planning* is valuable when it forces product managers to examine the context of their decisions. In fact, many people believe that the process is more important than the plan (i.e., the document).

When companies contact me to work with their product managers, the concern I hear more often than not is that their product managers "are not strategic thinkers." They would like their product managers to be focused more on the long-term future rather than on devoting all their energies to short-term tactics. That's a challenge for product managers charged with both upstream and downstream responsibilities. But in most cases it's doable.

ROAD MAPPING: DEFINING THE PRODUCT'S FUTURE PATH

The term *road map* is used in many different ways. It may be used as a tool for technology management, strategic planning, product development and launch, feature prioritization, release schedule, product marketing, or project planning. As an analogy, the technology and strategic planning versions are broad "interstate" maps (to help define direction) whereas template-driven versions are narrower "city" maps (to aid scheduling and manage complexity). In a sense the strategic versions are upstream road maps, and the template-driven ones are downstream road maps. It's important that product managers recognize the type of road map needed or expected by the company to attain their goals. In general road maps will be most appropriate when the product line is important to the company and/or requires significant resources, or when there is a recognized perceived threat in the marketplace.

While there are different types of road maps, a very common one (and the kind described here) is for future product line/portfolio planning and is more of the "interstate" or *upstream* variety. Product managers building this type of product road map must balance technology *push* against market *pull*. At the simplest level, road maps are time-based charts linking knowledge about technology, markets, and business strategy. While the concept is fairly straightforward, its application is not. It requires significant estimation about when specific technologies will be available for commercialization, when markets are ready to accept these technologies, and when appropriate resources and commitment will "fit" a firm's business strategy. No matter how sophisticated the numbers are (and no matter how detailed and glitzy the templates used), it's important to realize they are built on a variety of *assumptions* and are therefore subjective.

Road mapping is a process of compiling information (i.e., planning), whereas the ultimate road map is the output (i.e., the plan). As suggested earlier, the *process* may be very valuable even though the resulting document may require constant revision. The value of the process is in forcing individuals to articulate their assumptions and in *integrating* information. As a result, it encourages consensus, contributes to better forecasting, and provides a framework for thinking about the future. The process may uncover promising new technologies, "repurpose" parts from different products and designs, and/or help align technology road maps with suppliers. Motorola, for example, tries to select components and suppliers *before* design takes place. By developing multiyear technology road maps, Motorola is able to source suppliers that have the needed capabilities and willingness to invest in technology alignment.[1]

A starting point for the process of upstream product road-mapping may include regular innovation meetings with suppliers, technology experts, lead users, market experts, and others who may be able to contribute to a futuristic road map. A Frito Lay product manager once shared with me that she used gourmet chefs as part of her innovation meetings to identify potential future ideas for retail food products. Harley-Davidson, Motorola, and others solicit the input of suppliers to identify potential components or technologies that may be used in future products. At a minimum, product managers should solicit cross-functional internal perspectives while going through the process.

These are the possible steps to developing a road map to support a company's global growth strategy. The team members may have expertise in (or knowledge of) the competitive landscape, market drivers and trends, corporate resources and vision, international product/regulatory requirements, operational capabilities, technology trends, and product architecture. Each would provide, on a timeline, general information about his or her area of expertise. This may include anticipated dates for new competitive products, tipping point dates for changes in customer product usage, dates when new regulations will be in effect, dates when the company is intending to penetrate specific global markets, and similar factors. Then the group would attempt to align all the factors and dates in a way that provides direction for the product portfolio.

Shifting from the process to the result, road maps are both forecasts of what may happen and general plans that define a course of action. The format may include tables, graphs, flow charts, bubble charts, or basic text. The output may be a table with dates as column headings, and rows for different target geographic markets. The intersecting cells (of target market/date) will indicate (at a high level) the product variation to be launched at that time. Each cell will have a related and more detailed plan of action.

INNOVATION: BALANCING BREAKTHROUGHS AND INCREMENTAL CHANGES

While road maps can be useful for both breakthroughs and incremental changes, the innovation and ideation processes can be somewhat different. Ideation is the process of exploring diverse and potentially "hidden" ideas for new products and services. It should flow from (or at least not be inconsistent with) product strategy initiatives. As a process, ideation is ongoing and actually exists separate from new product development. Product managers should be continually tuned in to potential idea sources and keep looking for opportunities when the time is right.

There are numerous sources of product ideas, and product managers must always expand their idea network. Road maps and product strategies are an obvious nucleus for ideas. Brown-bag lunches with R&D, sales force input, customer service, supply chain partners, competitive comparisons, and customer requests could yield possibilities for revenue generation ideas. Market and technology trends may open up new opportunities that you had not previously considered. Be open to both market-pull and technology-push ideas that might have merit for your product portfolio.

Incomplete ideas need to be enriched and converted into revenue opportunities for further evaluation. Customer research is one obvious way to enrich ideas. This can take several paths. Input from *typical* customers through surveys or sales force input can highlight current product deficiencies (but is less likely to identify totally novel products). Customer visit programs are a form of ethnographic research that might uncover unarticulated product gaps, needs, or opportunities. Some of the changes might be simple product modifications, while others might be innovative breakthroughs. Ideas for breakthroughs are more likely to come from lead user research or open innovation.

Lead user research, championed by Professor Eric von Hippel from the MIT Sloan School of Management, focuses on gathering ideas from people or industries that are already solving problems you are grappling with. For example, von Hippel explained how the automotive industry obtained several ideas for antilock brakes from the aerospace industry. His Web site, www.leaduser.com, contains several videos describing the process of lead user innovation.

Open innovation—a term coined by Henry Chesbrough, author of the book by that title—is another approach to broadening the scope of ideas and solutions for new product development. (Note that Chesbrough has a brief YouTube video on the concept.) The intent of open innovation is to leverage the external sources of technology and innovation to either contribute a solution to a part of a product you are developing, or occasionally provide the complete product solution.

During the past decade Procter & Gamble has made a concerted effort to increase the percentage of its products that have elements that originated from outside the company. In fact, it renamed their R&D group C&D for connect and develop. While some of the connections occur as a result of current interpersonal networks, there are several companies that exist to facilitate the process. NineSigma helps its clients prepare technical briefs and find people who can solve identified technical challenges (somewhat analogous to the approach used by headhunters to find appropriate job candidates). InnoCentive posts scientific challenges from its *seeker* clients and pays *solvers* a monetary award for a workable solution. YourEncore is composed of retired scientists and engineers who can work with clients on specific short-term innovation assignments. Yet2 acts as a channel to acquire, license, and/or sell unused patents. There is more detailed information on all these organizations on their Web sites.

Cocreation is a variant of open innovation whereby companies create products along with their customers. The most explicit example is perhaps Facebook. The company provides the platform, and individual customers create their own unique products and user experiences.[2] While not all cocreation is this direct, customer-driven product development is being aided through the use of social media. Unilever, for example, solicits feedback on ideas and prototypes through two online communities.[3]

The best research for idea generation captures insights within the context of the customers' realities. That's why ethnography can be such a useful tool. Paula Gray (in her interview at the end of Chapter 4) and Dave Franchino (in the interview toward the end of this chapter) explain how ethnography can contribute to providing a better voice of the customer for new products. Not only do product developers observe customers, but they also consider the needs of various other influencers in the purchase decision. IDEO, the design consulting firm from California, has a YouTube video describing its "deep dive" approach to product innovation. In this video, the company redesigns the shopping cart by studying how people use them in stores, gathering statistics on the risk of child injuries, and talking to retail owners and security personnel.

STRATEGIC PRODUCT THINKING

Strategic product thinking is a precursor to new product development because it forces product managers to envision a future that does not yet exist—to lead the market and create products before customers ask for them. This requires a certain level of risk and creativity. Product managers must ask themselves: How will the customers of tomorrow be different from the customers of today? What products/services will these customers expect? What existing capabilities can we expect to use in the future, and what new abilities will we need to develop? The emphasis is not on projecting the present into the future. Rather, the emphasis is on trying to understand how the future will be different from the present and the impact this will have on present planning.

Fostering a Customer Mindset

Fostering a customer mindset requires the product manager to step back and redefine the business in terms of customer functions. It may also require redefining what it means to satisfy the customer. When David Whitwam became CEO of Whirlpool, his vision was to transform the company into a customer-focused organization and to shift thinking from product to customer, as indicated in the following excerpt from an interview in *Harvard Business Review:*

> *The starting point isn't the existing product; it's the function consumers buy products to accomplish. When you return to first principles, the design issues dramatically change. The microwave couldn't have been invented by someone who assumed he or she was in the business of designing a range. Such a design breakthrough required seeing that the opportunity is "easier, quicker food preparation," not "a better range."*
>
> *Take the "fabric-care business," which we used to call the "washing-machine business." We're now studying consumer behavior from the time people take off their dirty clothes at night until they've been cleaned and ironed and hung in the closet. What are we looking for? The worst part of the process is not the washing and drying. The hard part is when you take your clothes out of the dryer and you have to do something with*

them—iron, fold, hang them up. Whoever comes up with a product to make this part of the process easier, simpler, or quicker is going to create an incredible market.[4]

Core Growth, Adjacency Growth, and Breakthrough Growth

Products can have varying levels of risk, and it is usually wise to have a portfolio of new products to balance the risk/return equation. New products with the lowest risk are line extensions—slight modifications (new and improved versions) of an existing product. Larger or smaller package sizes, stronger or weaker flavors, and lighter or heavier components are all examples of line extensions. Most of these modifications are intended to increase usage among or provide more options for current customers. This is generally referred to as core or organic growth, as shown in Figure 6.1. Most of these options have a short-term planning horizon and would be part of either the existing products portfolio or the new products portfolio.

FIGURE 6.1 ➤ Categories of new product growth

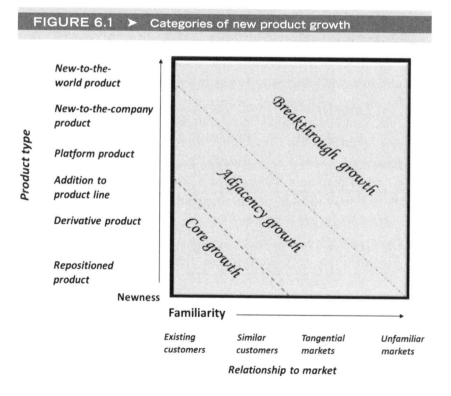

Sometimes the same (or a slightly different) product can be repositioned to reach tangential markets. The classic example of this is baking soda, which has been repositioned for numerous applications beyond baking. Bayer pain reliever extended to five models to increase usage among tangential markets such as people with arthritis or heart-attack victims. Finally, taking the existing product to a new market can be potentially profitable, but it must be marketed correctly. For example, the Bendix brake division of Allied Signal decided to increase its brake sales in the do-it-yourself (DIY) market. It discovered that its packaging didn't connote high quality, so it redesigned its packaging to incorporate a strong color blue as part of the repositioning strategy. In one year its sales moved from less than a 1 percent market share to more than a 20 percent share.

Products that are more than line extensions are also new and can be marketed to the same customer segments, tangential segments, or totally new markets. Of these three alternatives, the least risky is reaching the existing customer base through franchise extensions. A franchise extension (also referred to as a brand extension) refers to taking what the product (or brand) connotes and applying it in a different product category. For example, Arm & Hammer baking soda extended its brand franchise to detergent, toothpaste, and similar products for which the concept of "clean and fresh" was appropriate. Castle & Cooke found that its Dole brand connoted more than pineapple and used the brand name to launch Dole Fruit & Juice bars. These types of extensions can have definite benefits, but they require some strategic thinking and planning. Most of these would fall into the adjacency growth section of the new product categories.

Flanker brands are used when a company wants to enter a slightly different market segment (e.g., the cost-conscious segment) but does not want to dilute its current image. Flanker brands allow a company to retain its current position with existing customers, while still expanding into different segments. Marriott has used flanker brands to extend its position. Fairfield Inn is a low-price, low-frills product of the Marriott chain. (See Business Brief 6.1, "The Power of Line Extensions.")

Business Brief 6.1

THE POWER OF LINE EXTENSIONS

Most products will die if they are not reinvented as the marketplace changes. Since consumers now cook less (reducing the amount of aluminum foil and plastic wrap used), Reynolds and Glad Wrap introduced line extensions to revive their products. Reynolds discovered that one of the biggest complaints customers had about aluminum foil was that it stuck to food. This research led to Reynolds Release, the first variation of the product since 1947, causing an increase in usage. Clorox found that its Glad plastic wrap did not provide the leak-proof seal that consumers wanted, and soon thereafter launched Press 'n Seal.

Extending a franchise offers a number of benefits that *new-to-the-world* new product development does not. The major one is that extension capitalizes on the company's most important assets—its brand names. Thus the company moves into a new category from a position of strength. A further benefit is that investment outlays typically necessary to establish a new brand—a significant expense—are minimal. However, line extensions must offer new value to customers. Companies that are successful at line extensions tend to regularly rotate the brand assignments of their product managers to prevent them from getting stuck in ruts. This reduces the likelihood of proliferating virtually identical products.

A consumer is exposed to hundreds of brand names every day. Being a well-known brand is not sufficient to be a good brand extension. Few consumers want JELL-O shoelaces or Tide frozen entrees. A brand can be successfully extended to a new category when the brand has both fit and leverage.

- *Fit* is when the consumer accepts the new product as logical and would expect it from the brand.
- *Leverage* is when consumers, by simply knowing the brand, can think of important ways that the new brand extension would be better than competing products in the category.

Since a brand's meaning can change over time as brand extensions are introduced, management needs to develop a brand plan—what extensions are introduced short term and what others become possible long term. Note the changing possibilities Ocean Spray faced as it moved from cranberries to cranberry juice to being a full-line bottled juice supplier. Companies must develop a long-term scenario to avoid diluting important elements of the brand and to improve the odds of pursuing more remote areas where the brand could have leverage.

Source: Adapted from Edward M. Tauber, "Brand Leverage: Strategy for Growth in a Cost-Control World," *Journal of Advertising Research* (August-September 1988), p. 28; and Eileen Roche, "Product Development: Why Line Extensions Often Backfire," *Harvard Business Review* (March-April 1999), pp. 19–21. Micheline Maynard, "Wrapping a Familiar Name around a New Product," *New York Times* (May 22, 2004), p. C1.

The riskiest approach is to create a new product for a new market, especially if the product is not just new to the company but also new to the world. Unless the new market can be reached through existing distribution channels and/or the product can build on core competencies, this is a questionable endeavor. The company must carefully assess whether the risk is worth the effort, whether it will be possible to develop and protect a competitive edge in the future, and even whether the idea is best left for the competition. This would fall into the breakthrough growth section of new product categories. They would be part of either the R&D portfolio or new products portfolio, but they would have a longer-term planning horizon.

CREATE A NEW PRODUCT CHARTER

The net result of a product manager's strategic product thinking should be a long-term charter or strategy for the product line. Rarely will a product manager develop this strategic plan in isolation, or without input from others in the organization. Rather, it will be a multiperspective effort—especially if technology road-mapping or new organizational capabilities are part of the process.

The charter should define the new product objectives, such as *penetrate a new market, alter an image*, or *provide a complete customer solution to some problem*. There should be an effort to reduce risk by balancing short- versus longer-term horizons, and line extensions versus products with greater degrees of "newness." It's also advisable to stagger the new product pipeline so that there is a slow stream of new products rather than a logjam of several to be launched at the same time, followed by a vacuum.

Product development involves many functions within a company, not just the product manager. But because product managers are frequently charged with the ultimate success of a new product, it is important that we discuss their involvement in the process. Although new product development goes beyond the fiscal year planning horizon of the marketing plan for a product line, certain portions will need to be addressed each year. For some years, researching and submitting product proposals will be the extent of new product efforts. At other times during the development project, milestones should be written into the annual plan. And, finally, as commercialization draws near, launch documentation will need to be developed and possibly integrated into the annual plan.

UNDERSTAND PAST SUCCESSES AND FAILURES

To improve the potential for new product success, it helps to calculate your company's "hit rate" in new products and determine the reasons for it. Compare successful product launches with unsuccessful ones. What were the common elements of successful development efforts that were different from unsuccessful development efforts? Was there a difference in R&D investment and shared communication? The number of ideas generated? The sequence of steps in the development process? The understanding of the market? The application of core competencies? All of these can be significant factors and must be part of the strategic thinking process. The medical products group of Hewlett-Packard, for example, uncovered 14 critical internal processes that differentiated successful and unsuccessful products:

When executives at Hewlett–Packard's medical products group studied 10 of their new product failures along with 10 of their successes, they were surprised to identify a total of 14 essential tasks that determined which products worked and which didn't. The steps covered a wide range of corporate skills. Among them: figuring out which new products play to a company's core strengths, understanding how a new product should be sold, and getting an early fix on a project's costs.[5]

Research and development and manufacturing personnel are important contributors to successful strategic product planning. Product managers should determine with manufacturing how wide a product line can be without putting a strain on efficiency. This includes understanding how future products can be developed from a common platform. When Whirlpool (the appliance company) went global in the 1980s, it spent over half a year looking at appliance markets around the world. It felt that consumer needs were similar enough to justify a common platform. That allowed the company to significantly reduce costs and bring innovations out faster. This moved Whirlpool from a $3.5 billion company to a $13 billion company in 2005.[6] Prevent product proliferation by deciding which products can be dropped when new ones are introduced. If products are not to be dropped, the product manager must lobby for increased R&D and/or operations funding to attain the strategic product goals.

PREVIEWING THE NPD PROCESSES

Stage-Gate is a process pioneered by Dr. Robert Cooper. It divides the development effort into distinct time-sequenced stages separated by management decision gates. At each of the gates a decision is made as to whether to move on to the next stage, request refinements, or table a concept—thereby *incrementalizing* the decision process. Multifunctional teams complete each stage prior to their obtaining approval to proceed to the next stage. This is a variation of project management applied exclusively to product development. The gates are a bit like quality control checkpoints on an assembly line. They assess whether everything is progressing according to plan or whether corrective action should be taken.

In addition to the project reviews just described, some companies also have portfolio reviews, generally conducted by the management team two to four times per year. During these reviews the team may reprioritize projects to balance the overall portfolio and improve resource allocation. Some of the questions asked at this review include the following. Does the project improve the overall value of the portfolio? Does it improve the portfolio's strategic alignment? Does it negatively affect other projects?

While there is a generic flowchart for NPD, the reality is that it should be scalable. Line extensions and low-risk projects may be best suited to an abbreviated version by combining steps and/or using some self-managed reviews. Breakthrough and platform projects may require additional substeps throughout the process. In either case, the process should be customized to fit the organization.

To better understand the product manager's role in the process, it is useful to collapse the process into a product manager's 3C development process: concepting, creating, and commercializing. (See Figure 6.2.) During *concepting* there's a strong emphasis on data capture, with the product manager taking a lead role in gathering and evangelizing market insights. As the process moves into product *creation* (design and development), emphasis morphs slightly from *product* management to *project* management. Whether team leadership stays with the product manager or shifts to a separate project manager depends on company procedures, product complexity, and role expectations. Either way, the product manager must stay actively involved in oversight, ensuring that the new product/project effectively passes gate reviews (or occasionally making the recommendation to kill a project). If the project moves into the final C—*commercializing*—, the product manager should again take the lead including pre- and postcommercializing activities.

Note that the flowchart in Figure 6.2 has several activities plus decision points. The activities include product strategy; ideation; business case creation; definition and design; prototype formation and testing; development; and launch. The decision points include a strategic filter, business screen, definition checkpoint, development readiness appraisal, and process review. (The last is more of an evaluation than a decision, but it is separate from the action steps and may

FIGURE 6.2 ➤ 3C framework of new product development

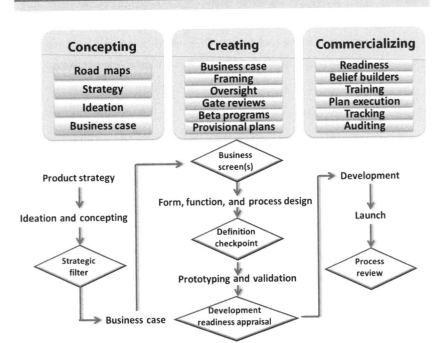

lead to decisions on future improvements.) Always remember that this is a generic flowchart, and there may be additional steps for innovations and a compression of steps for line extensions. Platform and technology products may require further modifications. That's why product managers should recommend adaptations of the process to meet the unique needs of their companies and situations.

Strategic product planning requires an understanding of corporate and divisional strategic goals. Most long-term visions have some implicit (or explicit) statement of the future "picture" of the company and its product offerings. The product manager has to understand the role his or her product(s) play in this vision. It is not enough to know the percentage of profits expected from a new product line, although that is important information. The product manager must also know what new markets, new technologies, and new directions to incorporate into the long-term product plan.

After a product strategy is spelled out, the first step of a specific new product development project is idea generation. Ideas are fleshed out into a proposal and filtered using questions of fit with existing product and corporate strategy. Major product ideas/concepts that pass screening move to a multifunctional team. The product manager (with team input) establishes a business case, providing the rationale for the company to develop the product. Note that this step is the bridge between the "concepting" phase and the creating phase. Once the business case is complete, it's shared with the new product review committee (often composed of key executives from all functional areas). If it passes the business screening, there is a shift from exploratory evaluation to project management. The company authorizes the use of resources to more fully define the concept and begin the activities of design. For some projects, such as those involving highly technical or complex products, team leadership might shift from the *product* manager to a *project* manager. In other cases team leadership is handled by the product manager (who serves as the de facto project manager).

During definition and design, the team works to convert market requirements into product specifications in a way that is reasonable and producible for the firm. This means that service-product companies have the requisite capabilities and that physical-product companies are able to manufacture to the specifications.

This leads to the next decision point—the definition checkpoint. Here the project review committee decides whether to invest resources to build prototypes. If approved, the project moves to the next activity—prototyping.

Prototype formulation, testing, and evaluation start with the creation of a working model or preliminary version of the product. This model is then put through use tests either inside the company's facility or by customers. Alpha tests refer to having the product used by employees or a department in the company. For example, a food item might be tested in the firm's cafeteria before being tested outside the company. Beta tests refer to having a select group of customers use the product under actual usage conditions. These tests can uncover potential defects that necessitate product elimination or redesign. If the tests go well, the product may proceed to prelaunch scale-up and production planning.

During this prelaunch time period, product managers are working on provisional plans for launch. They pull together details for the marketing plan, while engineering and production complete final product drawings and tool debugging. It's worth noting that although prototype development is presented after definition and design in this flowchart, these stages may be handled concurrently or even in reverse order. There are circumstances in which customers cannot assess a concept in the abstract, such as when they're evaluating the taste of a new food product. In these situations, a prototype is required early in the process.

After prototype testing yields positive results, the last decision point before ramp-up and development is the development readiness appraisal. Here the company determines whether there is appropriate design available to allow manufacturing to occur, if the business case is still valid, if the product specifications truly fit the market requirements of the business case (including any revisions or modifications), and if the provisional launch plans are complete and ready.

During launch the product is taken to the market, possibly through a planned rollout. After launch, the new product project is evaluated with a goal to either take immediate corrective action or to improve the process for the future. The activities and decision points of creating and commercializing are covered in more depth in the next three chapters. First, let's return to concepting and the activity of ideation.

DEVELOPING PRODUCT IDEAS

The number of ideas generated can affect successful product commercialization by increasing the likelihood of uncovering the best product concepts. Although many argue that there is no shortage of ideas per se, it can also be argued that many good ideas never surface because the available ideas are accepted as "good enough." Product managers are frequently under pressure to generate new products quickly. Because they also juggle existing products at the same time, they do not allow themselves the luxury of thoroughly examining all alternatives. They resort to line extensions or me-too products. This is why strategic gestation of ideas and having a portfolio plan can be a useful prelude to product development.

There are several sources of strategic product ideas. An important source is customers and potential customers. Unfortunately, too many companies don't use a disciplined approach to obtain futuristic ideas. For business-to-business products, a useful research approach is a systematic customer visit program. A *customer visit program* is a structured approach to data collection through which specific customers are targeted for their expected contributions to an issue being studied, company personnel are recruited to participate in the program because of their importance to the decision being made, and written objectives are established for the data collection. Customers who are futuristic thinkers, who are industry leaders, or who have unique applications for the product are asked to participate in the program. These lead users often provide more innovative ideas than the more representative customers. A small group of people from R&D, operations, and marketing are briefed on the goal of the project, and arrangements are made to call on the selected customers. The resulting insights from the customer visit program are then synthesized into potential long-term product ideas. Trade shows are another vehicle for reaching customers. Conducting a focus group at a trade show can be a lower-cost alternative for obtaining new product ideas.

Brainstorming sessions focused on a particular goal can be another tool for product development. During the sessions, participants are encouraged to think in terms of metaphors and analogies. The application of analogies was used successfully when Canon was attempting to develop a drum for its minicopiers:

> *Canon designers realized that 90 percent of all maintenance problems are related to the photosensitive copier drum. Therefore they wanted to make the drum disposable, but at acceptable price and quality levels. Coincidentally the team ordered out for beer, triggering a discussion on whether the process for making an aluminum beer can be applied to a copier drum. This led the team to a process technology that could manufacture aluminum drums at an acceptable cost.[7]*

Product managers must also be aware of the company's core competencies and be willing to work with other functional areas and other product managers to leverage these skills into future products and markets. (See Business Brief 6.2, "Innovating Innovation.")

Business Brief 6.2

INNOVATING INNOVATION

How does innovation happen? For many product managers, competing demands on their attention cause short-term needs to be more pressing than long-term possibilities. Or alternatively, they are exploring so many opportunities that they don't focus enough on any one. That's why a product portfolio plan or a product innovation charter, which actually sets boundaries, paradoxically encourages innovation.

Nokia Group, for example, focuses its innovation efforts by "studying user needs, emerging technologies and the changing business environment within the mobility and communications space." By limiting new ideas to these customer-need categories, extraneous pursuits are minimized.

Similarly Air Liquide shifted focus from product innovation to what it termed *demand innovation*—meeting existing demand in a new way. As a supplier of industrial gases to the pulp and paper industry, the firm's income dropped as the product became a commodity in the 1990s. After unsuccessfully investing R&D resources into an ozone-friendly alternative to bleach for paper and pulp, the company discovered a need for gas-management services. These services, which accounted for 7 percent of its revenue in 1991, grew to 30 percent of Air Liquide's revenue by 2004.

GE Healthcare encourages an active involvement of lead users who are referred to as *luminaries*. Most are well-published doctors and research scientists from leading medical institutions. GE brings them together for regular medical advisory board sessions to assess the evolution of GE technology.

P&G encourages innovation through cross-pollination from one product to another rather than inventing from scratch. Tide StainBrush, an electric device for removing stains from clothing, uses the same basic mechanism as the Crest Spinbrush Pro toothpaste. P&G also encourages thinking in terms of generating more solutions for customer needs rather than in terms of extending products. P&G gained a greater "share of mouth" with its spinbrush and Whitestrips, while Colgate was focused on toothpaste.

These best practices at P&G became popularized as "open innovation"—as in the book by the same name by Henry Chesbrough. Some of the philosophies of this concept include:

- There is a need to work with smart people both within and outside your company.
- Commercial and technical innovations should be integrated more seamlessly.
- A better business model is superior to getting to the market first.
- Share and benefit from intellectual property.
- Make the best use of internal and external ideas, and you will win.

Source: Adapted from Liisa Väualikangas and Michael Gibbert, "Boundary-Setting Strategies for Escaping Innovation Traps," *MIT Sloan Management Review* (Spring 2005), pp. 58–65. John Teresko, "P&G's Secret: Innovating Innovation," *Industry Week* (December 2004), pp. 26–32. "Business: The Rise of the Creative Consumer: The Future of Innovation," *The Economist* (March 12, 2005), p. 75. Nanette Byrnes, Robert Berner, Wendy Zellner, and William C. Symonds, "Branding: Five New Lessons," *BusinessWeek* (February 14, 2005), pp. 26–28. "Special Report: Don't Laugh at Gilded Butterflies," *The Economist* (April 24, 2004), p. 81.

Although ideas can come from a variety of sources, both internal and external, the product manager should actively be looking for new product concepts. (See Figure 6.3.) Do not believe that there are already too many ideas. It is not just the number of ideas but also their quality that is important. The product manager is best suited to determine whether a flanker product is necessary to offset a competitive entry, or if a group of customers has adapted a product to a unique application that can be extended to other market segments. Attend technology-sharing meetings (either within the company or through trade associations). Keep communication open with salespeople to

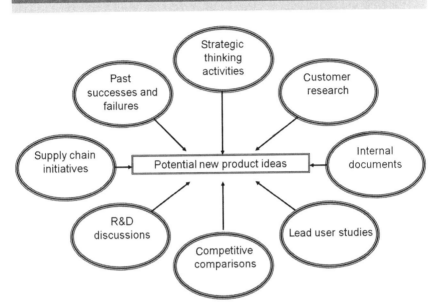

FIGURE 6.3 ➤ Sources of new product ideas

identify opportunities. Monitor shifts in market size or composition that could suggest changing needs.

If there is no repository for product ideas in the company, create a database of ideas related to the product. Even ideas that didn't pass screening may turn into winners in the future. Skim the database on a regular basis (perhaps quarterly or semiannually) to determine whether any ideas should be dusted off and reexamined.

The ideas should be subjected to a preliminary screening to determine whether more effort is justified. Strategic filters might include the following[8]:

- Fit within existing product mix
- Patentability
- Risk of competitive entry
- Ability to sell through existing distribution
- Compatibility with strategic plan
- Acceptable payback period
- Growth potential
- Cost of tooling and machinery
- Compatibility with core technologies

The criteria for a specific company could include all or none of these factors. However, the act of listing them forces the issues to the surface and provides a forum for discussing product concepts. The criteria should be developed separate from, and in advance of, screening particular ideas.

Many different approaches can be used for this screening process. Some companies simply indicate "must have" criteria for new products to be considered. Others list several criteria that can be evaluated on a yes-no basis. Still others use criteria with weights and ratings as shown in Table 6.1. In the table, the most important screening criterion was "compatibility with strategic plans" as designated by the weight of 0.20. The committee rated this particular idea 0.7 for "compatibility with strategic plans," yielding a weighted rating of $0.20 \times 0.70 = 0.01$ (rounded from 0.014). Each row is calculated this way and then added together to arrive at the total weighted rating. Note that the product idea being evaluated obtained a final weighted score of 0.44. If several other ideas being evaluated simultaneously obtained scores of 0.56, 0.62, and 0.70, the relative priorities would become clear. The real value of these priorities is that it provides you the ability to decide how to best allocate developmental resources.

A mathematical rating device such as the one shown in Table 6.1 does not necessarily quantify results because the evaluations are still subjective. However, a screening checklist like this provides the opportunity for individual members to evaluate new product ideas according to consistent parameters prior to meeting as a group. It also fosters discussion within the new product development review committee and focuses the conversation on project-review metrics considered important to the company.

Whatever type of screening tool is used, it is important that it allow a reasonable balance between being too strict and too loose. A too-strict approach can cause potential winners to be killed. A too-loose approach results in mediocre products being pursued. Having criteria for screening that functions like a funnel makes it possible for the better ideas to be approved for further development. Without good screening, too many ideas may continue into the development process, taking up resources and reducing the probability of success. It shifts from a funnel to a tunnel, as shown in Figure 6.4.

Table 6.1

Product Screening Checklist

Requirements for a successful product	Relative weight	Rating of product concept 0.0	0.1	0.2	0.3	0.4	0.5	0.6	0.7	0.8	0.9	1.0	Rating
Fit with existing product mix	.15					X							.06
Patentability	.05				X								.02
Low risk of competitive entry	.10								X				.07
Ability to sell through existing channels	.10									X			.08
Compatibility with strategic plans	.20								X				.01
Acceptable payback period	.10										X		.09
Growth potential	.10						X						.05
Low cost of tooling and machinery	.05			X									.01
Compatibility with existing technologies	.15				X								.05
Weighted score													.44

FIGURE 6.4 ➤ Use a funnel rather than a tunnel approach to screening

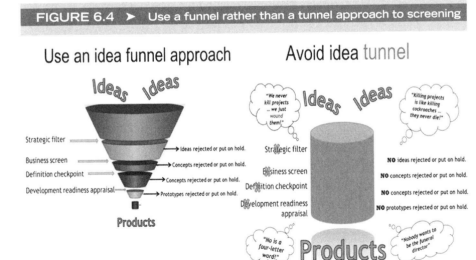

Use an idea funnel approach

Avoid idea tunnel

Ideas Ideas

Strategic filter → Ideas rejected or put on hold.
Business screen → Concepts rejected or put on hold.
Definition checkpoint → Concepts rejected or put on hold.
Development readiness appraisal → Prototypes rejected or put on hold.

Products

"We never kill projects ... we just wound them!"

Ideas Ideas

"Killing projects is like killing cockroaches ... they never die!"

Strategic filter
Business screen
Definition checkpoint
Development readiness appraisal

NO ideas rejected or put on hold.
NO concepts rejected or put on hold.
NO concepts rejected or put on hold.
NO prototypes rejected or put on hold.

"No is a four-letter word!"

Products

"Nobody wants to be the funeral director"

After the product idea passes screening, a cross-functional team is established to work on the product. The team is usually composed of the product manager and counterparts from operations, design, and, in some cases, procurement, a key customer, legal, finance, customer service, and sales. The role of the salesperson will vary by company. Although sales input and up-front support are critical, not all salespeople can identify with the top 10 percent of potential or targeted customers that represent leading trends. A recent study by AT&T comparing salespeople's judgments with customers' judgments about an innovative new product concept found that the sales force was "consistently more optimistic and exhibited different preference patterns."[9] In this case, it may be more beneficial to solicit input from a *variety* of salespeople than in having sales as a core member of the team throughout the process.

The next chapter focuses on taking these (sometimes still raw) ideas, developing a business case for them, and guiding them into products that can be commercialized.

CHAPTER CHALLENGE

Think about innovation and product development in three time horizons and categories including core growth, adjacency growth, and breakthrough growth. Manage them as separate portfolios. Also, consider adding various design thinking efforts to your repertoire of skills.

INTERVIEW WITH DAVE FRANCHINO: USE DESIGN THINKING TO HARVEST UNTAPPED POTENTIAL

Dave Franchino, President and Principal, Design Concepts, Inc., www.design-concepts.com

Dave, before we get into the nitty-gritty, can you tell us a bit about Design Concepts, as well as the career path that got you there?

Design Concepts, Inc., is an award-winning, innovation and design consultancy. We use our experience in product and service design to help clients uncover new opportunities, build brands, and build business. We've been around for more than 44 years delivering strategy, research, industrial design, human factors, engineering, and prototyping services. We're fortunate to have collaborated with companies worldwide to uncover needs, find opportunities, and design solutions that create business success for our clients.

My background might be a bit unusual for the innovation industry as I came to it by way of engineering. I spent 12 years in the automotive industry with Saturn Corporation prior to joining Design Concepts. When I started with Saturn, I had a pretty engineering-centric perspective on where "innovation" came from, but I quickly realized that business success seldom came solely from pure technical execution—no matter how clever or innovative. Later as I went on to study at Stanford University, I became increasingly intrigued with the unique blend of technology, marketing, design, business, finance, and strategic planning required to drive innovative businesses forward. While at Stanford, I had the opportunity to work with another design innovation firm—IDEO—which was my first introduction to the field of innovation consulting. At Design Concepts I've been lucky enough to work with a remarkable team of researchers, strategists, designers, engineers, prototyping specialists, and innovators. They are constantly pushing the boundaries of the way in which we help our clients build and grow their businesses.

Lately this approach has become known as design thinking, and I'm proud that our firm has been on the leading edge of rethinking the methods and processes that help firms deliver new innovation, customer satisfaction, and business success.

So, you consult on design thinking with a number of firms. How do you define the term "design thinking," and what's the significance to companies?

Design thinking is simply a way of thinking—a broad way of approaching problems—that draws on many of the methods and processes designers are trained to use when approaching a new design challenge.

We like to say that design thinking changes business as usual. What we mean by that is that design thinking breaks away from the linear, additive, purely analytical, traditional thinking that has come to define business; it brings a new approach to business.

Design thinking combines a rational, analytical approach to problem solving with an empathetic and creative approach. It's that combination that brings balance and perspective to problem solving for the purpose of designing products, defining business strategy, creating services, or tackling social issues.

It's somewhat of a misnomer to call this design thinking. It makes it sound as though it's an approach exclusive to the design field. In truth, it's an iterative, qualitative approach that product designers embrace daily—but with much broader applicability than just traditional design problems. Our toolbox includes stage-gates and milestones, but it also includes discovery, ethnographic research, team ideation, rapid prototyping, and informed intuition. Where traditional business takes a straight path toward a predefined goal, design thinking takes a circuitous route and often a roller coaster ride without the preconceived thoughts on where the best solution might lie. The process itself gives you permission to explore and create and fail and start again. It's a replicable process that moves innovation away from being an elusive concept or intangible business goal and instead demonstrates innovation as a reliable and repeatable process.

It's significant to business because it's a strategic direction and approach that leverages greater value from innovation teams than traditional approaches.

Can you share a couple of specific success stories?

I think some of our best design-thinking successes have come from guiding our clients into taking a completely fresh approach to the problem at hand.

Design thinking helped one of our medical device clients take a step back and realize they had significant strategic opportunities adjacent to their traditional product offering. Historically, they had been intensely focused on improving the features and functionality of their core product. Traditional market research and business analysis had driven ongoing improvements in their equipment but failed to recognize significant customer pain points in the overall landscape in which their products functioned. We led them on an internationally focused design-thinking project including deep ethnographic research in more than a dozen countries. By mapping the overall user experience, it quickly became apparent that there were significant opportunities to leverage their credibility in that specific piece of equipment to provide a broad range of products *and* services that the marketplace desperately needed and eagerly sought. Most exciting for us and the client was that it created not just new product opportunities but strategies with a new business model.

In another instance we had a client who was offering a highly sophisticated medical product which had been tailored for the U.S. marketplace. Outside the U.S. and Western Europe most countries used devices with a far lower level of design features. The prevailing theory within their company—and in the competition—was that other markets would eventually embrace the same level of sophistication, complexity, and cost. Once again we led this client on a multination ethnographic discovery and ideation process using design-thinking principles. Through direct interaction with customers, brainstorming, and prototyping, we realized there was a significant business opportunity to introduce a transitional product—one that took a step beyond traditional feature sets, but without the level of cost and complexity present in their current offering. It wasn't simply that the U.S. product was too expensive and complex, but rather that the cost and complexity inherent in their base product was addressing needs that simply were not present in these other markets.

Like most good business ideas, when you're done the solution seems straightforward. But without the freedom that a design-thinking process brought, neither of these companies would have overcome the internal inertia and capitalized on these business opportunities.

Are there any differences in design thinking for services compared with products? Or breakthroughs compared with line extensions? Or consumer products compared with nonconsumer products?

For me, one of the real epiphanies of design thinking is how transportable these tools and techniques are across traditional business frontiers. As consultants in the field of innovation it is remarkably common for us to be asked to work in a field we have had no prior exposure to. This has given us a healthy appreciation for the value that discovery research, team-based ideation, rapid prototyping, iteration, and informed intuition can bring to a host of industries and opportunities. Every field has its nuances, but most can benefit from a fresh perspective and customer-focused approach to innovation.

Over the years we've found that our process makes it possible for our work in consumer products, for example, to inform our perspective on medical devices. Our work in service design might reveal an insight that readily applies to a commercial product. Design thinking as a process and a way of thinking leverages the creativity of the team regardless of the industry.

We currently have a mechanical engineer, an ethnographic researcher, a Ph.D. in linguistics, and an M.B.A. working together on a project exploring a drug therapy. It may sound like an unlikely team, but they all bring a perspective of both rational and creative thinking to the project. The process of design thinking gives them the freedom to work outside their traditional fields and brings amazing solutions to the table.

The repeatable process and the reliability of the results are valuable for any industry or field.

What are the specific takeaways for product managers?

The business landscape is certainly getting more competitive. More and more is expected of each business and each product manager. Innovation is becoming a mandate rather than an approach. I believe that while success for product managers will still involve managing the current portfolio and product road map, there will be an increased emphasis on new opportunities and spaces.

Some of the basic tools in design thinking aren't standard parts of the skill set normally associated with product management. Traditional quantitative market research is an invaluable tool for most product managers but not necessarily the most productive way of identifying breakthrough opportunities. Ethnographic discovery research requires approaching the market without any preconceived notions or hypotheses—looking for deep understanding of customers' needs and wants in areas that are often completely tangential to current product offerings. We've found that some product managers are so intimately connected with their current customers and current product offerings that looking at the market with a completely fresh set of eyes can be a challenge. Design thinking can help formalize a process for taking the time and effort to look at mature markets from a new perspective.

Likewise, the skills of team brainstorming, rapid prototyping, and iteration can be leveraged in a broad range of business areas. Design thinking makes it possible for product managers to break out of traditional ruts and demystify the process of innovation.

Aside from its role in new product development, we feel design thinking has applicability for product managers across the entire product life cycle. A challenge for many businesses is getting product managers—who are generally on the front line of opportunity—to look for and embrace new business opportunities and strategies that might not lie directly within the path of their current product line. Design thinking can be an important tool for harvesting untapped potential both within and adjacent to existing offerings.

CHAPTER 7

Creating—and Getting Approval for—Business Cases

TRUE OR FALSE: The more precise a business case is, the more accurate it is.

Ironically, this is not true. Business cases rely on assumptions and estimates about the future: forecasted sales, customer intent, and expected costs. Adding more decimal points may provide the appearance of precision, but the reality is that there is still a lot of subjectivity to the numbers.

TRUE OR FALSE: A successful business case is one that gets funded.

Again, this is false. A successful business case is one that helps people make the right decisions. Keep in mind that the business case step is the process of proving or *disproving* the business potential for a product concept. Some product managers approach this step with the belief that success is defined as getting approval for the business case. As a result they are tempted to pad projections or become wildly optimistic on their assumptions. While this doesn't guarantee that you are setting yourself up for failure, it certainly increases the probability.

I start this chapter with two true/false questions because the questions represent very common misconceptions. Developing and defending a new product business case can be an intimidating task for many product managers. That's why it is so important to think about the whole process of building a business case as well as the document that results from it.

Before going further, it may be useful to talk a bit about terminology since companies use all these terms in different ways. For purposes of this chapter, I am defining *business case* as a structured proposal for investment in a new product. It will contain market requirements (i.e., needs or benefits), a general statement of the feasibility of building a product that addresses the requirements, a discussion of the targeted market and opportunity, as well as a financial overview. In other words, it provides the case (i.e., rationale) to support economic investment in the new product project. Companies that refer to this type of document as a market requirements document (MRD) or business plan or proposal may use the term *business case* to refer strictly to the financials. Which terms are used is not important as long as everyone understands how they are being used in the organization.

In the previous chapter I mention that the three core components of new product development from a product manager's perspective are concepting, creating, and commercializing. During early concepting a product manager might generate and evaluate numerous product ideas at a high level. Most will be discarded almost immediately, and a few will require further data collection and analysis to determine which idea should be built into a concept for the business case. (See Figure 7.1.) So ideation is a predecessor to (and flows into) the process of building a business case for a given product concept.

THE IMPORTANCE OF THE BUSINESS CASE

It's important to approach case building as ammunition for decision making. It starts with gathering data on market potential, realistically assessing what factors might make it easier or harder for the product to gain market acceptance, and then forecasting accordingly. In other words, the business case should predict the *outcome* if the decision is made to pursue it. Determine reasonable cash flow projections with

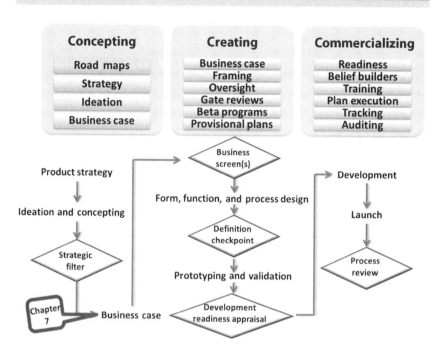

FIGURE 7.1 ➤ The business case phase of the 3C framework of product development

rough probabilities of achieving various cash flows during an acceptable payback period. (A two-minute tutorial on Monte Carlo simulation of probabilities associated with new product forecasting can be found on the Palisade Corporation's Web site—www.palisade.com—in the section describing their @Risk add-in module for Excel.) If the management team is examining several new product proposals and cannot fund all of them, the combination of expected revenue *and* probabilities provides more ammunition for making the right decision for the company.

Beyond the forecasted revenues and costs, there may be soft benefits to consider. These could include increased brand awareness, referrals, or higher customer satisfaction. While soft benefits cannot be directly translated into hard dollars and cents, they can be linked with carefully articulated assumptions. For example, if the assumption is that a new product will prevent defection to the competition, then the financial value of this business can be estimated.

The business case is a skeleton plan that provides the financial, competitive, and market justification for the project. It is essentially an economic proposal for an investment and should be built from data. It is sometimes helpful to think of a business case in the context of an entrepreneur compiling a business plan in an effort to get venture capital.

Since the quality of a business case can have a direct impact on people making correct decisions regarding the acceptance or rejection of a product concept, it's worth doing right. This doesn't mean simply following a "best-practice" template to magically give you a perfect case. Rather it means objectively evaluating the positives and negatives of the concept for the organization. It might also require explaining why other concepts were rejected in favor of this one.

The process of developing the business case begins with answering the question *why* you are considering this concept at this time. Carefully consider its fit with the business strategy, product strategy, and/ or product road map. Is this a proactive or reactive product? Will it fill a gap or open new opportunities? What is the size of the opportunity and the expected financial performance? Will it be possible to manufacture this product, and do we have the capabilities to do it? What might be the consequences of *not* pursuing this concept? What are the risks and how will they be mitigated? Don't assume that the answers to all these questions are obvious. They might not be.

COMPONENTS OF THE BUSINESS CASE

Companies will require different content for different business cases depending on the type of industry or product and the needs of the individual business. (The Web site of Solution Matrix—www.solutionmatrix. com—contains some useful white papers and articles on business case analysis.)

Figure 7.2 shows the primary components and subcomponents of a business case. Note that underlying all the components are your assumptions. Clearly state important assumptions and "pressure test" them against other people's perspectives. What would happen to the outcome if these assumptions changed? Look at best- and worst-case scenarios. Challenge yourself as you examine your beliefs about each component of the business case.

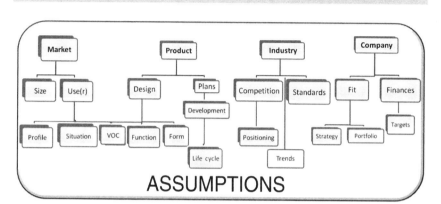

FIGURE 7.2 ➤ Business case components

Market Components

Ideas that make it to the business case phase are refined and converted into realistic product concepts. Here the product manager is heavily involved in (1) determining the appropriate features and attributes that will maximize customer satisfaction and acceptance, (2) identifying the target price, and (3) revising estimates of sales potential and profitability. It's important that these activities be integrated. Changes in attributes may cause a target price to be unattainable, and the realized price may change customers' willingness to buy (a key factor in sales volume). There must be a holistic perspective of these factors in defining product features to minimize future change orders. Otherwise, conflict between product managers and project managers is likely to occur.

Start with secondary data. Conduct Web searches to get more information on market characteristics, trends, and competition. Look for any purchasable marketing research studies that have been conducted. If relevant, conduct patent searches to ferret out potential future competitors. Talk with industry experts and potential customers to assess attitudes toward the product idea. Getting market input from "typical" customers is appropriate for many line extensions, whereas getting input from lead users is important for innovative products. But both are important for attaining voice of the customer. (See Business Brief 7.1, "Customer Input in Identifying Market Opportunities.")

Business Brief 7.1

CUSTOMER INPUT IN IDENTIFYING MARKET OPPORTUNITIES

Lead users, companies, or individuals with *extreme* or *demanding* needs for a product are important sources of innovative product ideas. More representative customers provide more input for line extensions, concept development, and life cycle sales forecasts. But all contribute the voice of the customer to new product development projects.

Toshiba America Medical Systems has developed strong relationships with leading U.S. medical institutions to better understand the market opportunities for medical imaging products. Toshiba took advantage of a physician advocate and ally at Johns Hopkins to establish a group of thought leaders and leading medical experts. The team sits on Toshiba's advisory board, reviews beta products, and pushes innovation.

Procter & Gamble, on the other hand, is interested in both innovations and improvements to existing products and marketing strategies. In April 2005 it instituted its first annual "Consumer is Boss" event to solicit new product ideas. One idea from a 7-year-old girl was to have consumers vote for the next flavor of Crest. As a result, P&G had a Web vote to select between lemon, berry, and tropical fruit flavors to extend Crest Whitening Expressions.

The Iams managers of P&G also learned that some pet owners added treats (table scraps) to their dry dog food to induce older pets to eat it. Follow-up quantitative research revealed that 40 percent of owners used such methods. So the brand launched Savory as a more nutritious alternative to table scraps.

While multiple approaches can be used, product managers should continually challenge themselves to focus on why people do the things they do—and the relevant competition at those times—and use the information in product development and marketing. Clayton Christensen, author of *The Innovator's Solution,* suggests that the reason many products fail is that managers don't look at markets the way customers experience life. For example, when a manager of a fast-food chain wanted to improve milk shake sales and profits, he first asked customers whether the shakes should be thicker, chunkier, or have different flavors. The changes requested by customers were made but nothing happened. Another group of researchers discovered that most of the customers consumed shakes to make a long, boring commute easier. Since it could take 20 minutes to sip the shake through a think straw, it relieved the boredom of the trip. The competition was not just other shakes but also "boredom, bagels, bananas, doughnuts, instant breakfast drinks, and, possibly, coffee." The new perspective changed the new product concepts.

Source: John Zimmer, "How to Win a Marquee Account," *Sales and Marketing Management* (February 2004), p. 72. Jack Neff, "P&G Kisses Up to the Boss: Consumers," *Advertising Age* (May 2, 2005), p. 18. Clayton M. Christensen and Michael E. Raynor, "Creating a Killer Product," *Forbes* (October 13, 2003), p. 82.

Table 7.1 shows a sample spreadsheet that defines the market opportunity for high definition television (HDTV). The second column lists the market potential by year as calculated from a variety of key variables. The third column contains the total population as defined by relevant demographics in census data. The technology realization column lists the probability that technology would be available that year to enable an acceptable level of product quality. HDTV awareness was a subjective estimate of the percentage of target customers aware of the product. Program availability refers to the estimated percentage of broadcast time devoted to HDTV programming. The intention to purchase at a given price was based on survey data. Given that this spreadsheet was developed when HDTV was an innovation (as opposed to a line extension), it was reasonable to look at the yearly market penetration of an analogous product (in this case color TV). Multiplying all the variables together yields a projection in the second column that is a calculated estimate of market potential by year.

Table 7.1

Example of Market Opportunity Forecasting

Time period	Market potential	Population base	Technology realization	HDTV awareness	Program availability	Intention to buy	Average price	Market growth penetration
	TV households, 000		Judgmental indexes			Market survey data		Color TV growth
Model	pot =	pop ×	tek ×	awr ×	avl ×	buy	price	% of pot	pen
Year 1	698	93,000	0.50	0.25	0.50	0.12	2,000	.50	349
Year 2	1,488	93,930	0.55	0.40	0.60	0.12	2,000	.52	774
Year 3	3,287	94,869	0.60	0.55	0.70	0.15	1,800	.48	1.578
Year 4	5,232	95,818	0.70	0.65	0.80	0.15	1,800	.51	2.668
Year 5	10,452	96,776	0.80	0.75	0.90	0.20	1,600	.47	4.912
Year 6	17,281	97,744	0.85	0.80	1.00	0.26	1,400	.48	8.295

Condensed from Robert J. Thomas, *New Product Development: Managing and Forecasting for Strategic Success* (John Wiley, 1993), p. 174.

Concept Refinement and Voice of the Customer

To refine your understanding of the market need, solicit input from key customers who are knowledgeable and cooperative. These customers don't have to be representative, but they do have to be willing to suggest improvements and modifications to the initial concept. Probe for specific modifications that could affect the sales potential of the product. What if certain features were enlarged? Minimized? What if the product was harder? Softer? What if the dimensions were more standardized? More customized? Is color important? How about location? Get as much input from these key sources as possible. In some cases, this type of qualitative research with a small sample is sufficient to develop the concept. In other cases, a larger sample is required so that you will fully understand the needs of the market.

Once the concept is more fully developed, it is important to test it among a large group of customers. This group will be more representative of the target market. There is no one best approach to concept testing, but most are variations of qualitative research and focus group discussions. Generally, several versions of a concept (possibly including competitors or placebo concepts) or several different product concepts that address the same need (i.e., substitutes) are explored in one concept test. This is because people usually provide better information when they are comparing alternatives, and the resulting information is more reliable than absolute evaluation. Mock ads, product descriptions on cards, drawings of the concept, and rough prototypes can all be used as part of the research. In some cases, the product's technical documentation and owner's manual is part of this analysis.

Some of the questions to be addressed during the concept test include the following: Does the proposed concept make sense to the customers? Is it preferred over what is currently available? How much value do the improvements have over existing alternatives available to the customer? Is the product consistent with the way customers currently perform the function, or will it require a change in mindset? Would they be willing to pay more? What are the flaws? Are there changes that would make the product viable (or more viable)? What is the basic need that this product would satisfy? Has the brand name or trademark been included in the concept test?

Intention to Buy

The concept tests usually include some indication of intent to buy at some specified price. "Intent to buy" refers to the respondents' indication of the probability that they would buy the product if it existed, usually expressed along a scale (e.g., 1 = "definitely would not buy" to 5 = "definitely would buy"). This is an important component of the concept test but should not be projected literally as the actual sales forecast. Customers will almost always overestimate their willingness to buy in an artificial setting such as a focus group. Obtaining pricing information is difficult at best. However, determining a target price is critical for establishing a target cost for the product development process. Although no research method is infallible, there are a few techniques that are worth trying.

One approach is to ask customers to supply a price range: What is the highest price you'd pay, above which you'd feel you were being gouged? What is the lowest price you'd pay, below which you'd question the quality of the product? Another approach is to split the concept test groups into experimental and control groups. Give each group a different price for the same described concept and determine whether there are differences in the willingness to buy at the stated prices. A third strategy is to ask customers what value (in monetary terms) the new product would have over what they are currently using. (See the estimated economic model in Chapter 3.) A final approach is to ask customers what they would be willing to pay for the product and what features they would be willing to give up to attain that price. In each case, an intent-to-buy question should be included.

At this point, the product team should attempt to establish a target price. The target price is necessary for estimating target costs for the developmental process. "Design by price" is an approach used by several companies in industries with rapidly changing technologies, short life cycles, and pressure on pricing.

The target price depends on the value perceived by the market. Determining value will be different for low-unit-value, frequently purchased items (e.g., consumer packaged goods) than for high-priced, infrequently purchased goods (e.g., capital equipment). The purchase of consumer packaged goods has an element of habit and inertia in the decision-making process. Higher-priced products may have groups or committees involved in the process. The differences in decision making, as well as the different decision makers, need to be taken into account in the analysis.

Market Requirements Document

By this time, the team should be able to list and display all the potential product features in a market requirements development table similar to Table 7.2. The table shows an example of a bicycle frame. The first column lists the needs as identified through customer and lead-user research. Note that the needs are what the customer wants to get out of using the product (the benefits) rather than how it is to be designed. The second column contains the ranking or rating of importance of each identified need. The third column converts the benefits into targets or goals for the designers to use in developing the frame. For example, the desired mass in kilograms provides direction (i.e., a goal) without specifying materials or production techniques. Also, the target cost range is determined by starting with the target price(s) and deducting an acceptable margin. Columns 4 and 5 list the metrics for the major competitive products. By comparing the initial and competitive metrics with the importance ratings supplied by the market, adjustments may need to be made in column 6. The final revised metrics are the output of the concept development and testing phase. Since this point represents a milestone in the new-product development process, there should be a sign-off by the initial review committee to indicate its acceptance of the metrics, in effect freezing the benefit set (although actual product specifications won't be frozen until after prototype development).

It can be difficult completing the market requirements development table for breakthrough products. Customers (whether consumers or industrial buyers) do not have competitive products to use as their benchmark. Therefore, the analysis has to start with the function being provided by the product. How is that function being handled now without the benefit of the new product or service? What benefits and costs are related to changing the way it is done now? Then both the rational and emotional motives for switching to the new product have to be considered and valued.

Table 7.2

Market Requirements Development Table

1. Needs	2. Importance*	3. Initial Metrics†	4. Competitor A	5. Competitor B	6. Revised Metrics†
Lightweight	Must	Total mass in kg.	Competitor A will be lighter than concept	Equal	Need to reduce the mass
Can withstand rain and water contamination	Must	Time in spray chamber without water entry	Concept is better than A	Concept is better than B	Continue with initial metrics
Safe in crash	Must	Bending strength of materials	Competitor A has superior bendability	Competitor B breaks sooner	Improve bending strength to match or surpass that of Competitor A
Easy to install	Should	Average time to assemble	Concept has quicker time than A	Concept has quicker time than B	Good performance as long as it does not add to cost
Works with a variety of attachments	Should	List of attachments and sizes	Similar product-line fit	Similar product-line fit	Continue with initial metrics
Competitively priced	Must	Target cost range	On track to be competitively priced	On track to be higher priced	Maintain target cost range and determine how to help customers perceive value

Profile: Define the tatget users in demographic and psychographic terms. Include a statement on the impact of influencers on the purchase decision.
Use Situation: Describe where and how target customers would use the product. Incorporate any insights from observation and design thinking activities.
Nonfunctional Requirements: List any aspects of the product that may be important design parameters (such as appearance or feel) that may be necessary parts of the product even if they do not provide functional benefits.

*Note that the importance column should suggest what benefits (functionality) are required, nice to have, or in some cases, critical to avoid.

†Note that metrics deal more with functionality than with features.

Adapted from Kent Ulrich and Steven Eppinger, *Product Design and Development* (McGraw-Hill, 1995), pp. 54–65.

To estimate a target price, several things need to be considered, specifically the possibility of competitive attack, the price sensitivity of the market, and the degree of competitive differentiation. Figure 7.3 shows a tree diagram with the considerations in new product pricing. For example, if the target customers are not price sensitive, the product is highly differentiated, and competitive response is not expected, it is conceivable to charge a relatively high price. On the other hand, if price sensitivity is high, product differentiation low, and competition heavy, a low price will be necessary.

The appropriate technical people should be involved in the concept testing to assess the technological feasibility of any suggestions that customers might make. The concepts that appear to have marketing, technical, and financial feasibility are then subjected to a more detailed business analysis.

Product Components

The product section of the business case should include the product definition in terms of form and function, the product development plan, and the launch and life-cycle plan. The product definition will incorporate the revised metrics from the market requirements development table

FIGURE 7.3 ➤ New product pricing decision tree

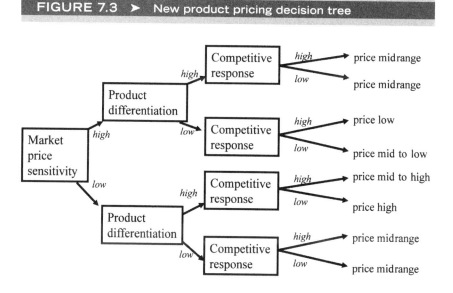

(referencing any relevant usage information), along with competitive positioning from the industry section. Although having a prototype is unlikely at this point, there may be concept descriptions or illustrations.

The product development plan discusses expected resource requirements and a general timeline. The composition of the core team may be included if it's known. A rough commercialization strategy will highlight the major tactics expected for the launch, and the life-cycle plan will highlight the road map for line extensions and potential derivatives.

Industry Components

If the new product will be launched into a new industry (e.g., when a company generally selling into a government market reengineers a product for a commercial market, or vice versa), information about required performance standards, regulatory restrictions, or channel expectations should be included. And regardless of the newness of the industry, competitive positioning must be addressed. For a directly competing product, do a function-by-function (rather than feature-by-feature) comparison. How will the new product improve functionality and provide value for the targeted customers? On a perception basis, how will the proposed product be positioned against the competition? Will it be perceived as a more complete solution? Easier to use? More attractive design?

Company Components

In the company portion of the business case, describe how the product will fit within the overall corporate strategy and goals. If the firm's growth goal involves global expansions, how will this product drive business in other countries? If the corporate goal is increasing customer satisfaction through convenience, how does this product enhance customer convenience? Also explain how this product is a substitute for, a complement to, or an enhancement of the existing product portfolio.

Projected Financial Analysis

A rough business case may have been prepared prior to the preliminary idea screening, and it will have been refined concurrently with the concept testing. It should be continually evaluated and made more definitive as new information becomes available. At minimum, it should be updated whenever a significant milestone has been reached. The skeleton business plan presented at the beginning of the process can now have some of the gaps filled in. The product description should now be more detailed, with marketing and cost objectives included. The market analysis should have more specifics on potential segments and niches, customer applications and key customer identification, and competitive benchmarks. The product development plan should include the composition of the project team, product specifications, a critical path chart with key milestones and target dates, and implementation schedules. The marketing plan should specify planned rollouts, short-term and long-term resource requirements, identified risk factors, and suggestions for minimizing risk. The financial analyses should be expanded to include more detailed income statement and cash-flow information than was available at the proposal stage. Table 7.3 shows a simplified projected financial analysis for a hypothetical industrial product.

Table 7.3

Projected Financial Analysis

	Year 0	Year 1	Year 2	Year 3	Year 4	Year 5
Revenue	0	10,700	13,843	17,689	25,428	29,242
Less cost of goods sold	0	3,583	4,635	5,923	8,515	9,792
Gross margin	0	7,117	9,208	11,766	16,913	19,450
Development costs	−3,150	0	0	0	0	0
Marketing costs	0	7,200	5,814	7,430	10,679	12,281
Allocated overhead	0	1,070	1,384	1,764	2,548	2,924
Gross contribution	−3,150	−1,153	2,010	2,572	3,691	4,245
Supplementary contribution	0	0	0	0	0	0
Net contribution	−3,150	−1,153	2,010	2,572	3,691	4,245
Discounted contribution (15%)	−3,150	−1,003	1,520	1,691	2,111	2,110
Cumulative discounted cash flow	−$3,150	−$4,153	−$2,633	−$942	$1,169	$3,279

The revenue line is based on the market analysis and resulting forecast. The cost of goods sold is obtained from technical and manufacturing personnel on the product development team. The accuracy depends not only on their best assessment of per-unit costs, but also on the precision of the product manager's sales forecasts. The difference between the revenue and cost of goods sold is the gross margin available to cover fixed costs and contribute to profits.

The development costs include any costs already incurred for R&D and concept testing, as well as anticipated costs for prototype development, equipment and materials, labor, product testing, and additional marketing research. If the rollout requires additional capital expenditures, they should be included here as well.

The marketing costs start at prelaunch. These would include advertising, distribution, sales force coverage, sales promotion, and any miscellaneous selling and communication costs.

Allocated overhead refers to administrative costs allocated to various products. Some companies will assess a lower (or even no) overhead cost to new products until they have established themselves, while other companies believe that all products should provide an equal (or greater) contribution to fixed costs (i.e., a type of "hurdle"). Regardless of the company's attitude toward cost allocation, it is imperative that the estimated *revenue* (either price or number of units) is not artificially inflated simply to cover these costs.

The gross contribution is the amount of revenue remaining after development costs, marketing costs, and overhead costs are subtracted from gross margin. This is the amount of money that the product is expected to contribute to indirect fixed costs of the firm and to taxes and profit.

The supplementary contribution is used when new products have an effect (positive or negative) on existing products. The resulting cash flows should be included on this line and either added to or subtracted from the gross contribution to arrive at the net contribution. In Table 7.3, gross contribution and net contribution are the same because the new product was not expected to have any impact on existing product sales.

The discounted contribution line shows the net present value of each net contribution figure, discounted at 15 percent per year. The last line shows the cumulative cash flows over time.

FRAMING AND SELLING THE BUSINESS CASE

Assuming you truly believe in the proposed product concept, the business case you put together should persuade management to pursue it. In other words, the information should be presented in a way that informs and encourages an affirmative vote. Carefully define the market requirements for the product: who, what, when, why, and where.

Depending on the risk and/or financial requirements of a prospective new product, the product manager may need to make a formal presentation of the idea to management. In that case, it's important to identify the "hot buttons" of each manager prior to the meeting in order to come prepared to address them. Top management will be interested in the return, expressed by NPV (net present value) or IRR (internal rate of return), and payback. Sales executives will want to know the strengths of the product as compared with the competition. Operations executives will be concerned about design complexity and manufacturability. Consequently, the product manager must present a clear opportunity assessment, proposed benefits and costs, risks (and measures to contain them), assumptions, alternatives, and an implementation plan. The goal is to provide a rational basis for making the decision as to whether or not to invest in the new product concept.

Communicating with all relevant individuals during the case-building activities of this phase can certainly reduce the criticism during the presentation for case review. The most important factor in disarming adversaries is to get their involvement and buy-in prior to the final review.

CHAPTER CHALLENGE

Stop thinking that a business case is simply a financial plan and that success is defined as getting approval. Reframe your perspective to view a business case as an investment proposal and your role is to be an objective evaluator and recommender.

INTERVIEW WITH KEVIN BOOTH: BOOST YOUR ABILITY TO BUILD AND SELL BUSINESS CASES

Kevin Booth, president,
The Hines Group

Kevin, it would seem that your varied consulting and turnaround positions have really given you a perspective on product development that few people have. Can you talk a bit about your background and how that has shaped your thinking?

My practical experience is in sales, marketing, operations, engineering, and general management. A portion of my career has been in consulting, specializing in sales, product and marketing planning, and strategy development. My consulting work was substantially focused on new product research, competitor intelligence, planning, as well as "revenue due diligence" in acquisitions. The turnaround experience is an extension of my work improving marketing, sales, and new product performance. In many ways, the essence of a turnaround is cash and value (that is, valuation). My work in turnarounds has provided a unique, critical eye on the impact of new products and product development as they impact cash and valuation.

In turnaround situations, product development can be a critical operational (and cash consuming) activity that affects company survival. New products can resuscitate revenues, but the investments are competitive to other essential and immediate uses of cash (such as payroll). Weak companies often face the challenge of substantial and short-term revenue declines (perhaps a few weeks or months), while new revenues (via new products) take months or years to be realized.

Because cash is so very precious, a critical evaluation of NPD opportunities is essential for a company in recovery. That said, two competing biases affect the evaluation of product opportunities. The optimism (call it *hope*) that a new product might *save the company* is often at odds with fiscal conservatism (perhaps fear) that cash will run out before the new product provides a positive impact.

Given your background, I'd like to focus specifically on the business case. How do you (personally) define what "business case" means?

First and foremost, a business case is a *proposal*. It's an investment pitch. It contains a rigorous assessment of potential profit and risks. A business case should have summary measures of return and cash flows, as well as pro forma income and balance sheets.

A business case is also a *plan*. A complete business case includes a plan for execution: personnel, distribution, licensing, tooling, billing, and so forth. The thoroughness of the plan provides credibility to the proposal.

The process of developing and "selling" a business case is complicated. Can you explain some of the factors product managers should consider in developing a business case?

All good business cases have a few basic *components* and require essential *competencies* by the business case team. The basic business case components include: a precise definition of the product concept, detailed specification of the target user (and channel) segment, a realistic projection of revenues, a comprehensive estimate of product costs (direct and indirect), support and compliance costs, and an assessment of technical feasibility. The essential competencies that are required include: market sizing, channel management, forecasting, product costing, compliance, and a basic grasp of manufacturing or service delivery.

All business cases contain *uncertainty*. No one has enough money to achieve certainty in their business case. Product managers should be constantly aware of "how certain" each of their estimates is, and which of the estimates (such as costs, revenues)

are worthy of additional investment (during the plan development) to improve the credibility of the business case.

One of the common mistakes made by novice product managers is neglecting the importance of *time* in their plans. For
example, market opportunity is often measured as X percent of
the total potential. A weak business case will assume to capture
the X percent without regard to *when* the sales materialize. Some
products require years to reach their potential. In that time, any
plan is subject to the realities of, for example, inflation, competitor reaction, substitute technologies, and obsolescence of the
installed base. Time also contributes to estimation error. Time
lowers the reliability of any forecast, so the longer the product
takes to earn its return, the less likely it is that it will.

One common challenge in developing a business case is
incorporating the less tangible factors in execution, such as a
new product's benefit of convenience, or a target segment decision maker's personal risk in purchasing a new product. My
suggestion is an attempt to find a way to put a quantitative
monetary value on the intangibles. An intangible that cannot
be monetized should be removed from the business case. When
I see justifications, such as, "We'll make it easier for the customer to …, " I immediately discount the credibility of the plan.

*Assuming that a product manager has developed a solid business
case, let's shift our attention to selling it to management. What tips
can you provide?*

Like any other sales activity, it is critical for product managers to
understand their audience. This bit of wisdom is so common that
it is a cliché. That said, I believe it is the strongest advice for selling the business case. In practical terms and as examples: a CFO
will want to know when the investment (the cash) is returned;
the VP of engineering will want to know which resources are
allocated to complete the product development; the VP of manufacturing will want to know the production resources required,
capital funding available, and production volumes envisioned;
and so on.

Learn the *values* of the management team. As examples: if the management team values strategic fit, be sure to have a clear vision about how the new product fits the product strategy and speak in terms of how the new product complements the existing portfolio. If the team values cash recovery, focus on the cash flows and return on invested capital, and be sure to have the appropriate performance estimates, forecasts, and assumptions available.

Learn about the behavior of the management team's *decision making*. There are many aspects to decision making, and that is a topic all by itself. I recommend that the product manager be aware of whether to provide, for example, scoring matrices, decision trees, summary measures of financial performance, or whatever is most useful to the management team. For the organizations that rely on "gut," the product manager should be more aware of the need to walk the business case around the management team to build acceptance. Like any group, there are probably one or two individuals who sway an entire management team.

As with any "sale," always provide the decision makers with a clear expectation of the "next step" and their responsibilities if the project goes forward. The next step provides comfort that the plan has been well considered and lets all individuals know what they are committing to.

What pitfalls should product managers avoid as they work on their business cases?

Five behaviors come to mind that product managers should avoid:

1. Avoid "magical thinking." While it is useful to be optimistic about the potential for a new product, it is equally important to be the "devil's advocate" and consider the many ways that the new product can fail. Usual areas to consider include: competitor reaction, resistance by sales channels, higher manufacturing costs, and slower market acceptance.

2. Avoid reliance on market *numbers* in lieu of market *understanding*. Many product managers rely on estimates of market size, for example, as if the market is a homogeneous opportunity. It is a failure of convenience. Understanding the market is expensive. The Internet has accentuated the risk of using publically available data to substitute for in-depth knowledge.

3. Don't rely on a single measure of performance to prove or disprove the value of a new product or line of business. Some organizations rely on a single measure (usually a financial measure), such as NPV, to rank opportunities. A healthy business case will report the many ways a product can provide value to the company, such as blocking a competitor, line-fill within the channel, entry into a new user segment, and utilization of excess manufacturing capability.

4. Avoid the comfort of planning. Instead, think like an owner. Planning should be difficult because it is essentially a series of tough decisions. Sweating the details of implementation—before you need to—will enrich the plan. When a planner begins to sweat like the person who will execute the plan, he or she will better appreciate the many aspects of successful product design, development, launch, and management.

5. Unless proven otherwise, suspend *faith* that the management team has a rigorous, deliberate method of making investment decisions. If a product manager suspects that decisions are the slightest bit whimsical, it is essential that the product manager provide the management team the tools to help with their decision. That is, to help team members say yes. The easiest approach is to provide a list of criteria to evaluate the project (assuming that the managers don't have their own).

Do you have any final words of advice?

Apply the "smell test" regularly. One of the greatest attributes of a strong product manager is the ability to periodically pause and consider whether there are logical inconsistencies in the plan or items completely forgotten. As examples, it is easy to forecast large revenue growth without budgeting sales channel costs; or plan for instant acceptance by the market when customers' engineers will take years to evaluate the product's value; or forecasting full market penetration for the new product in a year or two when the last five new products still have not met plan.

Always keep an objective perspective about the business case. If a particular new product doesn't go, there will be another, so there should be no fear about killing an idea before it wastes resources.

CHAPTER 8

Overseeing the New Product Projects

TRUE OR FALSE: Scope creep is a result of poor up-front planning.

Actually this is true and false, depending on the situation. There are definitely many examples of poorly defined market requirements that translate into unnecessary rework. However, there are also situations in which unforeseeable changes occur during the project that require product changes before launch. Product managers should try to eliminate the first cause and reduce the severity of the second.

At this point the product manager moves to the middle of the "concepting-creating-commercializing" components. (See Figure 8.1.) Early in this phase the team should strive to freeze the market requirements as boundaries for designing the product specifications. In fact, some companies (e.g., 3M) establish a team "contract" signed by all team members specifying the target market and freezing the high-level product definition. Subsequent changes require the signatures of all team members and possibly management, as well.

So the emphasis is now on *project* management. In some situations (or companies) project leadership stays with the product manager, and in others it shifts to an appointed project manager—often depending on both product complexity and product manager experience.

FIGURE 8.1 ➤ The creating phase of the 3C framework of product development

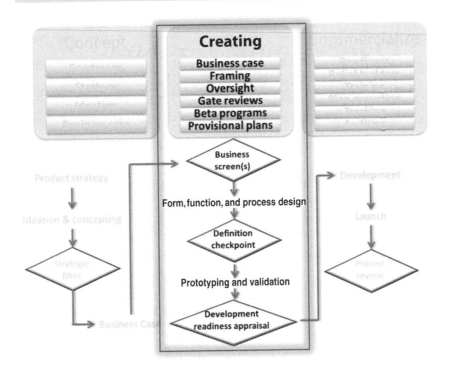

PRODUCT MANAGERS AS PROJECT MANAGERS

Kim Clark and Takahiro Fujimoto, in their *Harvard Business Review* article, "The Power of Product Integrity," differentiate between "heavyweight" product managers and "their lighter-weight counterparts." According to their research in the automotive industry,[1] many product managers are functional workers rather than cross-functional leaders. They lack influence outside their own functional area, have little or no contact with working-level engineers or with marketing, and act primarily as facilitators and coordinators. As a result, they spend much of their time going to meetings, reading reports, and writing memos.

Heavyweight product managers, on the other hand, function as the product's general manager. Clark and Fujimoto explain:

In addition to concept-related duties, the responsibilities that come with the job include: coordinating production and sales as well as engineering; coordinating the entire project from concept to market; signing off on specification, cost-target, layout and major component choices; and maintaining direct contact with existing and potential customers. Heavyweight product managers have a broad knowledge of the product and process engineering required to develop an entire vehicle. Years of experience with the companies give their words weight and increase their influence with people over whom they have no formal authority.[2]

Honda's "large product leader" is such a position. It combines the generation of a strong product concept with the ability to carry it through development to the final product experience for the end customer. When the product manager for the Honda Accord began the third-generation design, he was challenged with maintaining the concept "man maximum, machine minimum" throughout the development process while still repositioning the Accord to fit future customer expectations. Starting with a series of small-group brainstorming sessions, the product leader and his team decided to personify the car's message to consumers with the image of "a rugby player in a business suit." The next step was to break this image down into specific attributes of a car. Five sets of key words were chosen: *open-minded, friendly communication, tough spirit, stress-free, and love forever. Tough spirit* was translated into maneuverability in difficult conditions. *Love forever* translated into long-term customer satisfaction. *Stress-free* led to efforts in noise and vibration reduction.

To capture all these elements was a challenge for the Accord design team. In an effort to allow maximum space and visibility for the occupants, a low engine hood and a larger-than-usual front window were part of the design. Unfortunately the large window meant that the car could get uncomfortably hot in the summer unless there was a large air conditioner, requiring a large engine. And the large engine was contrary to the desire for a low engine hood.

Rather than allowing this to develop into an either-or decision, the product leader reminded the team members to look at their work through future customers' eyes and to maintain the integrity of the initial concept. The result was the development of a new engine that was both compact and powerful.

As the Honda example shows, being market-oriented is a critical role of the talented product manager. However, as Clark and Fujimoto also point out, it requires more than that:

> *It begins with customers, to be sure, since the best concept developers invariably supplement the cooked information they get from marketing specialists with raw data they gather themselves. But strong product concepts also include a healthy measure of what we call "market imagination": they encompass what customers say they want and what the concept's creators imagine customers will want three or more years into the future. Remembering that customers know only existing products and existing technologies, they avoid the trap of being too close to customers and of designing products that will be out-of-date before they are even manufactured.[3]*

The product manager must juggle numerous details and ensure that the subtleties of a product concept are not lost in development and marketing. Although creating product and marketing plans is part of this effort, an essential task is the interpersonal communication of the somewhat intangible ideas. Daily communication with functional engineering departments during the design phase and with plant personnel during the development phase is a necessary role of the product manager. Similarly, product managers in a sense must test-drive the vehicles and continually strive to attain strong product integrity:

> *The product manager's job touches every part of the new product process. Indeed, heavyweight product managers have to be multilingual—fluent in the languages of customers, marketers, engineers, and designers. On one side, this means being able to translate an evocative concept like the pocket rocket into specific targets like "maximum speed 250 kilometers per hour" and "drag coefficient less than 0.3" that detail-oriented engineers can easily grasp. On the other side, it means being able to assess and communicate what a "0.3 drag coefficient" will mean to the customers.[4]*

Outstanding product management organizations depend on the consistency between the formal and informal organizational structure. Honda demonstrated this consistency in some important ways. Communication lines were open and direct rather than indirect. Functional specialists were respected but not put on a pedestal. And the product concept was infused throughout the product team.

Heavyweight product managers in other industries have some of the same characteristics as they have in the automotive industry. As Jean LeGrand stated in her *Bankers Magazine* article, "A Product in Need of Management,"[5] "[a successful product manager in the banking industry] must be a senior-level professional, widely regarded in the profession." This individual must understand "complex portfolio management programs and such quantitative models as cost accounting and return on equity (ROE) computations." And, as in the automotive industry, the position requires market knowledge and the ability to translate technical concepts into customer-appropriate terms.

In fast-moving consumer goods (FMCG) companies, product managers (frequently called "brand managers") are less likely to have industry experience, but rather will have strong management and marketing skills that typically require an MBA. They are expected to create strong brand recognition for their products through their ability to command respect, maintain momentum throughout a product-related project, and motivate everyone toward the same goal. As with heavyweight product managers in other industries, the FMCG brand manager must strive for and champion product integrity.

TEAM STRUCTURE, COMPOSITION, AND PROJECT PROCESSES

A critical resource for a new product project is the right people to do the job. Specific engineers, designers, marketers, and others might personify the qualities most necessary for a given project, but they need to be "borrowed" from related departments. The product manager must negotiate with the various functional department managers, and sometimes with the individuals themselves, to obtain the appropriate staff for the task.

Match Structure with Type of Project

Teams may range from a few members to hundreds. The majority of U.S. firms use cross-functional teams with members representing the most important stakeholders on the project. Different team structures (see Figure 8.2) may be appropriate for different types of projects. Line extensions or simple products may use a straightforward transparent matrix structure in which the product manager ushers the development project through functional departments. In this type of structure, functional team members probably spend less than 25 percent of their time on a given project. The product manager is very likely junior or midlevel. As complexity increases, the structure may change to heavyweight with the product/project manager working with a team of functional experts who may be dedicated full time to (temporarily) work on a new product. Finally for some

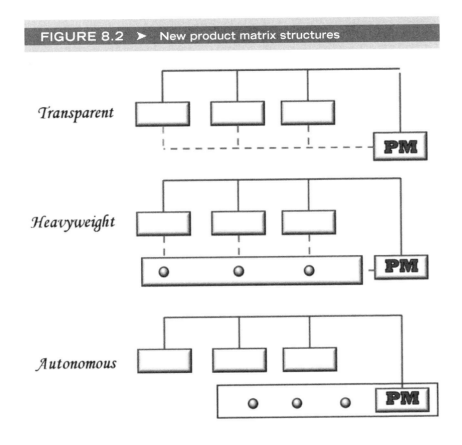

FIGURE 8.2 ➤ New product matrix structures

breakthrough products, an autonomous team (occasionally colocated) might be appropriate. In this structure the reporting relationship shifts from the separate functions to the project. This final structure is the least common of the three. (Smaller firms may not have the "luxury" of using different matrix structures since everyone might be involved on all projects.) Regardless of the structure, product managers must establish the best team integrity possible.

Different functional perspectives are critical, but you might also consider diversity in organizational tenure, culture, gender, and personality. While this may cause increased difficulty in coordination, it may also result in new ideas and solution perspectives from the interaction of divergent perspectives. Teams with a higher degree of shared mental models can be susceptible to groupthink. Therefore, there is value in having team membership change from project to project—but it comes at the risk of inefficiency. To reduce this risk, the product manager should try to preserve knowledge across teams. There are a few tools to help with this. (1) Seed newly formed teams with members from successful past teams. (2) Have new team members attend meetings of successful teams to learn from them prior to participating on a new project team. (3) Appoint members of successful teams as mentors. (4) Ensure that the entire team membership does not change simultaneously.[6]

Establish Team Ground Rules

Product managers as team leaders for product development are responsible for directing the team's activities, maintaining alignment with goals, and communicating with senior management. Start by establishing a team mission statement. While it may seem obvious that the team exists to develop a new product, it's useful to clarify that everyone is in agreement as to the functionality, timing, and goals of the product development effort. This mission statement should be at the top of all meeting agendas and minutes. After commitment to the mission statement, develop a shared set of ground rules for team meetings. This may include items such as, "Everyone comes to meetings fully prepared," or, "All meetings will start and end on time," or, "No cell phones or other distractions allowed during meetings," or, "Responsibility for minutes will rotate among members." Be sure that all team members are aware of their contribution to the deliverables expected for the various gate reviews.

Using Work Breakdown Structures and Activity Charts

As the project team is forming, so is the project schedule. The starting point is the identification of the major activities required to complete this particular new product project. Each of the major activities is further broken down into specific tasks and subtasks to create what is referred to as a *work breakdown structure,* or WBS. The information in the WBS is then used to estimate the time and resource requirements of the project. Therefore, the work tasks must be broken down to a level sufficient to allow acceptable estimates. Without the WBS, any estimates of time and resources will be nothing more than ballpark figures that may be substantially different from actual requirements. Following is an example of a WBS for a product recall. While it is not a new product development project, it provides a simple example of the process:

1000 Conduct comprehensive safety analysis

1001 Classify risks according to industry/government standards
1002 Plant visits
1003 Employee interviews
1004 Product and equipment tests
1005 Determine speed of recall

2000 Inform employees

2001 E-mail all employees
2002 Establish relevant landing page on intranet
2003 Workshop for salespeople on handling the recall in the field

3000 Inform intermediaries and customers

3001 First-class or priority mailing
3002 Phone contact with key accounts
3003 Toll-free hotline for answering questions
3004 Dedicated landing page on Web site
3005 Press releases to relevant media

4000 Recover the recalled product

4001 Channel inventory program
4002 Channel assurance for customer returns
4003 Direct customer returns

5000 Ensure repair or replacement in a timely manner

5001 Internal procedures
5002 External procedures

Once the particular activities and tasks are identified, capture their sequential and parallel relationships. What activities can be done simultaneously, and which ones can happen only in a specific order? This is frequently shown in a flowchart, such as the one shown in Figure 8.3. In this example, Activities A and B can be completed at the same time as C and D, although Activity A precedes B and C precedes D, and all must precede E.

The estimated times for each activity indicate that C-D-E takes the most time and is therefore the *critical path*—the sequence of activities that has no slack and that will delay the entire project if not kept on schedule. The process of constructing a network diagram such as this is called the *critical path method* (CPM). When probabilities are added to the estimated times, the process is called the *program evaluation*

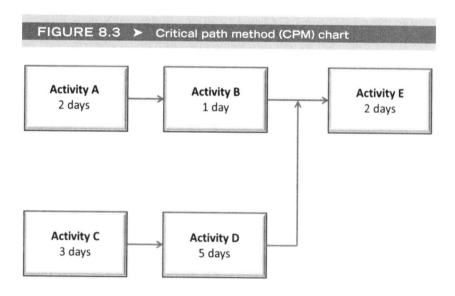

FIGURE 8.3 ➤ Critical path method (CPM) chart

and review technique (PERT). Note that even though the activities in Figure 8.3 were drawn in boxes (referred to as an activity-on-node network), the network could also be drawn with the activities on arrows connected by circles representing the completion of the activities (referred to as an activity-on-arrow network).

Simply constructing a CPM or PERT network is not the most challenging part of project management. Determining what inputs to put into the process and then managing them are the challenges. It's critical that the various individuals or functional areas that will be involved in the execution of the project provide input into the time and *resource requirements* of the various activities. The initial network developed from the preliminary inputs will define the expected budget and end point. If either of these is unacceptable, it's necessary to revisit the objectives, shift resources from noncritical to critical path activities, and/or substitute lower-cost alternatives into the process.

The project plan and schedule put in place prior to the execution of the project serve as tools of a *control system*. In this case, *control* refers to comparing the progress against the plan so that corrective action can be taken when deviations occur. Bar charts (also known as Gantt charts) are commonly used to visualize expected versus actual progress along the activities, as shown in Figure 8.4. Note that Activity B is ahead of schedule (since it was scheduled to be completed by Day 3 and has been

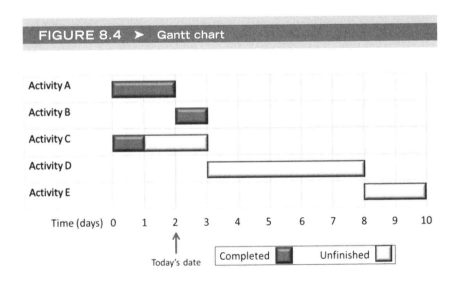

FIGURE 8.4 ➤ Gantt chart

completed by Day 2—today's date). Activity C is behind schedule by a full day. Since Activity C is part of the critical path, the project is falling behind schedule, and corrective action should be taken.

GUIDING GATE REVIEWS AND BETA TESTING

The product manager (along with the project manager, if responsibility is shared) should understand the role of gate reviews during the development process. Most decision reviews (also called phase exit reviews, business decision points, milestones, checkpoints, toll gates, and myriad other terms) are used to determine whether to proceed to the next phase of the product development project.

Different Requirements for Different Reviews

The major *business* reviews conducted with the product screening committee (most likely composed of the heads of each functional area) usually include variations of the business screen, definition checkpoint, and development readiness appraisal. The first review involves approval of the business case as described in the last chapter. The deliverables of this phase are the product definition (with market requirements), estimated revenues and costs, and the preliminary product development plan. The decision to move to the next phase is based on the project passing business screening criteria such as strategic fit and an acceptable risk of success.

Once the cross-functional team begins working on the new product in earnest, there will be continued efforts to better understand the target customers as well as design the best product or service to satisfy the conditions of the business case. Activities include customer visits, concept refinement and testing, and progress toward the ultimate product design. The deliverables include initial product specifications, a better handle on costs, and clearer market sizing and positioning. The next review is the definition checkpoint. At this gate the new product committee will assess whether the market and financial projections are still acceptable, whether the specifications appear reasonable and enable manufacturability, and whether the appropriate resources are available to move forward. If the answer is yes, the project may move into development for a line extension or to prototyping and beta testing for a novel product. Let's assume that the next step is prototype development.

Now the product moves into R&D and/or engineering to be developed into a physical product. Up until now it existed only as a verbal description or a rough mock-up. Now it must be translated into a technologically feasible product. This does not mean that marketing (or product management) is no longer involved. Rather, the product manager's job is to ensure that the core benefits that were the essence of the product concept are not lost during the development process and that progress is being made on the marketing plan, trade-name search, and other factors critical to new product success. This is why a project team approach is crucial.

Prototype Testing and Validation

After the prototypes have been developed, they should be put to rigorous functional and customer testing. The functional tests are conducted under both laboratory and field conditions to be sure that the products are safe and reliable (i.e., consistently perform as they are designed to perform). Customer tests are conducted to be sure that the design is appropriate. Market testing, in-home testing, and beta testing (customer prototype testing) are all variations of the types of tests to be performed at this stage.

Some manufacturers have built gigantic mechanical gizmos that can replicate almost any kind of abuse a product encounters. For example, a car takes a trip through Chrysler's huge climate-controlled lab where robotic drivers subject it to scorching heat and ice storms. Gerber recruits future customers of both sexes at birth and, with the help of enthusiastic parents, maintains a test panel of 2,500 toddlers through age three.

In order to make its PowerBooks even more customer-proof, Apple Computer puts all new models through common indignities. These include drenching them in Pepsi and other sodas, smearing them with mayonnaise, and, to simulate conditions in a car trunk, baking them in ovens at temperatures of 140 degrees or more.[7]

The selection of appropriate beta sites can have an impact on launch success for several reasons. First, the companies or individuals selected should have sufficient knowledge to thoroughly test the product and identify any potential problems or improvements. Second, they (the companies or individuals selected as beta sites) should have "reference value" to use as success stories at the time of launch. Third, they should have good relations with the salesperson in the territory as well as with the company to be able to withstand the risk of product failure without long-term damage.

Some questions to be answered during this stage are as follows:

- Does the prototype work as intended?
- Does it meet specs?
- Does it satisfy customer needs?
- Are there any anticipated production problems?
- Can they be overcome within a reasonable time and cost?
- Has production scheduling been finalized?
- Is it on schedule?
- Have costs been confirmed?
- Have raw materials been ordered?
- Are there minor modifications that can improve the product or its value without adversely affecting the project?
- Is there a need for a significant change that will necessitate a delay in the project?

In general, the product manager should validate the deliverables, the budget, the schedule, the risks, the resources, and the sponsorship of the new product project.

All these questions are part of the development readiness appraisal. If all these questions can be answered positively, the product specifications should be frozen, and the management review committee (i.e., top functional positions) should sign off on the product to indicate acceptance of the specifications and support to fund continuation of the project.

Note that during each of the reviews, product managers are expected to provide increasingly concrete "proof" of product viability. While the initial screen was based on high-level estimates and a "skeleton" of a business plan, product managers are expected to "add meat to the skeleton" as new information becomes available. To be most effective, remember to view the project from the perspective of the different stakeholders. Project team members are concerned about their own activities and the deliverables expected of them. The executive team is less concerned about the activities than they are about the deliverables and the *outcomes* or *results* of those deliverables. In other words, management wants to know the likelihood that the new product will attain the market share, profitability, payback, and other "promises" made in the business case. The product manager should come to the review meetings prepared to demonstrate that the project is on-track vis-à-vis the business case, and if it is not, have appropriate recommendations.

So far I have talked about the traditional (*hard*) business gate reviews for specific new product projects. There are two variations of gate reviews worth mentioning: soft reviews for specific new product projects and portfolio reviews for a batch of new product projects. Soft reviews generally refer to reviews with selected stakeholders rather than with the entire executive or new product screening group. The timing and frequency of these reviews is at the discretion of the product or project manager and are usually driven more by scheduling issues than business decisions. For example, if a product manager is concerned that a subcomponent may not be completed in time or if market information demands another look at functionality, it may be useful to review the select issues to get input on potential changes in direction that may or may not affect the overall project.

Portfolio Reviews

Portfolio reviews are more likely driven by top management than by product managers. While these are sometimes handled in concert with specific project reviews, the evaluation goes beyond an individual product. Rather the reviews are used to determine whether resources are being allocated most efficiently across all products currently in development so that they will attain maximum results for the company. Sometimes a decision may be made to shift resources from Product A to Product B, not necessarily because A is underperforming, but rather that the resources may result in a faster payback, thwart a competitive move, or have a similar strategic impact.

MANAGING AND PREPARING FOR SCOPE CREEP

In addition to managing the team and the gate reviews during new product development, product managers will also be on the lookout for scope creep. *Scope creep* refers to uncontrolled changes in a project's scope, such as additional functions, feature enhancements (featuritis), more expensive components, or other modifications to the initial business case. There are several possible causes: lack of clear product definition early in the process; lack of discipline in following through on the initial definition; and unanticipated market shifts.

To manage scope creep, each of the causes must be considered. First of all, ensure that your scope is clear in the business case. Specify the must-have market requirements and carefully check that they are understood and clearly translated into product specifications by the designer or engineer. Engineers consistently complain that product managers are not specific enough when providing voice-of-customer (VOC) requirements. While this should not encourage product managers to get too far into design, it's important to work with product developers to establish the best balance.

Next, work toward a "contract" of sorts, in which both the project team and the executive review committee sign off on first the market requirements and later the product specifications, thus effectively freezing these components. If all changes require that everyone sign off again, the changes will be carefully considered. If change is required because of quality issues, sign-off will be easy. If change is the result of whim, sign-off will be more difficult. If nice-to-have features are being considered, look into the possibility of incorporating them into a future line extension or an updated version to avoid the need for a change order for this particular project.

It is not uncommon for unavoidable uncertainty to exist at the time a project is started. For example, industry standards or regulatory requirements may be in a state of flux, requiring the ability to adapt as new information becomes available. Even though the plan is based on the best decisions at that time, product managers know that one or more components may need a future change in specifications prior to launch. In such cases it's best to design for uncertainty. Decide what options might need to change and delay freezing just those specs as long as is reasonable. Sometimes this requires "building around" the areas of uncertainty (such as a subcomponent) so that the total product will not require changes if the subcomponent changes. This may also mean that more and earlier prototypes will need to be developed (rapid prototyping) to accelerate learning. The flexibility of these approaches may cost a bit more up front, but save time and money in the long run if changes are necessary. It's sort of like paying for an insurance policy.[8]

Finally, if the scope creep is caused by unanticipated market shifts, such as new competitive products, recessions, or consumer behavior vacillations, a business decision will need to be made. Are the shifts significant enough to demand product changes? Can the product changes be minimized? Is it viable to defer the changes to a future product? If market shifts demand product changes, the sooner they can be addressed, the better it will be for the entire new product effort.

CHAPTER CHALLENGE

Think like a heavyweight product manager even if you are not the project owner during development. Continually strive to attain and maintain strong product integrity.

INTERVIEW WITH LAURA FARNHAM: WHAT EXECUTIVES EXPECT IN TERMS OF PROJECT OVERSIGHT

Laura Farnham, vice president, Johnson Controls, Laura.Farnham@jci.com.

Laura, you've had a distinguished career starting as a product manager at DEC and progressing to your current role as VP-Controls

Line of Business at Johnson Controls. In a nutshell, can you talk about your career path?

My first product management role was with Digital Equipment Corporation. At the time, it was a $12B computer products and services company, later acquired by Compaq and then Hewlett-Packard. They had a very formal process and time-tested discipline around product management. Because of the standardized process, it was relatively easy to move throughout the company. I began in semiconductors and moved into software, systems, and ultimately services. By the time HP acquired Compaq, I was vice president of marketing for Compaq Global Services. After that experience in the IT industry, I moved to building management systems (BMS) and heating, ventilation, and air conditioning (HVAC) with Honeywell, Trane, and Johnson Controls.

One of the great things about the role of a product manager is that it touches virtually every aspect of the business. It is so foundational to business success that it easily carries over from one business or industry to another. And it provides such great, cross-functional experience that the career path options are plentiful.

Tell us a bit about similarities and differences in product management across these companies?

Digital Equipment Corporation was by far the most mature in its process and cross-business deployment. That was partially a result of the industry (where the function was well-accepted), and partially due to the engineering culture of the company (which was very comfortable with standard, repeatable processes).

While the function of product management is maturing in the BMS and HVAC industries, the fundamental principles are equally applicable. The value of a mature process is that the whole business is engaged and understands the importance and impact of a strong product management function. It drives strategic alignment across functions—including sales, marketing, and engineering—in addition to ensuring that the right products are delivered to market at the right time and cost points.

Let's shift specifically to new product development. As one of the gatekeepers of the process, you are responsible for making recommendations on whether new product projects should move forward. What do you expect from your product managers to help you make these decisions?

It might sound a bit overwhelming, but I expect just about everything from the product manager. Whether it's a thorough understanding of the competitive landscape; trade-offs between features, cost, and time to market; implications of manufacturing locations and processes on cost and delivery; pricing and the trade-offs between margin and market share—you name it. The product manager is the single point of accountability for every aspect of the product.

Specific to the gate review process, the product manager will need to provide different information at different phases of the development process. For example, in an ideation or concept phase, the market information and customer requirements are at a relatively high level. As the concept matures and progresses to Phase 2 exit, a complete business case is required to support the go/no-go decision. This includes clear market sizing and growth rates, market share estimates, competitive positioning, pricing and margin targets, engineering and manufacturing investments, SG&A investments, etc. Additionally, scenario modeling should be included to illustrate the program sensitivity, for example, to changes in price, cost, or market share.

As development concludes and the team is preparing to launch the new product, I expect the product manager to validate the business case and market assumptions. Where product development takes an extended amount of time, market conditions may change which may affect the value proposition or competitive positioning. The product manager needs to monitor these factors throughout the development process. Adjustments to the marketing plans may be required to ensure that the program will deliver the financial returns promised at Phase 2 exit.

Can you cite a couple of specific product management success stories?

Most of my favorite success stories involve new or adjacent spaces. These are the hardest hills to climb because the organization is forced to think outside the box, and change is required on many fronts. But these are the most rewarding—similar to the "no pain, no gain" philosophy of exercise.

In one case, it was a new category of software. Some of the concepts came out of the R&D labs, which complicated the development process but ultimately gave us a leadership product. Our biggest challenge was forecasting sales since it was a totally new category of product. The good news was that it only ran on our operating system so we could make business case assumptions around penetration rates into our installed customer base. The next challenge was selling it—it wasn't our typical product and therefore required extensive training of the sales force and technical support teams. While it took a tremendous amount of effort to launch, it quickly became one of the company's top sellers and paid back not only financially but in the team's engagement level and overall professional satisfaction.

On the other end of the spectrum, it's as important to know when to *cancel* a project as it is to advance a project. Often it's difficult for product managers to recommend cancelling a product given the time and effort they have personally invested. But I recall one example where the organization was considering developing a new high-end product. The competition was limited, the market was well-defined, but the entry cost was very high, partly due to a long product development cycle. Emotionally the leadership team wanted to brand the industry's biggest system, but the financials simply did not justify the investment. Even though the product manager developed multiple scenarios to try to meet the financial requirements, he ultimately had to recommend cancelling the program. It might sound straightforward, but it was a very difficult decision for the company.

What advice would you give product managers that would help them do their jobs more effectively?

The role is very complex, and it's hard to identify one nugget of advice. So I'll leave you with three thoughts:

1. Plan thoroughly, deliver on your commitments, and communicate broadly.
2. Think holistically and proactively.
3. Build strong cross-functional, cross-organizational teams.

And, most of all, enjoy what you're doing.

CHAPTER 9

Formulating and Executing Launch Plans

> ***TRUE OR FALSE:*** Being first to market guarantees success.
>
> This is sometimes referred to as the first-mover advantage—and it does not guarantee success. In fact, many of the products we perceive as first-movers (e.g., Apple iPod, Amazon Kindle) were actually successful followers that fixed some of the mistakes of their predecessors. They also implemented superior launch strategies. Product managers are sometimes surprised to find out that their first-to-market new products were unable to sell themselves. Don't underestimate the value of a solid launch.

Now the product manager moves to the final phase of the concept-create-commercialize component of new product development, as shown in Figure 9.1.

CRAFTING A LAUNCH STRATEGY

The deadline is approaching. Stress is rising. There is a mix of excitement and worry as the launch date gets closer. Will the product be ready for shipment in time? Have all the ancillary activities been planned for? Will there be any surprises? This is a launch *process*—and the launch is actually a journey rather than the destination. The product manager is the tour guide who ensures that a strong new product doesn't fail because of a poorly executed launch. Think of a new

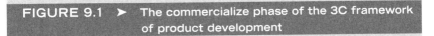

FIGURE 9.1 ➤ The commercialize phase of the 3C framework of product development

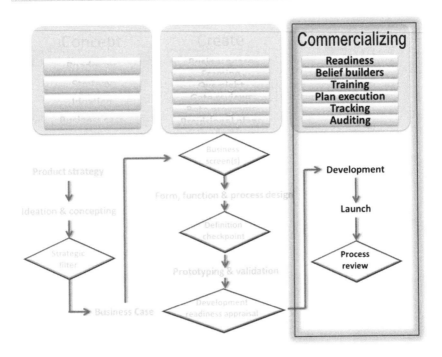

product project as climbing a mountain. The team is enthused and energized as progress is made toward reaching the summit (i.e., the product is developed). But the team members still have to trek down the hill (i.e., launch the product successfully). By then they are tired, hungry, and ready for the trip to be over. It's at this point that the product manager has to generate a new "buzz"—with salespeople, the channel, and with customers.

Although the launch is being planned from the first time the original idea *passes go*, the action now moves forward at a quicker, more deliberate pace. This chapter focuses on the prelaunch activities (which should have been completed by now), as well as the launch considerations when introducing the product to the sales force and channel, and the follow-through activities after launch to track progress and improve processes.

PRELAUNCH

The prelaunch is the period prior to commercialization when the product manager verifies that all preparations have been made for the actual product introduction. If market testing is necessary, it will be conducted at this point to evaluate the validity of the proposed marketing strategy. During this stage, the product manager must identify all stakeholders and determine their information requirements. Customer service must be prepared to handle inquiries and fulfill orders. Technical support personnel may require specialized training. The distribution channel may require advance notice of any unique requirements of the product or service.

Market Testing

Beta testing of the product, as mentioned in the previous chapter, is an effort to debug a product under real-world conditions. These tests should have determined the viability of the product, but they might not have addressed the best way to go to market. In this case, a market test or a simulated market test of the launch strategy (not just the product) may or may not be necessary. Test marketing helps assess whether the right price is being charged, whether the appropriate message is being communicated, and whether the proper distribution strategy is being employed. Of course, test marketing is expensive in terms of both money and time—and in terms of alerting competition to your launch strategy. Therefore, it should be undertaken only when the risk of not doing it is great.

For a typical test market, the product manager selects a geographic area that is as representative of the product's target market as possible and markets the product on a limited basis in that region. The key decisions to be made include: How many test markets? Which ones? And how long should the tests run? Most companies select two or three test markets that provide good representation of their target customers. Good representation refers to ensuring that critical demographic variables are dispersed in the target area in about the same proportion that exists in the total market area. The length of the test will vary depending on the type of product. Some will require six to nine months, and others will need two years. The factor to consider is the length of the buying cycle, with the ideal test market being at least as long as two buying cycles.[1]

Identify the "What If?" Items

Few launches occur without any glitches. So it's useful to go back to the beginning and retrace your steps to look for omissions. Develop a pre-launch checklist (perhaps like one shown in Table 9.1) to help you stay on track. The checklist should identify responsible parties and reaffirm launch readiness.

Start with a reality check on the product itself. It's almost a given that the end product is not exactly the same as the original idea. Determine whether the product still provides the benefits it was designed for. Make sure there is a clear understanding of the target market it is best suited for. If there have been changes in the market or the competition since inception, verify that your product still has competitive superiority.

For many products, especially consumer products, the packaging is one of the first contacts a customer has with the product; so you want to be sure it is appropriate. When the cholesterol-lowering Lipitor was launched in the late 1990s, it was considered one of the most successful pharmaceutical launches ever. And the company credits part of its success to the literature contained within the package:

> Look at the literature in the package insert that compares Lipitor with each of its major competitors in its power to lower cholesterol and tryglycerides. There is probably more food for comparative promotion than most products would have in a complete life cycle. This demonstrates the outstanding job performed by our clinical development and marketing teams working in collaboration, even up to the point of launch.[2]

Regulatory approvals are critical to most products in the healthcare industry and can delay a launch if they are not obtained on time. If a product is being launched globally, there may be separate approvals required for individual countries. Verify systems readiness from IT, production, technical support, and other operations groups. Be sure that your warranty program is clear and that claims can be handled if necessary.

Table 9.1

Prelaunch Checklist

	Yes/No	Contingencies
Product reality check		
• Does it fulfill the original idea? • Does it still fit the market? • Is there competitive superiority?		
Packaging		
• Will it facilitate storage, use, transport, and convenience? • Does it provide customer-friendly information?		
Regulatory approvals and standards		
• Have all country, governmental, and industrial approvals been obtained? • Can you demonstrate compliance and efficacy?		
Systems readiness		
• Is it ready for ordering and billing? • Are preliminary production runs complete?		
Service and tech support		
• Is infrastructure in place? • Warranty programs ready? • Service programs defined? • Spare parts, loaners, upgrade tools?		
Logistics		
• Process map for physical movement to customer's location?		
Marketing decisions		
• Pricing policies by market? • Rollout sequence planned? • Marketing communications on track?		
Marketing support		
• Sales and customer service training set? • Kick-off events and activities planned? • Collateral material ready?		

You should also verify marketing readiness. Pricing policies, including distributor discount programs and internal transfer programs, should be in place. Your rollout strategy should be finished, with priority markets identified. Your advertising group (whether internal or external) should be ready with the appropriate marketing communications at launch. Sales support—including training, kickoff events, contests, short-term incentives, collateral, and so forth—should be on track.

Launch Preparation Documentation

In addition to the prelaunch checklist mentioned earlier, other preparatory documents (as shown in Figure 9.2) might be important. Four to consider are: (1) market and product profiles, (2) a milestone activities chart, (3) the marketing strategy to support the launch, and (4) an early indicator chart with a control plan. All of these guide the launch and early commercialization.

The market and product profiles are critical components of the launch. The *market profile* should define the focused market of *ideal* customers, using as many segmentation variables as are appropriate.

FIGURE 9.2 ➤ Preparatory documents for launch

It should describe both the rational and emotional reasons the customer would be interested in buying this product. It should explain the customer's decision and purchase process(es), and it should possibly explain the role of influencers. Unfortunately, too many product managers list all markets that might someday buy the product in an attempt to build enthusiasm for its many applications and uses. But claiming that the product solves all of the world's problems and that everyone is a potential customer yields rolled eyes and cynicism in the sales force. This shotgun approach squanders resources and dilutes the sales effort.

Business Brief 9.1, Good VOC Helped Briggs & Stratton Design and Launch TransportGuard, offers several points worth mentioning here. First, Briggs & Stratton made a conscious effort to use both surveys and observation (ethnography) to gather information from customers in the commercial rental market. Second, the company identified a previously unarticulated need to create a highly desirable product feature. Finally, customer messaging focused on the theme of listening to customers, as highlighted in their "TransportGuard" YouTube video and on the page of sales collateral at the end of the business brief.

Business Brief 9.1

GOOD VOC HELPED BRIGGS & STRATTON DESIGN AND LAUNCH TRANSPORTGUARD

By Dan Roche, Marketing Manager, Briggs & Stratton Corp.

Dan Roche has worked in B2B marketing his entire career, starting as a marketing communications consultant with several Midwest ad agencies. Since switching to the "client side," he has been leading the marketing efforts for Briggs & Stratton Commercial Power, including managing the Vanguard brand. Dan enjoys spending time with his family, in the summers serving as the pit crew for his sons' go-kart racing team.

Briggs & Stratton enjoys high market share in consumer lawn and garden markets; however, the commercial power division is focused on growing market share in construction and rental equipment markets. The Vanguard engine line was created to differentiate the product, team, and value proposition to cater to the needs of people who use power equipment for a living.

Midway through the development of a new line of single-cylinder air-cooled engines, the team was at a crossroads in making a decision on commercial features that would be differentiated and valued enough to get the new engine line noticed among a sea of entrenched competitors.

Before getting customer feedback, the team needed to identify what voice it would prioritize in the VOC (voice of customer) process. Given the nature of the commercial rental business (tough environment, low end-user brand polarity), the team selected rental owners as a proxy to help team members understand the features that mattered most to commercial equipment owners and operators.

Then, armed with a list of feature options, the team did the next logical thing—it built an advent calendar. This tool (a large board with the engine photo in the middle surrounded by feature "doors") was the perfect concept screen tool to engage the customer and stimulate discussion about the features that made sense. Doors that were left open meant that those features were valued. Doors that were closed were not valued. The advent calendar also served as a physical prop to photograph and videotape during the VOC collection visits.

The other important part of VOC collection was to tour the locations of the rental owners. These tours offered countless opportunities to ask many questions and understand the real connection between the engine and the day-to-day task of keeping equipment running and keeping customers happy. During one of those visits, the team encountered a 55-gallon drum of motor oil in the maintenance shop of one of their VOC contributors. When asked why the owner had such a large volume of motor oil, it was learned that the engines he was using required hyperfrequent oil changes resulting from operator carelessness and a confusing shutoff procedure on the current engines. While the owner had long given up on his customers being more careful and following shutoff directions better, the team knew that one of the features on the advent calendar solved that problem for good.

This gave birth to the central feature of the new engines—TransportGuard. This feature makes for fail-safe shutting down of the engine using one operator touch-point, compared with the two switches (one for electrical and the other for fuel flow) on the current engines. TransportGuard combines both the electrical circuit and fuel flow into one lever actuation, thus removing operator error, protecting the engine, and saving the rental owner service time for oil changes.

The reason this is important is that when the engine is transported and the fuel valve is left open, fuel in the tank flows through the carburetor and into the engine. Fuel flowing into the engine during transport causes many problems that require changing the oil and cleaning out the engine. This costs the rental owner time and money to fix. It also jeopardizes the owners' ability to honor back-to-back rentals and costs them repeat customers because of the service time required to fix the engine.

The new Vanguard engines were launched at the 2010 World of Concrete trade show in Las Vegas, Nevada, in February 2010. The team used a combination of print and electronic materials and even a powered display to demonstrate the benefits of TransportGuard to communicate the advantages of this feature and the entire engine. At the show, the product won the Most Innovative Product award and has gone on to win similar recognition in the North American Rental and Turf markets as well as the European commercial industry.

The team developed a DVD to educate OEMs and rental owners on the challenges of transporting equipment and the hazards of oil dilution. Video segments from the DVD were converted for YouTube display.

Winning over the rental market gatekeeper has been a critical proof point for OEMs, who are ultimately responsible for engine placement on equipment. While work is still underway, the Briggs & Stratton team is confident that listening to the customer to discover unmet needs or unnecessary frustrations will reap long-term rewards of their commercial market customers. (See Figure 9.3.)

COMMERCIAL POWER

FIGURE 9.3 ➤ Example sales collateral.

YOU ASKED FOR DEPENDABILITY. THESE ENGINES DELIVER.

LISTENING LED TO THE DEVELOPMENT OF THE TRANSPORTGUARD™ SYSTEM — AN EXCLUSIVE ADVANTAGE ON THESE VANGUARD™ ENGINES.

You said fuel flowing into the engine during transport was a problem. You were right. During transport, engines are subjected to vibration, which can cause fuel to flow through the engine and into the oil. Fuel in the oil drastically reduces viscosity, resulting in more friction, increased wear and shorter engine life. Bottom line: oil dilution is costly and negatively impacts your business.

PROBLEM SOLVED.

Vanguard™ engineers went to work and now with a single flip of this red lever, your customers simultaneously shut off the fuel when they shut off the engine. Just that easy, no fouled plugs, hydraulic lock, cylinder wash down or crankcase oil dilution. Fuel stays where it belongs.

TESTED AND PROVEN.

To verify the performance of this technology, Vanguard engineers measured real transport conditions then precisely simulated those results in Briggs & Stratton's Engine Application Center. As this chart shows, competitor engines allowed up to five ounces of fuel to flow into the cylinder with the valve open. This can lead up to eight times the accelerated wear rate when compared to engines protected by the TransportGuard™ system.

With TransportGuard, you have the leverage to eliminate human error... minimize maintenance costs...and eliminate down time.

* Briggs & Stratton Engine Application Center testing 2/06.
** Fuel valve left open.

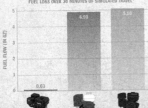

FUEL LOSS OVER 30 MINUTES OF SIMULATED TRAVEL*

VANGUARD WITH TRANSPORTGUARD™	HONDA™	SUBARU™
0.03	4.90	5.18

The product profile works in concert with the market profile to clarify the customer-based value. It explains what the product is and why it's better than the competition's product, and then goes on to provide proof of the claims. If there is different value for different markets, it's worth noting that here. Pharmaceutical brand managers realize the importance of establishing clear value by stakeholder, as explained in Business Brief 9.2, "Establishing Brand Value in Early Launch," which follows.

Business Brief 9.2

ESTABLISHING BRAND VALUE IN EARLY LAUNCH

According to conventional wisdom in the pharmaceutical industry, a new brand has 120 days after launch to create momentum. Therefore, product managers must establish a clear value proposition for all relevant stakeholders during the prelaunch time period. Patients who purchase the product in pharmacies are looking for relief from some ailment. Managed care professionals purchasing the product for in-hospital use are concerned with reimbursement issues. Physicians purchasing the product for clinic use want relief from paperwork and clear proof of efficacy. Value and benefits have to be expressed in terms relevant to these particular customer segments.

Product managers should also identify markets that may be resistant to the new product, and build in appropriate contingency plans:

In the 1990s, Merck promoted its new agent, Proscar (finasteride) as a way to enable primary care physicians to treat benign prostatic hypertrophy (BPH), thereby sparing older men a painful, invasive surgical procedure known as a trans-urethral resection of the prostate (TURP). The problem was that men with BPH were treated by urologists, a large portion of whose incomes came from performing the procedure. They refused to surrender their patients and fought against Proscar, which never fully overcame their resistance.

Similar concepts of segmented brand value can apply to other products as well. Tools aimed at do-it-yourselfers rather than professional contractors need to address different levels of competency, price sensitivity, and channel—even if the product is essentially the same. Products being launched into different countries must be "glocalized" to meet specific value requirements. And the roles of users, decision makers, payers, channel members, and other influencers will need to be considered as well.

Source: Adapted from Roger Green and J. Martin Jemigan, "Building Brand Value," *Pharmaceutical Executive* (September 2004), pp. 36–45.

The milestone activities chart lists the desired dates of completion for significant activities such as purchasing equipment for the launch, finalizing package design, obtaining legal clearance, subcontracting specialized labor, and preparing the owner's manual. Each of these may require several steps and may vary in importance depending on the project. Their potential impact on product success must be considered in assessing priorities. For example, electronic or high-tech consumer products require clarity in technical documentation in order to be successful. Customers are increasingly seeking simplicity in a complicated world. Unfortunately, as a *BusinessWeek* article stated, "Plain English is a language unknown in most of the manuals that are supposed to help us use electronic products."[3] The format of the milestone activities chart can vary from a simple list of activities and dates to more formal project schedule and control techniques like Gantt and PERT charts.

The marketing component of the launch materials details the branding, packaging, pricing, advertising, and related topics. As with the annual product plan, the new-product marketing plan should start with an objective such as, "Convert 25 percent of current customers to the product upgrade and obtain trial by an additional 25 percent." The marketing tactics would then be put into place to accomplish this objective. A streamlined outline for this new product marketing strategy is shown below. Some companies include all or most of the listed components; others will need to be more selective. Line extensions might require only an abbreviated outline, whereas breakthrough products will need extensive marketing strategy plans.

1. New-product objectives
   a. Sales volume
   b. Market penetration
2. Background summary
   a. Total industry sales volume and trends
   b. Major competitors and analysis
   c. Market segment and potential
3. Product overview
   a. Market requirements and specs
   b. Brand name
   c. Why is this better?
   d. Ideal customer profile
   e. Positioning
4. Entry strategy
   a. Timing
   b. Rollout strategy
5. Company preparations
   a. Internal preparations
   b. Sales force tools
   c. Customer service training
   d. Field seminars
   e. Policy statements
6. Marketing plan
   a. Targeting market
   b. Sales incentives
   c. Channel incentives
   d. Base price and discounts
   e. Special promotions
   f. Advertising
7. Resource requirements
   a. Training tools and costs
   b. Demos and tools
   c. Launch events
   d. Miscellaneous

As mentioned earlier, a decision will need to be made as to whether to price a product high initially to recover the development costs or to price it low to gain market share faster. Now you have more information than was available early in the process, and you are able to fine-tune the pricing. A number of factors affect this decision. First, how likely is it that competitors will enter the market soon? The ability of competitors to enter the market will be based on the investment required to enter, the ease of entering, and their own strategies. The faster that competition is likely to enter, the more appropriate a penetration (low) price strategy is. Second, is there a large enough segment of customers willing to pay a high price for the product initially? Third, is the company, product, or service positioned appropriately for the price strategy being considered? Finally, what are the payback period, hurdle rates, and return required by the company?

The final component of the launch documentation (after completing the milestone activities chart and the various event calendars and schedules from the marketing plan) is a calendar of early indicators of potential launch success. *Early indicators* refer to outcomes, such as the number of inquiries that can help predict or provide early indicators of the level of launch success. For example, history might indicate that 30 inquiries typically convert to one sale. In that case, tracking the number of inquiries could provide an early indicator of future sales. Other early indicators might include the number of sales calls made for the new product, the percentage of distributors willing to carry it, the awareness level of the market, the number of facings retailers give to the product, and so on. After identifying the early indicators, the next step is to set time-based (e.g., weekly, monthly) goals for each. The early indicator chart, then, lists the outcomes expected by the end of designated time periods (e.g., each month), thereby enabling the product manager to compare actual against expected performance without waiting for final sales data.

With launch documentation prepared, the product is ready to move to the launch phase. It's worth noting that sales training may sometimes be required during the prelaunch phase (perhaps six to nine months prior to the official launch), or it may be part of the launch process. The information on sales training is presented below in the discussion of the launch stage.

Timing

Whether relative to the competition or relative to seasonal or industry events, timing can be a critical component of new product success. If competitors might be (or are) entering the market, the product manager must decide whether to get there before, with, or after the competition. First entry usually provides an advantage, but if rushing results in a flawed product, the result can be more damaging than good. According to Fernando Suarez and Gianvito Lanzolla in their *Harvard Business Review* article, "first-mover advantage is more than a myth but far less than a sure thing."[4] They argue that the combined effects of market and technological change affect a firm's chances of first-mover advantage. Specifically, gradual evolution in both the technology and market arenas provides the best conditions for lasting impact. On the other hand, abrupt changes in technology (or changes in both technology and markets) will give later entrants weapons for attacking. The assessment of competitive response and market acceptance must be considered in timing and implementation decisions.

Timing an entry *with* competition can neutralize the competitor's potential first-mover advantage as well as possibly increase the potential market faster. Delaying an entry until after competition is in the market might make it possible to capitalize on competitive flaws as well as benefit from any competitor advertising that educates the market. Timing is also important if there are seasonal or cyclical aspects to a product or if success depends on visibility at a key "new products" trade show.

Decisions regarding timing should take into account what impact the new product may have on the rest of the company's product line. Launching a product before components essential to its usability are available is premature timing. Similarly, launching substitute products must be appropriately timed. If there is substantial pipeline inventory in the channel, you may want to postpone the launch until some of the old product has been sold. However, if a delayed launch risks a vacuum period when there is no inventory of either the old or the new product, it can create a period of potential advantage for the competition. In this case, plan a period of overlap, using pricing, and/or channel strategy to differentiate the substitutes and minimize cannibalization. Timing can become a significant issue in the pharmaceutical industry when products are going off patent, as explained in Business Brief 9.3, "Product Line Planning for Patent Expiration."

Business Brief 9.3

PRODUCT-LINE PLANNING FOR PATENT EXPIRATION

With more than $80 million worth of blockbuster drugs having reached patent expiration in 2008, it's not surprising that 71 percent of pharmaceutical companies are aggressively pursuing life-cycle management tactics. This may include introducing generic versions, flanker brands, encouraging Rx-to-OTC switching, and extending the brand through follow-on product, reformulations, or new delivery systems. A fundamental question is how quickly customers will switch to generics since that affects the timing of these decisions.

The acceptance of generics is growing. The Federal Trade Commission reports that between 1984 and 2002, the share of prescriptions that became generics has grown from 19 to 47 percent, with experts estimating it at over 50 percent today. According to Jon Hess, a senior analyst at Cutting Edge Information, "With so much riding on the right strategy, companies are really taking a closer look at what others have successfully been doing in the industry. Right now, of the patent-protection strategies available, line extensions appear to offer companies the greatest potential for lucrative returns."

BristolMyers Squibb, GlaxoSmithKline, Johnson & Johnson, and Pfizer have all explored generics or flanker brands during the first decade of the 2000s. As an example, before Prilosec went off patent, AstraZeneca was able to successfully transfer 40 percent of the users to its new acid reducer, Nexium. While not all companies face the type of impact affecting pharmaceutical companies when their products go off patent, they can learn from the thought processes used for life-cycle management.

Source: Jon Hess, "Line Extensions: Most Common Patent-Protection Strategy," *PR Newswire* (March 2, 2005), p. 1; and Edward Tuttle, Andrew Parece, and Anne Hector, "Your Patent Is About to Expire: What Now?" *Pharmaceutical Executive* (November 2004), pp. 88–92.

Geographic Strategy

It is also necessary to make decisions on a geographic strategy. On some occasions, a national or international launch is appropriate, but many new products start with a full rollout strategy. Prioritize the markets (e.g., regions, industries, or countries) and decide on an entry sequence. For example, it might be desirable to first enter the most attractive markets in terms of size and dollar potential. Or it might be more desirable to enter markets in which competition is weak, thus providing your company and product the opportunity to gain experience, exposure, and market position. The selection of rollout markets can also be based on different product applications, pipeline inventory in the markets, ability to gain distributor or retailer support, company reputation in the market, or a host of other factors.

Although the rollout might appear similar to test marketing, it differs in a couple of important ways. First, in a test market the product manager targets regions that are representative of the final launch. This is not the case with a rollout. The markets are selected based on their ability to provide an early cash flow or to gain commitment from a potentially influential market segment needed for the continued rollout. Second, the test market is a final test *before* the commercialization decision is made. The rollout occurs *after* the commercialization decision is made.[5]

LAUNCH

The next step of the new product development process—launch—results in the introduction of the product into the market. Here the product manager's job is to educate, motivate, and keep the momentum going. Implementation will require putting the timing and geographic strategies into action. It will require training and providing incentives for the sales force and the channel. And it will require executing the communications plan that was previously engineered.

Sales Training

Whenever possible, identify clients/prospects by name. The more detail that can be provided for the sales force, the greater the chances of encouraging salespeople to sell the new product. Work closely with members of the sales force to provide them with information that will help them sell. Prepare "how to sell it" booklets that discuss customers (not target markets), applications (not features), and useful questions to ask on a sales call. Make sure that customer service stays in the loop with sufficient communication through internal newsletters, informal and formal meetings, and various announcements.

The introductory marketing strategy details introductory pricing, base price, and option pricing; press releases and product announcements; direct mail and e-mail blasts to select customers; shipping policies and procedures; channel and end-user communications; and training for the sales force and/or customers. The sales training in particular should help salespeople *sell* the product rather than simply *pitch* the product.

The sales training that is part of the product launch should educate and motivate the salespeople to sell your product. In other words, why should the salespeople believe that the product will perform as claimed? What motivation is there for them to sell it? For a modification of an existing product, the best proof is past sales success. For completely new products, a bit more persuasion is necessary. Results from test marketing or beta testing, statements from sales managers or other salespeople indicating their success in a rollout region, sales that you (as product manager) have personally made, or trade shows and lead generation programs in place can help convince salespeople that the product is worth their time and effort to pursue. In addition, financial and nonfinancial motivators should be considered. Higher commissions, better bonuses, and desirable contests can work under the right circumstances. Nonfinancial motivators could include customer input suggesting that less sales effort is necessary to be successful, the ability to sell the product along with another product with a minimal increase in selling time, or unquestionable proof of superiority over the competition.

Sales training may also need to extend to the channel. Distributors, dealers, and other resellers don't have the same vested interest in the new product as internal stakeholders might. Yet they all play a crucial role in getting the product to target customers. Not only do these resellers need to believe that it is a good business decision to make an investment in your new product, but they must also be motivated to create the best environment to make the product a success. What training will their salespeople need? Will they need to provide technical training to their support personnel? How much inventory is necessary? Does the new product require minimum shelf space or specific shelf facings to be successful? Will the reseller need help in promoting the product? Some companies find that contests and additional funds are required to establish the "excitement" necessary to give the new product a chance to be successful. (See Business Brief 9.4, "Launching a New Product through a Dealership Network.")

Business Brief 9.4

LAUNCHING A NEW PRODUCT THROUGH A DEALERSHIP NETWORK

Many new products are sold through dealers, distributors, wholesalers, or retailers. These organizations have a significant impact on the launch process. They desire new products that can increase revenues and profits from their customers, but sometimes they need help in executing the plans. Chrysler, for example, stepped up its efforts to launch a stream of new products and establish closer cooperation with dealers. David Cole, director of the Center for Automotive Research in Ann Arbor, Michigan, recognizes the importance of these relationships. "Chrysler has a lot of new products. The real problem is that everyone else does, too. It's how companies and dealers execute the other things that is going to make the difference between the winners and losers."

Starting in 2003, Chrysler rolled out a more comprehensive program to support new product launches through its 4,400 dealers. These dealers are independent-minded entrepreneurs who have spent tens of millions of dollars on their operations and want assurance of the best future cars to invest in. Many dealers had complained that previous training and support materials were insufficient for their needs. The program, therefore, was designed with several components:

- Day-long ride-and-drive programs.
- Salesperson certification after passing online course at dealership.

- Competition with several $1,000 prizes.
- Internet-based contests, with best scorers posted on an online leader board.
- Collateral including pocket guides, laminated sell sheets, static-cling disks.
- DVDs and other point-of-sale materials.
- Programs to help dealers get customers back for future service.

Another example of a launch process is the one Cadillac used to introduce the Catera in the late 1990s. Even though the product was not as successful as had been hoped, there are nevertheless insights that can be obtained from the launch process. When Cadillac introduced the Catera (an entry-level luxury car), it had to shift from its existing market of older, loyal customers and appeal to a demographic segment unfamiliar to its dealers. To inspire dealerships to get behind this new product, it created Catera College. The college consisted of two-and-a-half days of sessions providing information about the new customer base and the vehicle itself. At the college, dealers drove the car and saw it taken apart piece by piece. For dealers who could not attend, Cadillac rented theaters across the country. On the big screen, dealers were presented with an up-close look at their customers, as well as the teamwork involved in selling the product. While the training itself was not an incentive to sell the product, it provided the tools necessary to make the incentives (such as a contest) work, and both were tied to Cadillac's Standards for Excellence (SFE) awards.

Dealerships were awarded points for success in such categories as technician training, salesperson training, and customer service. Every month, each dealership is notified of its standing in the contest. The grand prize is a trip to an exotic locale with a twist. Just sending winners to the beach to drink cocktails and watch the sun set is not part of Cadillac's game plan. The company has made intensive business seminars a major focus of the trip. In 1997 when the Catera was being launched, the grand prize was a trip to Germany to see the Catera being built.

SFE winners appreciate the dual purpose of the trip. "There are meetings in the morning to discuss ways to better your dealership. The goal is to get you to look at your store and find ways to improve it," says Ed Nimnicht, president and CEO of Nimnicht Cadillac in Jacksonville, Florida. "Then you get some leisure time to enjoy winning the contest."

Part of the product launch incorporated tests for dealers. They earned points for answering questions properly and had to demonstrate a minimum knowledge level to get into the program. In addition, selling the Catera was a requirement for dealers trying to win Cadillac's "Master Dealer Status."

It's worth noting that a successful launch will not "save" a product that is not inherently strong, but it's also true that a strong product can be hurt by an unsuccessful launch strategy.

Source: Adapted from Dale Buss, "Wheeling and Dealing," *Sales and Marketing Management* (February 2004), pp. 36–41. Kenneth Hein, "Preparing for the Launch," *Incentive* (April 1997), pp. 45–49.

Marketing Communications

The message and media strategy for a new product launch will follow many of the general issues for marketing communications. When possible, public relations and publicity should be the first step in the new product communications strategy and should *precede* the launch date. The more differentiated and unique the product is, the more valuable the public relations effort is. *Public relations* refers to the activities and events a company stages to attain media visibility. These can include, but are not limited to, open houses, tours, speeches, and sponsorships. The information presented by the media about these events, as well as the publishing of articles and press releases, is *publicity*.

Public relations and publicity should be the first communications tool used for products that offer *unique benefits* to customers. (In other words, these activities will be most effective for products that are more than minimally different line extensions or cost reduction efforts.) When Lipitor (an anticholesterol drug developed by Warner Lambert) was in the final stages of testing by the FDA, it teamed with the American Heart Association in a national cholesterol education program. Through this public relations effort, the company positioned itself as being concerned about cholesterol, thereby providing a solid position for the emergence of Lipitor.

Similarly, when Cutter launched the first insect repellent in the United Stated using Picaridin instead of DEET, it had a limited budget and relied heavily on public relations. To gain support for Picaridin, it worked with experts such as local health officials, the federal Centers for Disease Control and Prevention, and the World Health Organization. These associations gave credibility to the ingredient, and by association, to the product. The firm launched a nonbranded Web site touting Picaridin's benefits. Managers also attended a West Nile virus conference and encouraged the CDC and WHO to include Picaridin as among their recommended products.[6]

There are other components a product manager can incorporate into a new product public relations campaign. (1) Develop press kits to be used at trade shows and other events. At a minimum, these kits should contain beta test results (if available); white papers detailing the importance of the new product; corporate history, positioning, and background information; and copies of press releases. (2) Draft articles for select publications explaining how their readers will benefit from this new product. For publishers to be interested in these types of articles, the product must be truly novel, and the article must provide information value to the reader beyond a sales pitch. (3) Again, if the product is truly innovative, it may be possible to provide a demonstration as part of an educational session at a trade show. (4) Issue press releases to the appropriate media.

After public relations opportunities are exhausted, it's time to begin advertising in earnest. Although the public relations activities often precede the launch date, most of the advertising and other promotional activities coincide with launch. To be sure that this happens, the planning must be completed prior to launch.

To begin the promotional communications, go back to your "best-prospect" profile and determine the most critical benefit that you should emphasize. Lead the communications with *this* benefit for *this* particular market. Be sure to address the following in the communications: What will your product (service) do for the prospect? How will it do that? Why is it better than the competition? What proof do you have for making your claims credible? What can the prospects do if they are not satisfied with the purchase? Note that the first question identifies the benefit, the second question provides the features that supply the benefit, and the third question demonstrates the advantages. These communications contain the same components as the typical FAB (features, advantages, benefits) approach to sales training, but reorganize them so that benefits are the most important thing presented to the prospect. The product manager is responsible for translating the positioning strategy mentioned earlier into a communications message for the customers, and for keeping the message relevant and current. Be sure to capture testimonials from any beta sites. Then determine how best to convey the message: through trade shows, through the sales force and/or channels, through print media, through direct mail, through electronic transmission, or through other means. Targeted advertising in trade journals to coincide with the launch of the product at a trade show can be effective. Try to get your message in front of prospects multiple times through creative use of media.

Direct salespeople will need various types of communications materials including: internal (confidential) company information, sales tools they can use on calls, and marketing collateral they can give to customers. The internal documentation contains the product's sales objectives and positioning, along with competitive comparisons and very likely proprietary data. (This information may be placed on the corporate intranet as well as being distributed in print format.) The sales tools should be focused on helping the salespeople complete the sales call; therefore, the emphasis should be on *how to sell*. The collateral pieces should be written from the customers' perspective, following the FAB approach mentioned earlier. (If the customer is a distributor, the material should focus on how the distributor will benefit from the product. If the customer is an end user, the material should focus on end-user benefits.) Even when the customer is an end user, different types of benefits may be relevant depending on the individual's level. Top managers, for example, are interested in how the new product will affect their bottom lines, whereas technical people may be more interested in data sheets. Too often product managers provide only product features and benefits (relevant to technical people) and don't provide supporting material for salespeople to use with higher-level managers.

Indirect sales channels will have some differences. The company information will be focused more on the partnership or relationship between the manufacturer and the distributor and will not contain confidential information. For high-margin products, videos and electronic self-testing modules may be beneficial, but only if the channel perceives a true value in the time commitment. The sales tools will very likely be shorter, with less detail. The collateral pieces should focus on end-user benefits. The percentage of the budget devoted to communications material for direct versus indirect channels will depend on the channel prioritization that is part of the launch strategy.

POSTLAUNCH EVALUATION

After (or during) the launch stage, some type of project appraisal should be completed. The main objectives of this stage are to improve future product development efforts and to move the product from a new product status to being an ongoing product requiring long-term maintenance. There may also be a need on occasion to relaunch a product that is not meeting expectations. The relaunch should be considered as early as possible, and hopefully the need for it will have been uncovered by the early indicators as discussed in the prelaunch section of this chapter. If the product is still an acceptable product, changes to the marketing strategy may need to be made to make it a success. A contingency or control plan should be part of the launch materials. An example of a control plan is shown in Table 9.2.

In addition to evaluating the new product, it is also useful to evaluate the new product development process. The best way to make improvements for the future is to compare and contrast successful and unsuccessful projects. By documenting your insights, you can increase the probability of success for other new products.

CHAPTER CHALLENGE

Look for creative approaches to launching new products. Don't assume that a product will sell itself.

Table 9.2

Sample Control Plan

Potential Problem	Tracking	Contingency Plan
1. Salespeople fail to contact general-purpose market at a prescribed rate.	Track weekly call reports. The plan calls for at least 10 general-purpose calls per week per rep.	If activity falls below this level for three weeks running, a remedial program of one-day district sales meetings will be held.
2. Salespeople may fail to understand how the new feature of the product relates to product usage in the general-purpose market.	Tracking will be done by having thes ales manager call one rep each day. The entire sales force will be covered in two months.	Clarification will be given to individual reps on the spot, but if the first 10 calls suggest a widespread problem, special teleconference calls will be arranged to explain the product to the whole sales force again.
3. Potential customers are not making trial purchases of the product.	Track by instituting a series of 10 follow-up telephone calls a week to prospects who have received sales presentations. There must be 25 percent agreement on the product's main feature and trial orders from 30 percent of those prospects who agree on the feature.	The remedial plan provides for special follow-up telephone sales calls to all prospects by reps offering a 50 percent discount on all first-time purchases.
4. Buyers make trial purchase but do not place quantity reorders.	Track another series of telephone survey calls, this time to those who placed an initial order. Sales forecast based on 50 percent of trial buyers reordering at least 10 more units within six months.	No remedial plan for now. If customer does not rebuy, there is some problem in product use. Since product is clearly better, we must know the nature of the misuse. Field calls on key accounts will be used to determine that problem, and appropriate action will follow.
5. Chief competitor may have the same new feature (for which we have no patent) ready to go and markets it.	This situation is essentially untrackable. Inquiries among our suppliers and media will help us learn quicker.	Remedial plan is to pull out all stops on promotion for 60 days. A make-or-break program. Full field selling on new item only, plus a 50 percent first-order discount and two special mailings. The other trackings listed above will be monitored even more closely.

Source: C. Merle Crawford, *New Products Management*, 4th ed. (Irwin, 1994), p. 317.

INTERVIEW WITH ELYSE KAYE: CULTIVATE PRODUCT LAUNCH TECHNIQUES

Elyse Kaye, Senior Product Manager, HoMedics

Elyse, before we get started discussing product launch strategies, can you talk a bit about your career path? You've worked for some very different types of companies.

My career path is not a traditional one. As a communications major at Michigan State University, I didn't learn about product or brand management in an academic setting. In each zigzag of my journey, I gained so much knowledge that led down the product management path.

Upon graduation, I stumbled across a position as a marketing coordinator for a consumer products company most well known for manufacturing the Lava Lamp. The company was traditionally sales driven and had opted against putting a lot of weight on marketing (hence hiring a 22-year-old to manage their marketing and public relations!). Distribution was expanding rapidly due to resurgence in kitsch. I was hired to formulate a working marketing plan and budget to grow the business. Talk about a dream for a student entering into the workforce—I was given a blank page! Throughout my time there, I was given the chance to execute on many different facets of the plan including establishing a licensing department and solidifying our product development process. It was through that introduction I discovered this was what I wanted to do.

The challenge with working in entrepreneurial companies at such a young age is that they can often be void of structure and process. My next position with a classical marketing and finance-driven office products company gave me that structure. There I learned the importance of controlling a P&L, the dollar value of excess inventory, and navigation of corporate environments. My role involved the management of teams of engineers, designers, packaging experts, sourcing, graphics, and sales.

My next position led me into the world of design, sourcing, and factory management. It is my belief that anyone who works on products must be hands-on in each area. When I began working with Marlo Handbags, we had *37 different factories* working on our product line. Each time that there was a special request, we brought on a factory that fit that need. As a result, we meant nothing to any of the factories. On my first trip to China on the company's behalf, I met with each factory to understand their capabilities as well as their limitations. By my next trip, we were down to 13 factories and were meaningful to each one. This led to better pricing, logistics, and relief from strained relationships. It also gave me an opportunity to expand the lines utilizing the factory resources.

Currently, I am the senior product manager for HoMedics—one of the world's leading consumer product companies. It is a fantastic blend of the larger corporation blended with the entrepreneurial spirit that I began my career with. I utilize skills which I learned in each of my previous challenges.

How did your approach to product launch vary across these companies?

A successful launch begins early in the development process with a well-laid-out plan that has flexibility. So many great products never make it to market because they are launched improperly. Internally, the biggest mistake made is the lack of constant communication. Working in silos leads to mass amounts of finger-pointing and expensive air freighting! Depending on the product complexity, I try to bring in the necessary players as early as possible. This includes the development team (designers, engineering, research, packaging, sourcing finance) and the launch team (sales, advertising, merchandising teams, PR, the marketing gurus). Even though everyone wants a concise timeline, the reality is that the plan should be "padded" to allow for unexpected circumstances that can kill a launch.

Personally, I enjoy getting out to the buyers whenever possible to discuss concepts at the infantile stage. Buyers are the retail gatekeepers to shelf placement. There is a historical feud between sales and marketing. Which came first, the production plan or the sales order? This conflict will always arise. My least successful launches occurred when sales and marketing were not working hand in hand. Every product manager can tell you a horror story of a customer being promised an unrealistic ship date. There are key dates and price points in any planogram reset. (A planogram is a diagram or schematic illustrating where retail products should be displayed in a store.) If buyers are excited about the product, they will work with the company to get placement and marketing support. If they are not onboard, it is important to understand why.

Another factor that affects the success of a product launch is the exit strategy. Average shelf time at retail is about 18 months for a consumer product. The average product takes about 12 months to develop. Do the math. The successful launch only ends when the last of the inventory has been sold and another successful product is ready to ship in its place. As managers, it is our responsibility to separate ourselves from the products (our babies) that we are launching. In the end, it is still about the numbers.

Thinking about the launch team you just mentioned, how do you as a product manager "guide" its efforts during the launch?

My role as the "guide" is to set the strategy, collect the active team members, assign responsibilities, and overcommunicate bilaterally.

Can you cite any examples of guerilla marketing, product placement, sales and channel incentives, or any other launch techniques you felt were really valuable in your product launches?

Absolutely! One of my favorite examples is when New Line approached us to put Lava Lamps in a new movie coming out called Austin Powers. No one could have predicted the success that would come from the revival of retro. The company actually had to strategically turn down some of the largest customers in the world because of production capacity constraints. Our sales quadrupled in just a few years. Product placement can be an inexpensive method to reaching a lot of new consumers. Another example that is more recent is that *O Magazine* named one of our Black & Decker shredders as one of "Oprah's Favorite Things" in the December 2010 issue. A coupon code was given in conjunction with Amazon.com. Sales of the product more than doubled that month compared with what the product had sold during the duration of the whole year.

I'm sure you read stories about product launches from all sorts of companies and industries. Have you noticed any solid products fail due to a poor launch, or alternatively, any "okay" products succeed due to a superior launch?

Apple is the role model for product launches. However, they also are marketing phenoms when it comes to releasing superior generations shortly thereafter.

How do you think launch strategies are changing due to social media and Web 2.0? Do you think consumer and B2B products are impacted equally?

Launch strategies today must include viral marketing plans. The Web is such a fantastic tool for education and for building awareness. Depending on what success looks like to your company, it can also be a great sales tool. I work in the retail sector. Buyers are the gatekeepers and, as times have changed, they have become very risk-averse. What made companies like Sharper Image so successful was the ability to go out on a ledge to bring in innovation. Retailers continue to dwindle. The closing of Sharper Image, Linens-n-Things, Circuit City, and other huge retail chains has given so much leverage to the giants who are left standing. Social media is fantastic for building excitement levels, but if the products do not get distribution into retail for companies like mine, it is almost a null point. I have had several products that tested extremely well with consumers and have gotten huge social media buzz—but that does not equate to sales.

Can you think of any examples when an early knowledge of launch strategy changed a product definition?

My buyers are often the key drivers in my launch strategy. They work with me on pricing strategies, predetermining buying schedules, and merchandising programs. A product looks and feels very different depending on the channel of distribution. For instance, a specialty retailer wants 60 points, a mass retailer wants 35 points, and a club chain wants 13 points. I would like a product line to be as efficiently designed as possible using, for example, shared parts. I also would want to have brand consistency in my packaging and product aesthetics. However, I need to be developing three separate product lines with three separate launch strategies and timelines.

What would be your three most important launch tips—your words of wisdom—for product managers?

Surround yourself with the best of the best. I like to call product managers the CEO of a brand or product. We are not going to be experts in all areas, but we are great at seeking those specialists out. Another key nugget I picked up later in the game is to remove emotional ties. Emotions lead us to make mistakes. Keep your plans flexible as there will be changes and challenges that you cannot foresee. And, most important, we have the most fun jobs in the world.

PART III

DOWNSTREAM PRODUCT MANAGEMENT: ONGOING LIFE-CYCLE MANAGEMENT AND GROWTH

CHAPTER 10

Life-Cycle Management

> **TRUE OR FALSE:** Life-cycle planning is a downstream product management issue.
>
> I admit that this is a bit of a trick question. Life-cycle *management* is a downstream issue, but life-cycle *planning* can be more pervasive. That's why I would consider this statement false. It's not uncommon for decisions to retire a product, for example, to be linked to a decision to develop a replacement. Therefore, life-cycle planning is part of broad portfolio planning described throughout the book.

Part II focuses on upstream activities, but now the focus shifts to downstream efforts to manage life cycles, as shown in Figure 10.1. A significant portion of life-cycle management involves marketing strategy.

When dealing with existing products, product managers are expected to do one or more of the following: (1) reinforce and protect sales of "core" and secondary products; (2) renew and revitalize sales of products that should be strong but have begun to falter; (3) relaunch or resurrect selected products or concepts; and/or (4) retire failing products. This chapter introduces the definitions and strategies related to these approaches.

Product managers reduce risk by having portfolios of new and old products. The portfolio allows some latitude for the fact that product acceptance and revenue cannot be precisely forecast and planned. Existing products must be evaluated on an ongoing basis to determine

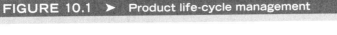
FIGURE 10.1 ➤ Product life-cycle management

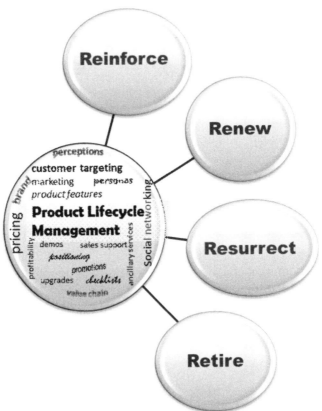

ways to increase revenue, reduce costs, generate new customer value, or eliminate obsolete products.

You as product manager should periodically compare your existing portfolio with competitive product lines or families. List all your products relative to the product offerings of your major competitors and look for gaps. Do they have products you don't have (or vice versa)? Do the differences represent a potential advantage (or disadvantage)? Does the analysis suggest the need for new products or the retirement of existing products?

Perform similar analyses relative to customer needs. Think about how the customer uses your products or services. Are there any complementary products or services that could augment your offering and make it more valuable to customers? Could these become part of your portfolio? If you haven't thought about your products in the context of customer needs, stop right now and do so.

CATEGORIZE PRODUCTS

Product managers, particularly those responsible for large numbers of products, often find it useful to classify products into categories to simplify or streamline decision making. There are a number of common approaches. One is the basic Pareto (80/20) rule: If a significant percentage of sales or profits comes from a few products, give those important products constant attention, with the rest receiving periodic attention. The Boston Consulting Group popularized a matrix in which products are evaluated in terms of relative market share and then identified as cash cows, stars, question marks, and dogs. Another approach is to define the products according to their position on the product life cycle: introduction, growth, maturity, and decline. A variation of these approaches categorizes products according to product life-cycle strategies including protect and maintain core products; renew underperformers; retire end-of-life products; and resurrect or relaunch concepts and products that may have a chance for a second life. (See Table 10.1.)

Table 10.1

Product Categorization within a Product Line

	Reinforce	Renew	Relaunch	Retire
Percentage of contribution to profits	High	Mid to high	Potential	Low
Brand value	High	Potentially high	Potentially high	Declining
Strategic fit	Solid	Can be grown	Can be grown	Declining
Growability	Self-sustaining	Growable	Growable	Unsustainable
Time-based potential	Solid current	Future growth potential	Future growth potential	Past performer
Strategy and resource commitment	Maintain: focused and steady resources	Grow: increase resource commitment	Grow: burst of supporting resources	Contract: reduce support

A "reinforce" product generates a good income stream but might not justify significant marketing expenditures. It may be a secondary product that doesn't face much competitive pressure, or it may be a core product that has strong brand equity. In either case, the product manager will look for ways to protect market share and prevent losses to the competition, preferably with minimal cost outlays.

Renewal products require revitalization; they can be at any stage of the product life cycle, but they are not performing at a level objectively determined as possible. These products require specific demand creation activities—to gain increased usage or market penetration—as described in the next few chapters.

Relaunch (or resurrect) products are those that have been ignored or even discontinued, but now seem to have value in the current environment. This could be to the result of technology growth, change in the competitive arena, or even a sense of nostalgia. These products might generate revenues through a relaunch campaign.

Finally, products that are either clearly not competitive in the product category or at the end of their life cycle are candidates for elimination (or retirement). These products are identified by a noted decline in sales, a lack of ability to achieve goals, or the development of a superior product that redefined functionality. Products in this category can pose unique challenges when a key customer "clings" to the product despite its unprofitability to your firm.

EVALUATE PRODUCT PERFORMANCE

The beginning point for a product performance evaluation is the audit conducted as part of your regular planning processes. It should uncover problems and opportunities related to features, potential new product entries, and/or quality issues to address in the upcoming fiscal year. Aspects of product performance to evaluate include sales/profits by customer segment, channel of distribution, or geographic region; the complementary value of the product to others in the line; seasonal fluctuations in demand; the awareness and preference level for the product; rate of repeat purchases (retention); and planned versus actual performance.

Product managers should avoid thinking about existing products as mature, but should rather treat them as "core brands." Think about the brands as if they were being acquired from another company; envision the possibilities. Study customers to find out not only their buying behavior, but also what causes that behavior.[1]

Product managers frequently use competitive matrixes to study their products. A *competitive matrix* (sometimes called a *perceptual map*) focuses attention on the relative competitive positioning a product has based on the most significant factors. (See Figure 10.2.) A competitive matrix is a visual display of one product compared to the competition along two axes. Each axis is a continuum of an attribute such as ease of use, comfort, price, and so forth. The selection of attributes should be based on what is important to customers.

Start by determining what is most important to a customer in making a buying decision. Ask customers to list and rank attributes in terms of priority and to assess how significant those attributes truly are in terms of affecting their purchase decisions.

Then select the top two or four attributes to determine the relative positioning of significant competitors along each attribute. For example, assume that Product A is compared with competing products X, Y, and Z along two important purchase criteria—perceived leadership

FIGURE 10.2 ➤ Competitive matrix (perceptual map)

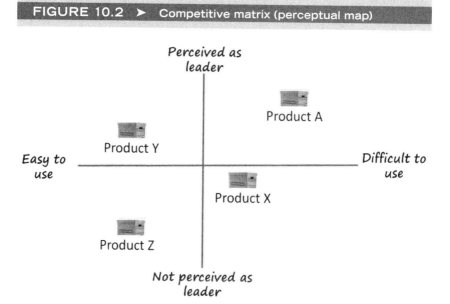

in the market and ease of use. Note that A is perceived as a leader to a greater degree than is the competition; this could be used as part of its positioning strategy. However, it is also perceived as more difficult to use than any of the competitors. This could suggest a strategy of providing clearer instructions and/or redesigning the product to make it easier to use.

When several factors are deemed equally important, another approach would be to list all factors as continua (i.e., adjectives along a scale, such as light to heavy) and ask customers to rate each product by factor. The average or mean responses for each competitive product can be joined by a line to indicate a "profile" of each. In Figure 10.3, three products are being evaluated against one another. Product A is perceived as slightly superior in terms of product consistency, Product B is easiest to use, and Product C has the best delivery.

Both the perceptual competitive matrix and product scaling profile approaches compare a product with its competitors along established factors. The typical objective is to improve attributes of your company's product that are competitively weak. What is generally missing is the internal cost of making the improvements. Sometimes a product can be made more profitable by reducing the cost of unimportant attributes. If this also results in a price reduction, the result can lead to more value for the customer. Therefore, it is useful to add cost information to the perceived importance and competitive performance of each attribute.

FIGURE 10.3 ➤ Product scaling map

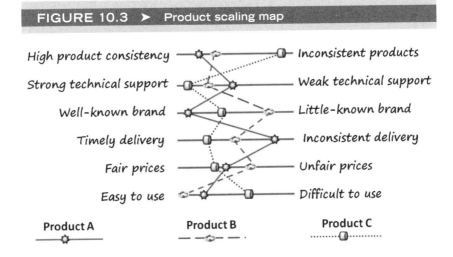

Start by listing the features and attributes of the product. Next convert these into customer benefits. Estimate the average importance of each benefit to the market and how well the product provides the benefit relative to the competition. Finally, assess whether the cost of the features related to the benefits is a significant proportion of the overall cost of the product.

Look for red flags. The benefits that are highly important to the market should come from features that perform at least equal to or better than the competition's product. If that's not the case, the product manager should improve on those features. If features provide benefits that are *not* important to the customer, their relative cost should be low. Otherwise, the feature should be evaluated for redesign or elimination.

This type of analysis might precede quality improvement and cost reduction programs. By working with teams from other parts of the company, the product manager can use value analysis, quality function deployment, or other techniques to increase customer satisfaction without a significant increase in costs, or the product manager should maintain customer satisfaction while lowering costs.

EVALUATE THE PRODUCT LINE

In evaluating a product *line* (as opposed to an individual product), the product manager can follow many of the steps already discussed. As product manager, you should maintain data on each item in the line and evaluate relative product performance. Examine customer behavior across the entire line. Try to determine whether customers will substitute a filler product if the core product is out of stock or whether they are apt to buy a competing product. Brainstorm ways to increase value to the product line by (1) adding products that enhance your competitive positioning and increase brand equity or (2) deleting products that are not important to the target market and simply increase costs. And as always, look for opportunities to increase market penetration through more insightful marketing.

You will probably find it useful to develop tools that will enable you to rank products. Choose the variables of most importance in evaluating the line and determine the best way to categorize the existing products. If your company does not have a product review committee, recommend that one be established. The committee should be composed of relevant stakeholders from marketing, manufacturing, and finance. The committee should develop a company-appropriate system for identifying weak products. The system would specify how frequently the committee should meet (e.g., quarterly, annually), what criteria to examine (number of quarters of sales decline, market changes, gross margin, etc.), and procedures for product elimination. Careful product line management and analysis—as discussed in Business Brief 10.1—is an important predecessor to establishing reinforcement, renewal, relaunch, and retirement strategies.

Business Brief 10.1

THE MANY ASPECTS OF PRODUCT-LINE MANAGEMENT

Product-line management involves conceiving and developing new products, but also extending existing product lines and building brand equity. Different companies emphasize different aspects of these product-line management activities, and a given product manager will emphasize different aspects as well, depending on specific needs at the time. Examples of each are presented in this business brief.

Developing New Products

In developing new products, product managers use a variety of techniques to reduce risk and increase chances of success. First, product managers (particularly in highly technical fields) have learned to begin next-generation products immediately after the launch of prior-generation products. Intel introduced this approach in 1990. Second, developing simultaneous products based on a corporate strategy leverages the success of the products by adding momentum. Intel demonstrated this as well with its ProShares family of products. Third, generating several products from a common platform spreads out development costs and allows products to be brought to market more quickly and at a lower price. Hewlett-Packard benefited from this in the introduction of its color DeskJet printer. Finally, establishing barriers to entry for the competition affords at least a temporary competitive edge. Here again, Hewlett-Packard discovered this in its work in inkjet printers.

In an effort to maintain its dominance in printers, Hewlett-Packard has beaten Japanese competitors by using their own tactics. Decades ago Japanese companies had taken the lead in handheld calculators, a market HP had pioneered. The success was a result of a mass-market strategy with low-priced, well-designed products. Then, HP followed that approach with inkjet printers, as Stephen Kreider Yoder explains in "How H-P Used Tactics of the Japanese to Beat Them at Their Game" in the *Wall Street Journal*:

> *H-P engineers adopted two Japanese tactics: They filed a blizzard of patents to protect their design and frustrate rivals, and embarked on a process of continual improvement to solve the inkjet's problems. They developed print heads that could spit 300 dots an inch and made inks that would stay liquid in the cartridge but dry instantly on plain paper. One engineer tested all types of paper: bonded, construction, toilet, and, for good measure, tested sandpaper, tortillas, and socks.*

Hewlett-Packard established a solid foothold in the black-and-white inkjet printer market using these techniques. However, it faced another challenge when its engineers were working on a color printer, intent on bringing out a full-featured, mechanical marvel. Marketing people suggested that they build on the platform they had already established, since they felt this approach, though less sophisticated, would satisfy the needs of the customers:

> *There was a near mutiny among the engineers until a product manager named Judy Thorpe forced them to do telephone polls of customers. It turned out people were eager for the product the engineers considered a "kludge." H-P learned that "you can tweak your not-so-latest thing and get the latest thing," Ms. Thorpe says. By sticking to the existing platform, H-P was able to get the jump on competitors in the now-booming color-printer market.*

One other thing, H-P's "blizzard of patents" set up a barrier to entry for competition. Competing engineers lost valuable time negotiating H-P's maze of fifty patents covering how ink travels through the head. By the time Canon became a serious competitor, H-P had sold millions of printers and had practiced continual improvement in manufacturing. Later, when Canon introduced a color inkjet, H-P was able to cut the price of its version before Canon even reached the market. As a result, Hewlett-Packard "owned" 55 percent of the world market for inkjets. And, like Intel, H-P is leveraging its knowledge of inkjets in other areas such as fax machines.

Extending Existing Product Lines: Successes and Failures

Sometimes products are not completely new, but rather they are product-line extensions. As a product manager plans for line extensions, there must be a careful balance between variety and redundancy. Fast-moving consumer goods are perhaps particularly vulnerable to this trap. In an effort to respond to competitive entries, to reach smaller market segments, to bolster short-term gain, and/or to gain more shelf space, many product managers offer too many variations of core products.

Numerous examples of extending product lines abound. When Nabisco introduced its line of Fat-Free Fruit Bars, the cookie category was growing at a modest 2 percent per year. Nevertheless, this line of offerings resulted in Nabisco's sales increasing three times as fast as the overall market. Similarly, when 7-Up introduced Cherry 7-Up, the new product variant was successful, and sales of the core product also went up.

Unfortunately there are pitfalls to line extensions. Introducing a product variation under the same name as a core brand could have the potential of weakening the brand equity. Line extensions can generally be easily matched by competitors. A number of hidden costs can arise resulting from increased production complexity, more errors in forecasting, and the loss of consumers because of potential out-of-stock situations.

As an example, John Quelch and David Kenny, in the *Harvard Business Review* ("Extend Profits, Not Product Lines") discuss the plight of a U.S. snack foods company they refer to as Snackco. Over time, Snackco's product line had grown, but its overall sales remained flat. In evaluating the situation, the company studied the effectiveness of core products, niche products, seasonal and holiday products, and filler products. The percent of the line as well as the percent of the sales volume accounted for by each type of product are shown in Table 10.2.

By looking at this analysis, it was clear that changes had to be made. Note that the core products generally followed the Pareto principle: 20 percent of the products accounted for 70 percent (instead of Pareto's 80 percent) of the volume. These were also the key products responsible for building company and brand reputation. Consequently, Snackco managers changed manufacturing and delivery schedules to ensure that core products were always in stock.

The niche products were holding their own, contributing 10 percent of the product line and 10 percent of the volume. These products were studied to determine in which market areas they had sufficient volume to continue and in which markets they should be dropped.

Seasonal and holiday items provided 10 percent of the sales volume even though they represented only 5 percent of the product line. These items were maintained with additional store displays provided for active selling periods.

Finally, filler products were evaluated. Even though the per-unit contribution was greater than it was for some of the other products, it wasn't enough to offset the fact that they were contributing only 10 percent of the sales volume despite the fact that they made up

Table 10.2

Snackco's Product-Line Analysis

	Percentage of Line	Percentage of Sales Volume
Core products	20	70
Niche products	10	10
Seasonal and holiday products	5	10
Filler products	65	10

65 percent of the product line. These products were carefully evaluated in terms of true costs and competitive need. The company decided to cut the number of filler products. The greatest cuts were in competitive areas where the company decided to use the shelf space to build share in core products. In leadership markets, the cuts were more selective with a goal of blocking shelf space from the competition.

Note the steps that Snackco took to perform this analysis. First, the sales/profit/contribution history of each of the items in the product line was collected and analyzed, along with data on customers and competitors. Part of this was based on internal records. But to be able to fully evaluate product performance, external research was also required. Random store checks indicated that the most popular items were out of stock up to 50 percent of the time and that when these items were out of stock, up to 40 percent of customers bought either a competitive product or nothing. The remaining customers purchased one of the filler products. The company also used consumer tracking panels to gather data on both household purchases and usage frequency.

After examining this information, Snackco managers were challenged to add value to existing products and to the product line, particularly for retail channel members. As Quelch and Kenny point out, they had to be able to prove that retailers would benefit from the product-line plan being proposed:

> Snackco's managers believed that the new strategy was on target, but they also knew that without the support of the sales force any efforts to implement the plan would fail. So, backed by Snackco's president, one of the sales regions undertook a four-month test to determine the impact of refocusing core products versus continuing line extensions. Not only did market share increase during the test, but sales-force compensation also increased because of the faster turnover of the more popular items in the line, which were given additional shelf space at the expense of the slower-moving items.

To boost market penetration, usage rate and/or the number of users had to be increased. Some of this was accomplished by scheduling manufacturing and delivery to ensure that core products were always in stock, as well as providing additional store displays for the seasonal products. However, some advertising changes were also necessary:

> *Snackco shifted from an umbrella advertising approach for the whole line to a strategy that focused on its flagship products. Advertisements for these products emphasized the Snackco brand and thereby promoted the brand's line extensions. Over the past two years, Snackco has made significant gains in market share and volume, which in turn have generated even higher margins.*

Adapted from: John Quelch and David Kenny, "Extend Profits, Not Product Lines," *Harvard Business Review* (September–October 1994), pp. 153–160; Stephen Kreider Yoder, "How H-P Used Tactics of the Japanese to Beat Them at Their Game," *Wall Street Journal* (September 8, 1994), pp. 1+.

REINFORCEMENT AND PROTECTION STRATEGIES

Reinforcement strategies are primarily defensive or self-sustaining in nature; they attempt to prevent loss to the competition and/or prolong a revenue stream. They could be applied to core products, fillers, or ancillary products. Maintenance strategies should require minimal oversight to free up time—and possibly resources—to devote to revitalizing other products. When a product manager handles numerous products, different ones could be in maintenance mode in any given year. The marketing of these products would be an appendix or footnote in the marketing plan, rather than a detailed discussion in the action plan. Common examples of maintenance strategies are:

1. Stay the course.
2. Reduce the scope.
3. Defend the perimeter.

Stay the Course

Some products remain under the radar all the time; they are supported by diehard customers. They don't require much push because of limited competition, and therefore they can be relegated to a footnote in your annual product plan. Also, if you have limited capacity for manufacturing a certain product, you may wish to maintain sales by doing what you have always done. Local breweries, for example, retain their uniqueness by limited production of beer. As the president of New Glarus Brewery (in New Glarus, Wisconsin) stated when demand surged for its product, "Eventually we're just going to throw in the towel and say this is all the beer we can make, and I think we're getting close."[2]

Reduce the Scope

Sometimes a product that might otherwise have been eliminated can be maintained by scaling back and focusing on a smaller niche market. This was the case with the Fisher Space Pen, better known as the astronaut pen. The growing economy in the 1990s provided the perfect environment for little indulgences such as a $50 pen that writes under extreme conditions—especially after it was featured on a Jerry Seinfeld episode. Unfortunately, the downturn in the economy in the early 2000s abruptly affected demand for the product. The only way to maintain sales was to focus on the truly core users—the "extreme professionals" in "extreme jobs." Police officers could use them to write vital signs on latex gloves at accident scenes. Therefore, the marketing for the product shifted to advertising in trade magazines for nurses, police officers, and paramedics.[3]

Defend the Perimeter

One of the risks of taking your eye off a core product is that competitors can begin to "nibble around the edges"—a phenomenon also referred to as "ankle biting." Therefore some efforts will need to be made to protect against competitive threats by maintaining the product's visibility in front of the customer, while still squeezing every dollar out of your marketing expenditures. While a disproportionate amount of funds may be invested in launching a product, a smaller amount could be spent on reminder sales promotions once "loyaltists" have been established in the customer base. For many medical products, a study by ACNielsen HCI found that reinforcement media—such as prescription pads, reference publications, and patient records forms—are effective vehicles for delivering reinforcement product messages. The study found three advantages to these nontraditional tools:

1. Point-of-purchase vehicles (Rx pads, patient record forms, reference publications, etc.) reach the physician at the prescribing moment.
2. They reach physicians when they aren't "expecting" to be exposed to a message.
3. Brand recognition is reinforced even though the sales rep is not present.[4]

RENEWAL AND REVITALIZATION STRATEGIES

The bulk of a product manager's work on existing products will be spent on renewal and revitalization efforts. There are several possible approaches. One is adding new value by either augmenting a product with more features and/or services or reducing costs. Another approach is repositioning, including brand refocusing and breakaway positioning. And still another is extending the base through new users, new uses, increased usage, and line extensions.

Add New Value

Value is the ratio of benefits to costs. The more benefits a solution provides (in terms of superior features, convenience, simplicity, trust, etc.) relative to costs (price, aggravation, inconsistency, etc.), the higher the perceived value. Market shifts (such as changing regulations) may affect the perception of value, and product managers need to make appropriate adjustments, as discussed in Business Brief 10.2.

Business Brief 10.2

PRODUCT LIFE-CYCLE MANAGEMENT IN THE FINANCIAL SERVICES INDUSTRY

By Wade Whitmus

Wade W. Whitmus is a product development manager for CUNA Mutual Group with nearly 27 years of credit union financial services and compliance experience. Prior to his current role, he served as product manager of several different financial services product lines, and as a vice president and chief operating officer with a service corporation. Wade is a certified product manager, and certified credit union executive.

From 2009 through 2010, Congress and the Federal Reserve Board (FRB) focused on new and expanded regulations that impacted open-end lending and more specifically credit card accounts. The regulatory change fervor by these two entities was in reaction to the recession of 2008–2010. The FRB and Congress felt consumers needed to be better protected with enhanced (clearer) disclosures; controlled terms and conditions of credit offerings; and pricing limitations on the product. The general sense by these two entities was that uninformed consumers may not be getting the best deal, thereby incurring higher fees and paying more than they should for credit.

The regulation changes had an impact on credit union operations, policies, card processing systems, and disclosures that were provided to consumers. In many cases, the regulatory changes impacted credit card program offering, pricing, and timing of statements and disclosures. During this time period, due to the fact that both Congress and the FRB were involved to advance consumer protection, there were initial regulations, new laws, revised regulations, technical fixes to the laws, and final regulations. Throughout this evolving regulatory process, financial institutions had to update their credit card disclosures at least once, if not twice, to accommodate timing requirements and compliance implementation dates from this ongoing battery of compliance changes.

It was within this market environment that CUNA Mutual brought additional value to its credit-card–document product line by a variety of tactics. As background, CUNA Mutual Group is a leading provider of financial services to credit unions, their members, and valued customers worldwide. With more than 75 years of market commitment, CUNA Mutual's vision is unwavering: to be a trusted business partner who delivers service excellence and customer-focused, best-in-class products and market-driven innovation. One product category that CUNA Mutual offers is a portfolio of documents that supports the daily operations of credit unions. We have a dominant market presence with this product line.

These documents support the opening of accounts and taking of deposits to granting different types of loans at credit unions. Our documents are available in both paper and electronic file formats (i.e., integrate with host processing systems, post to Web, or used in-house). Our value proposition is to provide customers with "compliance peace of mind" that extends way beyond the paper and ink or bytes and bits of our offerings. Documents are the end deliverable of the product we sell. We wrap around our "document experience" many value-added services to enhance the value of our documents for customers. These services include: training, Web-based resource library, e-mail alerts and other communications, reference guides/manuals, and access to compliance/operational experts. Our customers can access these services to successfully navigate through simple to complex compliance changes and the related impact they may have on a credit union's daily operations. Including value-added services positions our product to be less of a commodity with customers.

We utilized several different tactics and activities as part of our product-line management efforts to illustrate our value not only to customers but to our industry. Without this added-value, our products could be perceived by customers as commodities and thus subject to being price shopped. These activities to support our value-add included:

1. Compliance Alerts distributed to customers via e-mail that presented our assessment of the various credit card compliance changes and impact on credit card operations and disclosure documents;
2. Product Points (abbreviated technical pieces distributed to customers) provided insight and specific considerations of the compliance changes (*USA Today* type of compliance overview);
3. Webinars and conference call–based Q&A sessions to share insights and information (training), and respond to current issues and questions from our customers;
4. A special telephone hot-line to receive customer calls and orders for new disclosure documents (we also deployed outbound calling to targeted accounts to generate new business and follow up with existing customers);
5. A specific Web site where we posted information and updates on the credit card compliance changes;
6. We partnered with other organizations to move blocks of new and existing business to our new credit card disclosure documents (showcase our value);
7. Our field staff (outside sales) worked directly with customers to aid in their understanding of the compliance implications and how we could be a source for documents; and
8. Lastly, we created and sold updated credit card disclosure documents. We also made available to customers tools to make operational changes as well as learning aids to better understand the compliance changes and their impact to credit union operations.

Through both compliance updates, we effectively managed and enhanced our product line by delivering credit card disclosure documents to customers on time and as promised. The market responded favorably as we were able to nearly double our customer base and revenues through this process. We retained basically all of our existing customers. Our success with this compliance change was really driven by our strong market presence, external partnerships, and consistent brand touch-point management. We were able to enhance our overall product brand identity for truly providing compliance peace of mind and being a partner for "outsourcing" compliance issues.

The Customer Value Chain

It is important to continually rethink and redefine your product creatively to look for opportunities hidden behind the day-to-day grind. What changes to your value proposition are necessary to be relevant to target customers? Remember that value can come from any point along the customer value chain (CVC). Map your product's CVC (see Figure 10.4) and then look for opportunities to improve the total value experience.

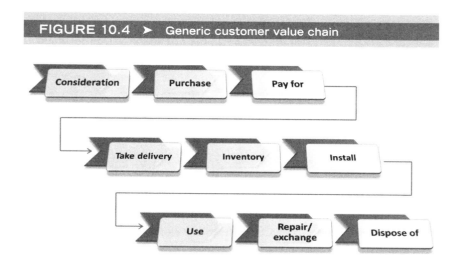

FIGURE 10.4 ➤ Generic customer value chain

Here are some issues related to each touch point that may generate ideas for value enhancement:

■ Prepurchase of education and information during the consideration stage can provide value—especially for complex decisions—by helping customers find the best fit for their goals and needs. Demonstrations, trials, and white papers can increase the customer's comfort in the purchase decision.

■ Streamlining the purchase through simpler paperwork or easier payment terms will increase the value quotient for some customers.

■ Simplifying payment through techniques such as pay-at-the-pump (for gas), fewer hidden fees, or smart-phone transactions might enhance value.

■ Delivery on the customer's terms (using, for example, straightforward appointments, drop-shipping, or expediting) might generate value.

■ The availability of access to inventory, perhaps as a result of convenient distributor locations or on-site inventory with pay-as-you-go contracts, can shift preference from one supplier to another.

■ Installation can be another area for rethinking value. Are there opportunities to add custom installation to a do-it-yourself product or vice versa?

■ Reducing the number of features (to make it simpler) or adding features (to enhance capabilities). This is an area where ethnography and customer visit programs can yield insights.

■ Are repair services valued? Can you increase value at this point, similar to Best Buy's Geek Squad?

■ If customers value the ability to return, exchange, or upgrade the product, it is possible to add value there.

■ With growing concerns about eco-friendliness, there may be a value opportunity in reducing the end-of-life impact either with environmentally friendly components or through a solid recycling program.

"What If" Analysis

Another approach is to use a series of "what if" questions. (See Figure 10.5.) What would happen if some features were magnified? For example, magnifying the screen on a television contributed to a new market for home theater. Increasing the size of sandwiches shifted the focus from one person to a group. Minimizing can also generate new ideas. Reducing the size of television screens created sports TVs. Twitter, as a form of microblogging, also fits this idea of miniaturization.

What if a new feature replaced an old one? Sony, for example, created the Walkman by replacing speakers with a headset. Cell phones have apps to act as credit cards. William McDonough's book, *Cradle to Cradle*, was manufactured with pages made of synthetic material rather than paper.

Can two existing products be combined to provide one with more value to the customer? The minivan combined the advantages of a station wagon with those of a van. The tent cot, available through sporting goods retailers, combines a portable cot with the coverage of a tent. Sometimes two product managers can bundle their products together to create more value than selling either one separately.

FIGURE 10.5 ➤ "What if?" thought starters

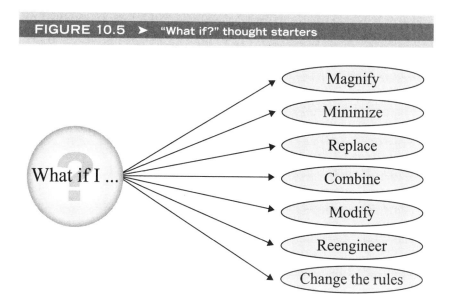

Can certain elements be modified? Can standard features become options? Can optional features become standard? This could include both product features and ancillary services. Modifications to sales approaches, contract terms, or technical support can change the product's solution and value.

Think about opportunities for reengineering. Can the development process be reengineered to reduce the overall cost of producing the product or service? Many training programs have been modified with e-learning modules to reduce time and travel costs. Companies such as GE have begun reverse innovation, whereby products are created in developing countries for use in that country as well as selected applications in developed countries.

Finally, some companies have begun to change the rules in their industry. Software as a service is shifting the purchase of software applications (via downloads and CDs for a given computer) to purchase of the *use* of the software (with the actual program housed on the supplier's computer).

Another avenue of exploring value enhancement is to benchmark features against the "best in class." Start by finding out from salespeople, customers, and industry sources what company or product is recognized as the best for the aspect under study. Then strive to uncover *why* it is perceived as the best. For example, when Ford redesigned the 1992 Taurus, it benchmarked more than two hundred features against seven competitors. Door handles were benchmarked against the Chevy Lumina, headlamps against the Accord, and remote radio controls against the Pontiac Grand Prix.[5]

Benchmarking should not be limited to the competition, and it does not have to be limited to product features. Improving processes used to deliver a product or service might provide more value for the customer. Mellon Bank in Pittsburgh, for example, undertook a benchmarking project to improve its credit card billing practices. By benchmarking seven other companies, including an airline, it learned about techniques and software technologies to improve the process. After adopting several improvements, Mellon cut outstanding complaints by half and was able to resolve problems in an average of 25 days instead of the 45 days it took previously.[6]

Product Versioning

Sometimes different product versions can be created to appeal more directly to specific market segments. Good-better-best product lines allow customers to select the price-value combination that works best for them. Adding features to (or defeaturing) a product may present a more "customized" solution for a unique set of needs. Since this approach may affect your brand strategy and/or pricing strategy, more information is provided in the brand and marketing chapters of this book.

Reposition

Creating a new competitive posture (in other words, repositioning) can give new life to some products. For example, Pampers' brand manager took a major step in 2004 to feature a man as a primary caregiver, contributing to the diapers' share growth from 49 to 59 percent. Red Bull extended its reach by targeting older consumers with a strategy centered on golf.[7]

Breakaway positioning refers to a more radical departure from the status quo. For example, rather than adding more features to a product, strip it to its baseline state. Then decide how you can augment it for specific customers.[8] Dow, for example, determined that many of its customers wanted to buy silicon in bulk without additional services (known as a naked solution). So in 2002 it created a new brand (Xiameter) and a business model to appeal to this set of customers. As another example, with the explosion of wireless capabilities being built into products and services, there's a minirevolution of antitechnology demand. Some coffee shops, for example, are bucking the trend and have sections outfitted with jammers to prevent cell phones from ringing and laptop computers from working.[9] Check out Chapter 11 for additional comments on positioning.

Extend the Base

Another renewal tactic a product manager could use is to boost sales volume by increasing the number of users and/or the usage rate per user. The number of users can be increased by winning competitors' customers, converting nonusers into users, and/or entering new market segments. Volume can also be increased by finding new applications for the product or by encouraging more frequent usage.

To increase the number of users, a product manager must collect three types of information: (1) why competitors' customers buy from the competition; (2) what, if anything, could convince nonusers to become users of the product; and (3) what market segments are attractive and accessible. Information on the first two items on the list can be obtained partly through sales input in the way of lost order reports. However, this is at best an incomplete picture because not all customers are contacted by the sales force. Therefore, if these are critical data, some additional research is necessary. Focus groups and one-on-one interviews can uncover new insights into why customers choose alternative products or choose none at all.

To identify what segments are attractive and accessible requires a combination of information and intuition. Start by profiling existing customer segments that have shown higher than average increases in sales. Determine whether these increases are unique to the product's customers or whether noncustomers with similar profiles have also exhibited a need for the product. Then assess whether the total segment (customers and noncustomers) is growing or declining in size. Also look for segments that have suddenly appeared and have specific needs not being addressed by the competition.

Sometimes the usage and users can be significantly different from the status quo—especially in the latter phases of the product life cycle. Superior Clay Corporation, for example, was a successful manufacturer of clay sewer pipes. As plastic pipes made most applications of clay sewer pipe obsolete, the company found it necessary to reinvent its product line. By reevaluating its competencies, it discovered it could transfer its clay-making capabilities to new products such as fireplace flue liners and decorative chimney pots. By extending its customer base to these new applications, Superior Clay became even more successful than it was initially.[10]

RELAUNCH

The relaunch of an existing product is a more extreme example of renewal and revitalization strategies (which can sometimes be incremental and subtle). If an unused brand is going to be reborn or if a product's repositioning is extensive, it might be useful to give it the same planning you would for a new product launch. An example of an extensive relaunch of this type is discussed in Business Brief 10.3.

Business Brief 10.3

SAFE DEPOSIT BOX DOCUMENTS REENGINEERING AND RELAUNCH

By Wade W. Whitmus

Wade W. Whitmus is a product development manager for CUNA Mutual Group with nearly 27 years of credit union financial services and compliance experience. Prior to his current role, he has served as product manager of several different financial services product lines, and as a vice president and chief operating officer for a service corporation. Wade is a certified product manager and a certified credit union executive.

For years CUNA Mutual Group (a leading provider of financial services to credit unions, their members, and valued customers worldwide) offered credit union customers paper and electronic documents to support their safe deposit box rental operations. Safe deposit boxes have traditionally been viewed as the ultimate place to store valuables, keepsakes, coins/stamps, and other heirlooms. Credit unions use vault space for this purpose. Not much changed with this credit union service over time, and our documents worked fine with minimal maintenance and updates.

Then events in recent times created the need for changes. Natural disasters (e.g., flooding in New Orleans after hurricane Katrina), terrorist attacks (e.g., the 9/11 attack in New York), and the potential threat of biological warfare or dirty bombs have shifted the landscape of safe deposit box operations in a relatively short period of time. Vaults that were once viewed as impenetrable were now being flooded, outright destroyed, or compromised (fire and water damage). A simple and valued service at financial institutions was now more complex and posed a new set of operational risks.

After reflecting on these new factors, as CUNA Mutual Group's product manager for the document line, I determined it was time to update our safe deposit box documents. The documents needed to be reengineered to support safe deposit box rentals in a new world, and it needed to be done in a way consistent with the overall company brand and product portfolio. With more than 75 years of market commitment, CUNA Mutual's vision is unwavering: to be a trusted business partner who delivers service excellence and customer-focused, best-in-class products and market-driven innovation. Our value proposition is to provide customers with "compliance peace of mind" that extends way beyond the paper and ink or bytes and bits of our documents.

We utilized a cross-functional team to approach this opportunity with two separate but linear work streams. First, we conducted a state-by-state legal search to identify and assess updated laws and regulations impacting safe deposit box operations. Simultaneously we engaged the services of a nationally recognized authority on safe deposit box issues. Both efforts would aid design and rollout of the new documents to the market.

Our legal team worked with our document design staff to update and redesign our safe deposit and disclosure documents. New contract terms and disclosures reflected the threats and risks associated with safe deposit box services. We combined state compliance considerations so our customers could use a multistate document in the event they had branch locations that crossed state lines. This eliminated the need for the creation of individual state versions of the document. Once drafted, our outside expert was engaged to review the documents and offer final edits and insights to strengthen the documents. The new risks and issues were somewhat beyond our customers' awareness.

Since we were in the position of having to get our customers caught up with this new world, we opted for a known expert to provide direct market input rather than traditional voice of customer input. The expert allowed us to move ahead of the market and be better positioned for a relaunch of this product.

Then it was time to relaunch the documents to our customer base and prospective new customers. The first step was to provide an educational Webinar conducted by the outside expert. The Webinar focused on new threats, risks, and considerations in running a safe deposit box rental program. The expert covered many key considerations and wove our documents in throughout the presentation (used as examples of how to address the issue or risk with our documents). Remember, credit unions are our target market, and we want to sell our documents (in compliance) for use with their safe deposit box program. This soft sell approach gave our documents credibility and an implied endorsement from a national expert—someone from outside our industry. At the end of the Webinar, attendees not only experienced learning and had takeaways to use back at their credit union, they also had the sense that they should use our documents to support their operations and cover all of these new service offering considerations and risks.

The end results of this document reengineering and relaunch included:

1. An updated, reengineered, and relaunched product for the market;
2. Pricing consistent with the enhanced value of our documents—expanded intellectual property and function (increased margin for us);
3. New, one-time, revenue from the Webinars (attendees paid a registration fee); and
4. Alignment with a national expert to provide enhanced credibility.

Through these steps we accomplished our mission of reengineering our documents, attracting new customers, and generating new revenue.

RATIONALIZATION DECISIONS AND RETIREMENT STRATEGIES

Note that this section has two components: a decision-making process followed by strategies. What criteria do you use to identify candidates for pruning? It's not uncommon for product managers to be unable to answer this question. Often when I ask them about their process for rationalization (i.e., the decision-making process) they will tell me how they announce product elimination to the market (i.e., the strategy or process *after* a "sunsetting" decision is made). Not all product managers give much thought to improving the decision process of rationalization. This is often challenging because they don't want the reputation of being "quitters" or "funeral directors." The use of standard criteria and perhaps a product rationalization review committee (similar to a new product review committee) can streamline the process.

Nearly all product lines could benefit from rationalization, which is the systematic analysis and modification of product lines to better align them with long-term goals. In fact, most firms would become more *profitable* if they eliminated weak brands and products. The bulk of Nestle's profits in 1996 came from around 2.5 percent of its brand portfolio. Procter & Gamble discovered that 66 percent of its growth between 1992 and 2002 came from its 10 biggest brands. Of Unilever's 1,600 brands in 1999, more than 90 percent of its profits came from 400 brands. As Nirmalya Kumar stated in his *Harvard Business Review* article, "The surprising truth is that most brands don't make money."[11]

The starting point, therefore, is to examine your existing products and product lines to look for pruning opportunities. David Anderson has developed the following typical criteria that can be used in the process of review and consolidation.[12]

1. *Sales volume:* List sales volumes in a bar chart format over time, in Pareto order.
2. *Sales revenue:* Similarly plot sales revenue.
3. *Part commonality:* Plot products by percentage of common parts.
4. *Cost of variety:* Determine and plot variety costs as a multiplier of baseline products.

5. *True profitability:* At minimum plot profit contributions without artificial allocations.

6. *Polls and surveys:* Collect input from various experts.

7. *Factory processing:* Are products compatible with manufacturing processes?

8. *Functionality:* Look for opportunities to consolidate products with similar functionalities.

9. *Customer needs:* What is the impact on customers if product is eliminated?

10. *Core competencies:* These should be based on the firm's clear core competencies.

11. *Clean-sheet-of-paper scenario:* Would you have this product if you were a new competitor?

12. *Future potential:* Does the product offer leverage for the future?

After identifying the weak products, a product manager has to make decisions and recommendations about what to do with them. As is discussed in the decision-making section of the leadership chapter, it's useful to generate several alternatives for dealing with the defined weak product. Should the price be lowered to stimulate sales and empty the warehouse? Should the price be raised to encourage customers to shift to a substitute product? Should the product be sold or licensed to another company?

The final step is to develop appropriate strategies and processes to carry out the decisions. The planning process should identify the stakeholders affected by the decision, their roles (if any) in the retirement strategy, and the timetables and schedules to implement the plan.

CHAPTER CHALLENGE

Approach product life-cycle planning and management with the same creativity and enthusiasm you would have for new product development. It can generate solid streams of future revenue.

INTERVIEW WITH GREG DICILLO: MOBILIZE YOUR PRODUCT LIFE-CYCLE MANAGEMENT PROWESS

Greg DiCillo, President, Life Cycle Strategies, Inc.; e-mail: greg.dicillo@lifecycle. us.com; Web site: http://www.lifecycle. us.com

Greg, although you have a background in marketing, we both know that's not necessarily the case for a lot of product managers. What are some of the challenges product managers face in making the transition from engineering to business (sometimes referred to as "the dark side" by engineers)?

There are a number of challenges facing technical people as they transition into the product management arena. Two of the most common challenges include developing a marketing competency and adapting from tactical to strategic thinking. Marketing in many cases is not a competency that engineers have cultivated, yet it is a significant part of a product manager's role. Product positioning, market segmentation, and pricing are critical aspects of a product manager's role that are not necessarily part of the technical product manager's résumé.

Another challenge is transitioning to a more strategic role. In general, many technical product managers have a great deal of experience working tactically on specific projects and product designs. When they move into a product manager role, they often struggle with the need to balance short-term project ideas against a broader, more strategic view of where customers and markets are heading and how to look for opportunities to innovate and change the game.

Can you cite a few examples of tools and techniques you recommend to achieve greater market penetration for existing (as opposed to new) products?

The most common technique we recommend to product managers to achieve greater market share for existing products is having them focus on the "whole product." Product managers have a tendency to view their product as the "tangible" designed product while minimizing the service, support, maintenance and repair, and logistics which can be extremely valuable attributes of the product or service offering. That's part of the total customer value chain. Becoming astute in assessing markets for "soft" product benefits can provide payback in a short amount of time and at marginal cost to the company. And beyond that it can provide significant differentiation and sustainable competitive advantage.

Do you have any other stories about revitalizing products to extend their life cycle—or even examples of the "sunsetting" or retirement of products?

We've had the opportunity to work with numerous companies that were intent on realigning their product lines. While the task of sunsetting or retiring a product is not simple, it is crucial to product line performance and ultimately the growth and profitability of a company. We treat the "sunsetting" of products in the same way that we treat new product development because all aspects of product life-cycle activities are in play. Identification of products for sunsetting requires front-end idea generation. Business cases are required to assess the costs needed to eliminate the products as well as the potential risks associated with potential lost customers. When product development comes into play, product transition strategies must be outlined (how to migrate customers from one product to another). Things like form, fit, and functional equivalency all need to be addressed. In some cases modifications to other products may be required to make the transition more effective. Product launch activities must be clearly thought out and executed. The sales force must be prepared on how to sell the transition, and marketing will need to effectively market the sunsetting program. Sunsetting a product requires well-thought-out and collaborative effort to be successful.

With over 20 years of experience, what nuggets of advice can you share with product managers regarding life-cycle management?

My advice to product managers is to make life-cycle planning the core of what you do. Most product managers treat life-cycle management as an event rather than a process. Every decision a product manager makes has a life-cycle impact. New product development has to take into account existing products. Markets go through life cycles, requiring product managers to assess their viability. When life-cycle management and planning is at the center of a product manager's planning process, product-line decisions from new products, to enhancements, to end-of-life are much clearer and easier to understand.

CHAPTER 11

Managing Brand Equity

TRUE OR FALSE: A brand is a logo.

I'm sure that just about everyone reading this book would know that this is a false statement. While a logo is the visual representation of a brand feel, the essence of a brand goes deeper. It is built with every touch point with customers. A brand is a promise, a stereotype, and a means of connecting with customers.

BRAND ELEMENTS, STRUCTURE, AND STRATEGY

Is there any difference between a product manager and a brand manager? Yes and no. At one end of the continuum, the term *brand manager* is commonly used in the consumer arena for people who manage related products (such as toothpaste or detergent) under a specific brand umbrella (such as Crest or Wisk). The emphasis is on positioning the brand name in the minds of the end users (and possibly the channel) so as to create a consistent brand identity. At the other end of the continuum, the term *product manager* is commonly used in business-to-business situations where the individual is actively involved in ideation and product development (often working closely with engineering), and sometimes has a product line that may or may not have product brand names that are separate from the company brand. However, there is substantial overlap in the middle of this continuum. This chapter focuses most heavily on branding strategies in the overlapping middle.

THE BASICS

Product managers who are not in "traditional" consumer packaged goods occasionally feel that brands are irrelevant to their industries. That may be because of a common perception that a brand is somehow simply a marketing "gimmick" (a charge that may be true for some products). Nevertheless, a brand identity can simplify customer-buying decisions because the brand serves as a form of identification that connotes a specific level of quality, price/value, and support.

The term *brand* has been defined differently by a range of experts and organizations. The American Marketing Association defines a brand as, "A name, term, design, symbol, or any other feature that identifies one seller's good or service as distinct from those of other sellers. ... A brand may identify one item, a family of items, or all items of that seller."[1] Kevin Lane Keller, a noted branding guru, argues that, "A brand is a product ... that adds other dimensions to differentiate in some way from other products designed to satisfy the same need. These differences may be rational and tangible ... or more symbolic, emotional, and intangible."[2] Interbrand, an international consultancy specializing in brand strategies, defines a brand as, "A mixture of attributes, tangible and intangible, symbolized in a trademark, which, if managed properly, creates value and influence. ... [F]rom a marketing or consumer perspective [value] is *the promise and delivery of an experience*. ... Brands offer customers a means to choose and enable recognition within cluttered markets."[3]

From the above definitions it's clear that a brand encompasses a holistic set of tangible and intangible attributes, the embodiment of a promise customers perceive was made to them. As such, a brand is a sort of *executive summary* or *stereotype* that customers use to make purchase decisions. Just as people form stereotypes (good and bad) of sports figures, politicians, geographic locations, and so forth, they form stereotypes of products, services, and companies. Product managers should strive to understand and manage their brand's stereotypes. There are four fundamental questions to ask yourself. (1) What *image* do customers have of your brand? (2) What value (*brand equity*) does this image have for customers? (3) How do target customers perceive this brand image compared to that of the competition (*brand positioning*)? (4) Is the customer perception what you want it to be, and is it consistent with our goals (*brand management*)? See Table 11.1

Table 11.1

Fundamental Brand Issues

Brand Issue	Description	Product Manager Concerns
Image	Customer's perception	Define rational and emotional cues
Equity	Relevance and importance	Determine why customers should care
Positioning	Image vis-à-vis the competition	Define your differential advantage
Management	Ongoing strategies	Define future plans

What Image Do Customers Have of Your Brand?

Regarding the first question above, the *brand image* is the customer's perception of your products, services, and company. This image is developed through customer experience with the product (or service or company), through marketing activities controlled by the company, and through interactions customers have with sources of information outside of the company. Think about the following corporate brands: Apple Computer Inc., Harley-Davidson Motor Co., and Samsung. Apple is generally looked at as "the company that defines high-tech hipness."[4] Harley-Davidson has an "outlaw" aura of rugged individualism with a sense of freedom.[5] And Samsung has been transforming itself into a designer of *state-of-the-art cool.*[6]

Now think about how customers might describe offerings in *your* industry or product category. Some of these descriptors might be rational (such as *fast response* or *complete product line*), whereas other descriptors might be more emotional (such as *friendly* or *trustworthy*). Similarly, the descriptors could be positive or negative. Decide what descriptors customers would use to depict your product(s). Keep in mind that the image may be different for customers from what it would be for noncustomers and even between different groups of customers.

What Value (Brand Equity) Does This Image Have for Customers?

The second question assesses the value customers place on the image just described. How *relevant* and *important* is the image? Customers may have a solid image of a product but may or may not feel that it is relevant to their needs or in some other way is not of value to them. This is the concept of customer-based brand equity. Maintaining relevance in changing markets can be challenging. Let's return to Harley-Davidson. The individualistic image has been highly relevant for the "dreamer" subsegment of baby boomers. However, the median age of Harley buyers has been slowly rising, and Harley is challenged with making its brand and products relevant in new and meaningful ways as it pursues female customers and younger male buyers. Think back to your product's image that came to mind as you were reading the prior paragraph. How relevant and important is this image to your customers?

How Do Target Customers Perceive This Brand Image Compared to That of the Competition (*Brand Positioning*)?

The third question addresses the brand's position vis-à-vis the competition. How distinct is the brand image? Both Apple and Harley-Davidson are cult brands that have been quite successful in distancing themselves from the competition and creating brand loyalty. Samsung has also been quite effective in establishing an image, but maintaining it over time will require keeping competitors at bay. If a product manager has one product under one brand umbrella, the brand positioning and product positioning are the same. When a product manager is responsible for several products, all products might share the "essence" of the same brand image, individual products might have separate positions that remain consistent with an overall brand image, or specific products might have distinct brand identities. This is discussed further in the section on designing a brand strategy.

Is the Customer Perception What You Want It to Be?

The final question on brand management involves the ongoing *strategies* a product manager uses to establish and manage a differentiated brand image that is valuable and relevant to a significant market. Decisions have to be made on line extensions, on matching brand value to specific customers and market segments, and on ensuring that the product can deliver on the brand promises made. In the example about Apple, the introduction of products such as the iPod, the Mac Mini, and the iPad requires an examination of the relationship between the corporate brand and the individual product brands. For Harley-Davidson, it's important to understand the relevance that different market segments may place on brand values. And finally, in Samsung's case, continued investment in product design will be necessary for the company to maintain its position against Sony, Motorola, and emerging competitors.

DESIGNING A BRANDING STRATEGY

In designing a branding strategy, product managers must determine the relative importance of the company's image compared to the product's image in the purchase decision. Does the customer select a product independent of knowledge of the company, or in large part because of the company? Many B2C products will have brand names that are separate from the company name, whereas many B2B and service-sector products will incorporate the company name in some manner. (Yes, there are exceptions to this statement.) The relative emphasis placed on the company name should be driven by the customer decision process. Ask yourself what percent of the purchase decision for a given product is the result of customer familiarity with the company (or possibly business unit or division) name and what is the result of the product? If several of these factors influence the purchase decision, the product manager may need to build (or borrow) equity from several different structural hierarchy levels.

The corporate image or reputation is governed by factors beyond the control of most product managers. The resulting corporate brand is typically the responsibility of corporate communications. At this level, communication is with all shareholders (customers, suppliers, employees, stockholders). The image of the product and the responsibility for product brands rests with product managers. Here the communication is aimed at end customers and the channel.

Brand Hierarchy Relationships

Whenever a product brand is linked to the company, product managers must evaluate the influences of one on the other. Although the product managers may or may not be able to change or control the corporate (or divisional) reputation, understanding its influence will be necessary to properly position their product(s). Products geared toward a specific industry may find difficulty gaining widespread acceptance if the corporate umbrella brand is not perceived as "fitting" that industry. Low-priced products may be perceived as inconsistent with a company believed to be the "BMW" of the industry (or vice versa). Flashy products may strain a conservative corporate image. On the other hand, product managers who can leverage a corporate image to facilitate product marketing benefit from a strong company position.

Let's use a university example to demonstrate the hierarchy. The University of Wisconsin–Madison recently tried to better link the "corporate" (university) brand to the "business" units (colleges, athletics) brands as well as the "family" (department) brands. The image of UW–Madison, as a land grant, Big Ten institution, is one of research and forward-thinking *sifting and winnowing*, as well as dedication to athletics. The top-level brand promise states "UW–Madison provides a comprehensive educational environment in which intelligent, spirited students and scholars can work together to create change that influences Wisconsin and the world." The next level of the brand would include, for example, the School of Business. The school also strives to fulfill the image and brand promise of research and change that influences Wisconsin and the world, and it does it partly through its "family" brands, such as the Executive Education Center, the Small Business Development Center, the Family Business Center, and other centers. These family brands target specific types of customers (family business owners, small business personnel, or corporate managers and executives) with specific product offerings (e.g., seminars on product management and small business fundamentals). The university, the schools, and the centers are *endorsing* brands for the specific seminar products. In this case, the managers of these products rely heavily on the endorsing brands for positioning, even though specific product characteristics and marketing parameters play a role.

In another example, Apple Computers is the corporate endorsing brand for products such as the iPod family brand. Within this product family, the iPod is the full-featured product, and the iPod Shuffle is the entry-level *flanker brand*. Since Apple has a premium image, the marketing of the iPod Shuffle was handled carefully to avoid damaging either the family brand or the corporate brand. On the other hand, the premium image added prestige and credibility to the launch of the product.

When the corporate name is a potential hindrance, sometimes business units or family brands emerge as endorsers to a product brand. For example, when Cascadian Farms, a supplier of cereals and other products to natural foods retailers such as Whole Foods, was acquired by General Mills, it was clear that the General Mills image did not add value to the target customers. To this organic customer segment, the heritage of Cascadian Farms had more equity than the image of General Mills. Therefore, its cereal boxes identify the product (e.g., Oats & Honey Granola), with Cascadian Farms as the sponsoring company.[7]

Beyond determining whether the corporate brand should be an endorsing brand with the products being subbrands, a product manager needs to evaluate a host of other factors. What is the core positioning for the brand or product (as viewed by customers), and what do you want it to be? Can and should the brand be extended to other products or categories? Might a different brand be justified—or even required—to create a new position or appeal to a new market segment?

Core Positioning

The brand should be positioned to take advantage of your customer-valued strengths, while being different from the competition. There are many approaches companies can consider including price-value positions, usage positions, user-focused positions, alternative positions, secondary association positions, or attribute positions. The positioning can apply to a brand or to a brand-product combination as mentioned earlier. (See Table 11.2.)

Price-value positions run along a continuum from premier to mass market. A premier position is typically held by a market leader whose products have a higher price (and presumably higher quality) than the competition. Prestige products such as Rolex, and market leaders such as Caterpillar, are examples of premier brand positions. At the other end of the continuum, mass market brands rely more on efficiency (e.g., Walmart) or economy (e.g., Suave). If a product manager is going to compete at more than one price-value position, consideration should be given to a dual or flanker branding strategy where different brands are used for different positions.

Table 11.2

Positioning Approaches

Positioning Approach	Comments	Examples
Price-value	Establishes unique prestige or economy and may facilitate a good-better-best strategy or product range	Toyota Lexus vs. Toyota Camry
Usage	Highlights product applications	Excedrin (for migraines)
User-focused	Can be directly related to segmentation	Callaway golf clubs (for "serious golfers")
Alternative	An anticategory position (may sometimes be short term as competition in the anticategory increases)	Organic Choice (Scotts' brand of organic fertilizer)
Secondary association	Focuses on "borrowing" meaning from location, person, or another product	BMW (*German engineering*) Affinity credit cards (cobranded with an association, company, causes, etc.)
Attribute	Emphasizes specific features or benefits	Nexium (purple pill) Dell (customization) FedEx (guaranteed delivery) Tums (with calcium)

Usage positions are directly linked to applications or the way a product is used. Although not entirely by strategy, Apple computers were historically perceived as the computers for graphic design, while PCs were more IT focused. Excedrin established a position as *the* pain medication for migraines. Genetic reagents may be positioned for pure research rather than applied research functions.

Sometimes relevance is established (or implied) by positioning products toward *users*—certain types of individuals (e.g., do-it-yourselfers, parents), experts (e.g., professional golfers, engineers), or industries (e.g., water purification industry, hospitals). Brands may be associated with the type of individuals (or companies) the target customers *aspire* to be like. Nike, for example, is a brand that appeals to aspiring athletes. Harley-Davidson appeals to a rebel's self-image. (See Business Brief 11.1.)

Business Brief 11.1

HARLEY-DAVIDSON: THE GREAT AMERICAN COMEBACK BRAND

In one of the August issues every year, *BusinessWeek* publishes Interbrand's annual ranking of the world's most valuable brands—and Harley-Davidson is a consistent entry. But that hasn't always been the case. In 1975, when Jeffrey Bleustein joined the company as engineering vice president, the product was notorious for being shoddily built. Bleustein (who later became CEO) and his colleagues restored quality and introduced new models. In 2005 Harley had racked up 19 years of unbroken gains in earnings and sales.

Harley's success as a cult brand has been driven by the unshakable loyalty and advocacy of the Harley Owner's Group (HOG)—a 650,000-member club that lets folks "feed one another's rebel self-image." The brand image is one of rugged individualism, of freedom and rebellion, of a "little bit of bad." It is connected to American culture and values, beginning historically with its production being devoted to supplying U.S. and Allied troops during World Wars I and II. The company has reinforced this cult brand image with "360-degree marketing." It attempts to create a sense of community—an extended family, of sorts—through HOG events, plant tours, races, and bike rallies.

But there is a challenge to continuing the success of the brand. The median age of new Harley buyers increased to 46 in 2003, up from under 45 in 1997, and has risen more since then. Demand among the core baby boomers is cooling off. Now the brand must be extended to new markets and/or new products. To reach new markets, Harley is trying to make the brand and products relevant in new and meaningful ways to "dreamers" who may someday buy a Harley. Women have grown from about 5 to 10 percent of the retail buyers, and sales to Gen Xers are growing. The company has developed a branded driver's education training program called Rider's Edge. Dealers customize the program to appeal to their local market. Revenues are also generated through licensed items from leather pants to Harley-themed Barbie dolls. Harley-Davidson now has an advisory board of brand marketers that looks at "brand" from a total business perspective.

Source: Adapted from Joseph Weber, "He Really Got Harley Roaring," *BusinessWeek* (March 21, 2005), p. 70. Dale Buss, "Can Harley Ride the New Wave?" *Brandweek* (October 25, 2004), p. 20. Diane Brady et. al., "Cult Brands," *BusinessWeek* (August 2, 2004), p. 66. James Speros, "Why the Harley Brand's So Hot," *Advertising Age* (March 15, 2004), p. 26.

Brands use an *alternative* approach when they establish themselves as "anti" category products. During the 1970s, 7Up branded itself as the *uncola*, a soft drink that was the antithesis of the cola product category. Satellite television signal providers advertise themselves as alternatives to cable TV. It's worth noting that this approach might be successful in the early stages of the product life cycle—and can occasionally provide a continued first-mover advantage in, say, new technologies—but the entrance of competition into the "anti" category might reduce the effectiveness of this approach.

Secondary associations provide another potential basis of positioning. Product managers sometimes "borrow" meaning from a geographic location, a spokesperson, or even an object. Switzerland, as the home of Swiss watches, conjures up an image of precision. Germany is noted for automotive performance. Napa Valley is associated with wines. Products originating from such locations can sometimes benefit from an association with these strengths. In other situations products attempt to establish a connection with relevant locations or other factors to build a base for a secondary association. Athletes (e.g., Tiger Woods for Nike Golf), politicians (e.g., Bob Dole for Viagra), and actors (e.g., William Shatner for PriceLine) lend specific characteristics to the products they endorse.

Positioning by *attribute* refers to establishing a differential identity on the basis of some unique product or service feature or benefit. For example, if your product is the *only* one in the category to offer a titanium shaft, or a blue-tinted lens, or some other special feature, it might be possible to position it on that basis if there is some reason the competition will not copy that feature *and* if that attribute is visible and relevant to your target customers. Positioning on the basis of a benefit (as is the case for Volvo with safety) is a similar approach, but the attribute is less tangible.

There are several dos and don'ts with regard to positioning. *Do* position from strength. Without it, you have no ability to protect your difference from the competition. *Do* reinforce the positioning through all marketing. If your various customer touch points provide contradictory cues, the image becomes diluted and the market becomes confused. *Do* be consistent. Think of brand positioning as a long-term investment.

On the other hand, there are things to avoid. *Don't* try to be everything to everybody. This requires focus and discipline, because there is a temptation to stretch your funds as far as possible. Unfortunately, a lack of focus confuses customers to the point of pushing them toward the competition. Even though a position will not appeal to all customers, as long as it fits a large enough market segment, you will have an edge. *Don't* use different positionings for the same target market. If your product appeals to distinctly different customer groups that don't overlap, it's possible to position the offering differently. But if there is significant overlap, the brand image becomes convoluted. *Don't* position on price unless you have a true cost advantage. Even with a cost advantage this position can be dangerous if a future new technology makes your efficiencies obsolete. *Don't* position on a promise you can't fulfill. This is consistent with the first *do* of positioning from strength. Be sure you can follow through on your promises to customers.

Brand Extensions

When product managers add more products to their portfolio of offerings, they may need to evaluate both the fit of the products and the fit of the brand. As always, the moves should be logical from a customer perspective. For example, when dealing with technology products, the brand goes beyond a traditional promise of quality and carries over to line extensions. Customers want to know that complex products made by the same company work well together—quality is not enough in and of itself. That's why Sony, Apple, and Samsung opened "brand showrooms" to allow customers to experience the breadth of the product line.[8]

How far can a brand be extended before it dilutes its identity with customers and risks becoming meaningless? What are the advantages and disadvantages of extensions? How should brand extensions be executed? When should flanker and dual branding strategies be used? These are difficult questions for product managers. While there are no concrete answers, product managers should at least give careful consideration to the questions.

Given the expense of establishing a strong brand awareness, companies are always tempted to leverage the brand by extending it to product variants in the same product line (e.g., a different flavor, a different size, or a different color), or even to different product categories (e.g., extending the Jell-O name from instant gelatin mix to frozen pudding pops). To the extent that the essence of the brand (e.g., freshness, on-time delivery, fun) fits the new product, it can work. Daimler-Chrysler's Jeep introduced the Kolcraft Jeep Cherokee All-Terrain Stroller in 2001. The brand concept extended well, and the product sold briskly—even prompting a copycat entry from Ford's Land Rover. The stroller won the number two spot in the August 2004 "Top Branding Extensions" survey conducted by TippingSpring, a New York branding firm. Apple got the number one spot for its iTunes online music store brand extension.[9]

Of course, there are always risks to brand extensions. The new product may be perceived as significantly different from the original product, causing confusion in the marketplace. Also, if the new product fails, there may be a negative carryover to the first product.

Therefore, companies frequently try to benefit from a known brand while still keeping individual products somewhat separated. McDonald's carries its promise of speed and convenience to numerous products and links them with a common naming mechanism of the *Mc* prefix (McMuffin, McNuggets, etc.). Similarly, Hewlett-Packard extended its printer family brands through use of the *Jet* suffix (OfficeJet, DeskJet, LaserJet), and Sony extended its portable music players brand through the use of the *man* suffix (Walkman, Discman).

In cases where significantly different value propositions are inherent in the products, it may be worthwhile to use separate brands. Product managers offering good-better-best product lines might opt for different brands to represent each line. Or if two similar products are offered through different value channels (e.g., a big box retailer and a value-added reseller), a dual branding strategy might be employed.

BRAND ELEMENTS AND PROGRAMS

Once a strategy for hierarchy and positioning is developed, it will need to be implemented through selection and application of various brand elements. This may include (but not be limited to) creating brand names, defining the logo and related brand elements, and establishing the communications program to accomplish your branding goals. As mentioned earlier, customers form an impression of a brand from a variety of touch points, not all of which can be controlled by a product manager. Nevertheless a product manager should strive to control brand communications whenever possible.

Kevin Lane Keller has identified five criteria to use in evaluating various brand elements: memorability, meaningfulness, transferability, adaptability, and protectability.[10] *Memorability* refers to the inherent ability to be remembered and facilitate recall at time of purchase. *Meaningfulness* is the quality of being descriptive and/or persuasive, of capturing and enhancing the intangible characteristics of the brand. *Transferability* relates to the extent to which the brand element can be extended to different products, categories, or geographic markets. *Adaptability* suggests the ability to update the brand element over time, to remain relevant to the market without losing the long-term equity already established. The final criterion, *protectability*, refers to the extent to which the brand element can be protected either legally or competitively. These five criteria provide a checklist for product managers to use when beginning a new branding effort or when evaluating changes to an existing brand.

Brand Elements

What impact do brand names have on product success? That's a difficult question to answer since there is synergy between the two.

Before the *first* purchase of a *new* product, the product's name has not yet established value in the customer's mind. After purchase, however, the product name becomes important and is, in effect, the reflection of a successful product. Chemical product brands such as Teflon, Skydrol, Plexiglas, and Roundup are all long-established, highly successful products with significant sales volume. Once the product was purchased and used successfully, future sales were enhanced. In the absence of a name, there is little leverage in introducing related products, and even small changes in formulation, design, or function might prompt the competition to move in.[11]

Brand names can come from a variety of sources. Some are current usage words, such as People or Oracle, or word combinations such as Hamburger Helper or Janitor-in-a-Drum. These are easy to spell, pronounce, and remember, but they should not be descriptive of the category in which the products reside, especially if the category descriptor has been in common usage for a period of time. Hybrid words, such as ThinkPad or AquaFresh, are intended to be more descriptive of a product's benefits and overcome some of the difficulties encountered with registering common usage words. However, the escalation in the number of hybrids registered has reduced the pool of potential brand names using this approach. Neologisms are brand names that are meaningless in and of themselves, such as Tylenol, Pepsi, and Google. These types of brand names should be distinct, but will require more marketing communications efforts to establish a meaning in the customer's minds. Regardless of the method used to brainstorm names, the most common goal is to find a brand that communicates the positioning and fundamental benefits of the offering to target customers. When seeking new brand names, it's important to conduct a thorough search of existing brands to avoid infringing on another company's trademarks.

There are numerous trademarkable brand elements beyond brand names including logos, symbols, characters, packages, slogans, and jingles. These elements are used to stimulate brand awareness, establish a differential and memorable identity, and/or communicate a solid value proposition. Many product managers complain about the "logo cops" when their corporate marketing communications department enforces consistency in the typography, layout, and color of logos. Rather than fight the efforts, product managers should work within the guidelines and strive to draw benefits from the corporate brand for their product brands.

Characters are sometimes used to reinforce a brand's rational or emotional attributes. The Maytag repairman was used to communicate a message of reliability. The Keebler elves established a brand personality of magic and fun. Crest has revived its Crest Kid with the same theme of *no cavities*. (See Business Brief 11.2, "Character Icons Must Remain Relevant.") Slogans (such as GE's Imagination at Work) are also used to strengthen a brand image or promise. Product managers should consider the best ways to incorporate these into their product's marketing program.

Business Brief 11.2

CHARACTER ICONS MUST REMAIN RELEVANT

Companies generally attempt to keep their brand icons consistent. But that's not always possible or advisable. Sometimes change is necessary in order for the brand to be relevant to new audiences or expectations.

Dell began phasing out Steven (Dude, you're getting a Dell) in 2002 when it was determined that the message of customization was not clear enough in the marketing communications and was not relevant to the primary target of businesses. Although the character had high recognition, the approach was not as effective in cementing the brand position as desired. Similarly, Aflac insurance has launched a campaign "that partly muzzles its web-footed friend and instead seeks to better define what the company does." Customers said they remembered the duck and related it to some type of insurance, but weren't sure what Aflac could do for them.

P&G, while retaining the essence of the "Look Mom, no cavities" theme for Crest, has moved from the Normal Rockwell image of the 1950s to a Cuban-born girl named Enya Martinez. The modern-day Crest Kid is reflective of the surge in the Hispanic population in the United States.

There are other icons that have also had updates and make-overs. Aunt Jemima, the matriarch of pancakes and syrup, received a new hairstyle and modified dress in 1989. The Brawny man—the 1970s plaid-shirted muscleman on Georgia Pacific's paper towels—received an extreme makeover in 2004, being "replaced with a dark-haired younger character who might even be labeled a "metrosexual."

Source: Brian Steinberg, "P&G Brushes Up Iconic Image of 'Crest Kid' in New Campaign," *Wall Street Journal* (March 29, 2005), p. B9. Suzanne Vranica, "Dell, Starting New Campaign, Plans for Life without Steven," *Wall Street Journal* (October 16, 2002), p. B3. Suzanne Vranica, "Aflac Partly Muzzles Iconic Duck," *Wall Street Journal* (December 2, 2004), p. B8. Claire Atkinson, "Brawny Man Now a Metrosexual," *Advertising Age* (February 16, 2004), p. 8.

Marketing Program

Regardless of the specific brand elements used in contributing to a brand image, the related marketing program is even more critical. A strong product strategy is at the heart of a successful marketing program. The product portfolio must consistently deliver on both the tangible and intangible promises of the brand. The perceived value will depend partly on the correct pricing strategy. The channel used to deliver the product to customers must offer the appropriate identity and support. And finally marketing communications must promise only what can be provided on a consistent, ongoing basis.

Coca-Cola discovered the risk of running an advertising campaign in conflict with its brand identity. Long identified with touch-feely commercials such as, "I'd like to teach the world to sing," Coca-Cola wanted to be daring in 2000. It decided to test a new agency with an "edgy" campaign that turned its traditional "warm and fuzzy" image on its head. One commercial aired a crotchety grandmother in a wheelchair who goes ballistic at a family reunion when there is no Coke. Another presented friends fighting at a high school reunion for the same reason. Consumers and bottlers wrote in to complain that the ads were mean-spirited. The ads disappeared after a few weeks, scrapping a $72.9 million campaign.[12]

In general, the marketing program should be consistent with the desired brand identity and positioning as discussed throughout this chapter. However, product managers should continually challenge the status quo and decide whether the old rules still apply. Periodically visit Interbrand's Web site (http://www.brandchannel.com) to read the various features and papers that provide diametrically opposed ideas. Some just might work for you.

CHAPTER CHALLENGE

Dig deep to uncover the value of your brand that resonates beyond product features. Then strive to make this value visible through all customer touch points.

INTERVIEW WITH JEFF MIKULA: MAKE AUTHENTIC BRAND CONNECTIONS WITH CUSTOMERS

Jeff Mikula, Vice President, Global Branding & Marketing Communications, Hill-Rom, Inc.

Jeff, you have been involved in brand management and planning for over a decade. Tell us a bit about your corporate experiences in creating and managing brand value.

I have been truly fortunate to influence a broad spectrum of corporate and product brands ranging from startups to the Fortune 500, in both agency and corporate roles. My career has spanned 17+ years, and I have worked in many different areas including

brand integration, planning, brand expression/identity development, positioning, architecture development, product development, and commercialization. Great brands touch many parts of
the business and the customer experience. That I have so much
diversity in my background really has helped me take the brand
work to even higher levels of success. Currently, I'm working
to do just that with Hill-Rom, a leading worldwide manufacturer and provider of medical technologies and related services
for the health-care industry. The company is a strong and pro-
lific brand in hospitals, post-acute care, and other patient-care
settings around the world. I'm leading development of global
corporate brand and product strategies for Hill-Rom that will
enhance leadership, growth, and brand equity across new and
existing markets.

There are so many different definitions of the term brand. *How do
you define the term?*

A brand is really the promise of value that a company or a product makes to customers and other stakeholders. In health care,
we are in the business of trust, and that's a strong value connection or promise we make to our patients and our customers each
and every day. To have strong brand equity—particularly in a
space like health care—a brand has to deliver on the promise in
all aspects of the business. It's really far beyond a look and feel
or a tag line.

*What are some of the differences between corporate brand man-
agement and product brand management? How about differences
between B2B and B2C brand management?*

No matter what, the goal is always the same in branding—to
make a deep connection with customers and stakeholders, while
consistently delivering on the brand promise. Brand managers
must keep their focus on what the brand represents and how it
will live and grow. In a traditional B2B environment, a purchase
decision is multidimensional with many brand touch points.

The focus is more on customer relationship with the company than solely on the product, and the audience is more targeted. In a B2C environment, a purchase usually involves much more of an emotional appeal compared with the rational or intellectual basis of B2B. The focus is more on the relationship the customer has with the product than with the company, and the audience is much broader. In both instances, consistency is important, and integration with business operations and the entire marketing mix help to optimize the brand's value and influence.

There are several "hot" topics in brand management from brand archetypes to corporate citizenship to social media. How have those topics influenced (if at all) your work in brand management?

In today's environment, authenticity and trust are paramount to building successful and sustainable brands. Customers engage with brands in ways that help clarify their own values and priorities. They are looking for companies and brands to show that they share those values on some level. Customers expect a two-way dialogue and the opportunity to engage. Organizations strive to create engaging brands with more transparency by building trust and leveraging reputation. Regardless of whether it's brand archetypes, corporate citizenship, social media—or all of these—brand managers will continue to be influenced by opportunities for their brands to be more engaging, authentic, and transparent with customers. Brand managers simply can't approach branding in the same way anymore, because our customers don't associate with brands the same way. All of these topics have influenced my brand work in some way—and the brands and our customers are the better for it.

Do you have any favorite sources of information and new ideas as they relate to brand-related topics?

While not new, perhaps one of the most important tools for brand managers is experience mapping—the process of identifying all of the interactions between a customer and a company. Some of the best advances in innovation around a brand or brand promise (and the worst failures) are related not only to fulfilling customers' *current* needs but also in foreshadowing what they will be in the future as the marketplace inevitably shifts. Experience mapping allows brand managers the opportunity to get close to every step in the experience, to be open and proactive about all of the touch points in the business that influence the brand connection. As the environment for brands continues to change, thriving brands must stay current or ahead of the evolving digital, social, and traditional vehicles. And we must be prepared for the next big innovation or disruption that could change the important connections with our brands and the marketplace as a whole.

Do you have any tips on brand management for product managers?

Dig deep to find the unique meaning of a brand that will create a bond that is far more important than general product features. Differentiation is critical for sales and profitability. Look around at all the influencers and consider how they interact with each other because these interpersonal interactions can be as important as how they interact with your brand. Get intimate with all the touch points of the customer experience. And go beyond simple product or brand awareness as a market measure. While the connections between brand and customer are deeper, the perspectives of influence and experience need to be much broader in this environment. Successful brand managers need both micro and macro vision to take a brand from good to great.

CHAPTER 12

Marketing Strategy and Go-to-Market Efforts

TRUE OR FALSE: Advertising, sales, and marketing are synonymous.

Absolutely false. Marketing is a *before* activity focused on understanding customers and how well their needs/goals fit with your current and potential product offerings (and is consequently the planning phase). Advertising and sales are *after* activities that are elements of your marketing execution. However, they are all linked together, and product managers must assess their respective roles in accomplishing desired product goals.

TRUE OR FALSE: Good salespeople can sell anything to anybody.

This is a commonly held misconception—sometimes by even product managers and salespeople! If product managers arm salespeople with a good product, a solid value proposition, relevant collateral and/or demos, and a carefully defined target market, the ability to sell should be fairly straightforward. Both sides have to work together to attain the desired sales.

By starting with two true-false statements, this chapter focuses on two issues: marketing strategy components of customer messaging and pricing. It also covers issues surrounding support for go-to-market efforts.

MARKETING STRATEGY

According to the American Marketing Association's online dictionary, "Marketing is an organizational function and a set of processes for creating, communicating, and delivering value to customers and for managing customer relationships in ways that benefit the organization and its stakeholders." This is a bit of an evolution from the long-standing model of the four Ps: product, price, promotion, and place. Since these are internally focused concepts, many experts (as suggested in the AMA definition) have shifted to the external perspective of customers. Viewing the product as addressing customer needs rather than as a bundle of features is paramount to this viewpoint. Figure 12.1 shows not only a few additional components added to the four Ps mnemonic, but also the shift from the traditional Ps to an external look at Cs.

Using this perspective, *product* embodies a bundle of need-satisfiers for the customer. *Price* requires a look at the monetized benefits and costs of the product for customers. *Promotion* moves from a monologue to a two-way conversation; this is becoming particularly important with the growth of social media (as discussed in the end-of-chapter interview).

FIGURE 12.1 ➤ Marketing's shift from an internal to an external perspective

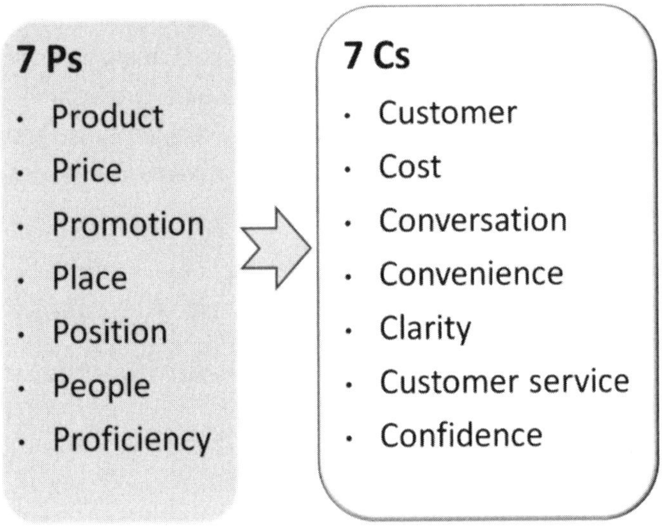

7 Ps

- Product
- Price
- Promotion
- Place
- Position
- People
- Proficiency

7 Cs

- Customer
- Cost
- Conversation
- Convenience
- Clarity
- Customer service
- Confidence

Place now adds some awareness of the convenience (or lack thereof) for your customer to acquire your products. Your *positioning*, if done well, translates into clarity from the customers' perspective. Do they really know and understand how you are different? Your *people* deliver the customer service that may be part of your brand promise. And finally, your *proficiency* and competencies in creating a unique, quality offering can be the proof statements, the "reasons to believe" that translate into confidence in your customers. That being said, each of the Ps has to be planned, managed, and controlled to be able to deliver on the promises of the Cs and to "benefit the organization and its stakeholders." Therefore, we dive into a few of the Ps and Cs in this chapter.

Target Customers

Knowledge about customers, segments, and markets has been discussed throughout this book, so I just want to make a few additional comments here. Product managers need both *hard* and *soft* market data to help them in decision making. Hard data refer to things like market size and growth rates; these are necessary for assessing financial market potential. Soft data refer to the less tangible elements of customer feelings and attitudes, which are necessary for brand equity and customer messaging.

Product managers should reframe their perspectives from *creating and selling products* to *helping customers make buying decisions.* And that means thinking about the customers' decision process. Is this a "considered purchase" or a simple purchase? Is this a first-time buy or a repeat purchase? Is the product being purchased by a new customer or an existing customer?

A considered purchase refers to a relatively complicated decision process. Capital equipment, for example, is generally a considered purchase which usually involves numerous influencers and is often a committee decision. To increase success probabilities, you should anticipate different personalities and "hot buttons" for the various people involved in the decision and try to provide the right "ammunition" to help them make a purchase decision in your favor. This means preparing financial "reasons to believe" for financial buyers and proof of feature-benefits for users. Even if people make these types of decisions on an emotional basis, they need rational data to "justify" the decision they have already made. Both intellectual and emotional drivers will need to be included.

A simple purchase, on the other hand, is more likely to involve a single individual and may lean more toward the emotional side of decision making. Your particular product could fall anywhere along the continuum from considered purchase to simple purchase, and you should adjust your messaging accordingly.

If the majority of your target customers are new, you will need to decide how much of your messaging to devote to introducing your company and/or educating them about the product category. Repeat purchasers may need more reminder types of communications.

Pricing Strategies and Tactics

The product manager must deal with both upstream and downstream pricing decisions. Estimated economic value modeling and the importance of understanding true product costs are covered in Chapter 3, and the new product pricing decision tree in Chapter 7, so they won't be repeated here. Rather I focus on the product pricing issues from more of a marketing perspective.

Focus your initial pricing efforts on the top (most important) products in your portfolio. These could be core products that generate significant cash flow or renewal products that could benefit from a stronger value proposition. Using historical sales records and sales force input, determine how price-sensitive the buyers are. If you raise the price, will you retain enough customers to maintain at least the current level of profitability? If you reduce the price, will you gain enough business to offset the lowered margin? While these are subjective questions, you can develop a spreadsheet for a breakeven analysis of the price changes similar to the example in Chapter 3 to give you a starting point for evaluation.

Manage your higher-velocity products more actively. These are products that are either more popular or have a larger potential market size, inviting more competitive price pressures. Let's say that you are a product manager for automotive aftermarket parts. Some of the specialized parts sold through dealers may command a higher margin simply because they are infrequent purchases and there is less ongoing price competition. High turnover parts facing competition from Walmart and other mass merchandisers may need to be evaluated and repriced as circumstances dictate.

Try to control price leakage (the difference between invoice and pocket price), as described in the pocket price waterfall discussion in Chapter 3. Product managers are sometimes asked by salespeople and others to authorize additional discounts and exception prices. If the exceptions provide additional unit sales or prevent loss to the competition, it might be worth it. But it pays to think about the bottom-line impact of price changes if unit sales stay the same, as shown in Table 12.1.

The first column in the table is the base case: 5,000 units of the product are sold for $200/unit for total revenue of $1,000,000 and net pretax income of $50,000. If the price of these products is reduced by 1 percent to $198 and nothing else changes, the bottom line drops from $50,000 to $40,000, or a 20 percent decline. Going back to the base case, compare the impacts of a 1 percent volume decrease, a 1 percent cost-of-goods sold (CGS) variable cost increase, or a 1 percent fixed cost increase. It should be clear that this 1 percent drop in price should be authorized only if additional unit sales can be expected. (To estimate how many additional units, refer to the information in Chapter 3.)

Table 12.1

Comparative 1% Changes

	Original	1% price decrease ($198)	1% volume decrease (4950 units)	1% CQS increase ($121.20)	1% fixed cost increase ($353,500)
Sales (5,000@$200)	$1,000,000	$990,000	$990,000	$1,000,000	$1,000,000
CGS (5,000@$120)	600,000	600,000	594,000	606,000	600,000
Gross margin	400,000	390,000	396,000	394,000	400,000
Operating costs	350,000	350,000	350,000	350,000	353,500
Net pretax income	$ 50,000	$ 40,000	$ 46,000	$ 44,000	$ 46,500
Percentage change in income		−20%	−8%	−12%	−7%

Develop a pricing strategy for substitutes and complements in the product line. When two products compete with each other as substitutes, it's important that the prices be evaluated concurrently. Are the products targeted at different customers with different value propositions? If so, price accordingly. If there is a rollover strategy when one replaces another, strive to time the rollover to minimize the need for differential pricing. When the products work together as a complete solution (such as equipment and replacement parts), decide whether it makes sense to price the equipment low to gain initial sales and generate more margin from future consumables. Business Brief 12.1 looks at some issues related to product-line pricing.

Business Brief 12.1

PRODUCT-LINE PRICING

Zebra Technologies Corp., a maker of bar-code printers, had developed a reputation among customers as a manufacturer of high-quality, top-of-the-line printers. But the company saw a lot of sales potential in the low-end portion of the marketplace. A low-priced, low-frills printer was a cinch to make. But offering such a model posed two risks: It might tarnish Zebra's image of quality with its customers, and, worse, it might cannibalize the existing product line.

The solution Zebra came up with was a no-frills version with a plastic housing that pleased its clients. But it didn't give away the store: It made sure that the stripped-down printer couldn't be upgraded which ensured that it wouldn't compete with its high-end model, which was faster and could print on different kinds of materials. The result: The new printer helped Zebra's sales climb by 47 percent in one year, and margins on the new printer matched those of Zebra's original line.

Apple took a similar approach with its move downstream. In an effort to bring out products for the low end of its two core markets, Apple announced the Mac mini and the iPod Shuffle. The Mac mini was a stripped-down version of the Mac and is the least expensive computer Apple ever released. The lower-priced product was an effort to convince users of Windows-based products to switch to the Mac. Apple felt that the lower price, along with Microsoft's vulnerability to computer viruses, could tempt some customers to reconsider their computer-buying behavior.

The iPod Shuffle was a simple, inexpensive version of Apple's standard iPod with less functionality and a lower song-storage capacity. It targeted a more price-sensitive, younger market. Both the iPod and Mac businesses showed brisk growth after the launch of the new products.

Source: David Greising, "Quality: How to Make It Pay," *BusinessWeek* (August 8, 1994), p. 58. Nick Wingfield, "Apple Scores with Cheaper Lines," *Wall Street Journal* (April 14, 2005), p. A3. Peter Burrows and Andrew Park, "Apple's Bold Swim Downstream, *BusinessWeek* (January 24, 2005), pp. 33–35. Nick Wingfield, "Apple Tries a New Tack: Lower Prices," *Wall Street Journal* (January 12, 2005), pp. D1–D5.

Regardless of the base pricing strategies, build your own tool kit of ideas to test. Use Table 12.2 to get you started. Not all these ideas will work for you, but they have all worked in appropriate situations. Most are self-explanatory, so the table contains an overview of the major categories.

The incentive pricing tools should be designed to "incent" specific kinds of behavior. Order-size discounts, for example, attempt to maintain a shipment size at an acceptable freight cost whereas cumulative discounts strive to encourage customer loyalty over a longer period of time. Ownership variations such as licensing may enable customers to enjoy the benefit of a product or service, even if they might have limited budgets. Pay now, benefit later (or its reverse) may allow a product sale to occur within a customer's specified budget requirements. Consumption pricing allows customers to pay for only the quantity of a product they use. Product-line variations (also known as product versioning) allow products to be priced according to the perceived value of a specific customer segment. Product innovation can be used to limit

Table 12.2

Pricing Tool Kit

Price Variation Category	Example Tools		
Incentive pricing	Rebate	Package pricing	Product mix discount
	Coupon	Penetration pricing	Step (or block) discount
	Promotional pricing	Every-day-low pricing	
	Sales	Order-size discounts	Deductibles
	Price match guarantee	Cumulative volume discounts	Preferential terms
			Buy one, get one free
Ownership variations	Leasing/renting	Layaway	
	Licensing	Metering	
Pay now, benefit later	Membership	Prepayment	
	Subscription	Lock-in pricing	
	Retainer		
Buy now, pay later	Financing programs		
	Credit		
Consumption pricing	Peak and off-peak	Usage	
	Metering/hourly rates	Two-part pricing	
	Price-per-project		
Product line variations	Versioning	Portfolio pricing	Free offers
	Private label	Bundling	Life-cycle pricing
	Good-better-best	A la carte-menu pricing	Loss leaders
One-size-fits-all	Flat rate/fixed fee		
	All-you-can-eat		
Real-time price variations	Negotiation	Competitive bid pricing	
	Dynamic demand	Auction pricing	

Price Variation Category	Example Tools		
Customer engagement	Loyalty pricing	Yield management	Customer segmentation
	Guaranteed rate	No haggle pricing	
		Protection pricing	Price assurance
	Priority access	Enhanced warranties	Minimum order size
		Bartering	Psychological pricing
	Location-based		
	Goal attainment		
Nonstandard revenue generation	Market expansion		
	Sponsorship/ advertising fees		
	Controlling price leakage		

© Linda Gorchels 2010. Reprinted with permission.

price sensitivity as discussed in Business Brief 12.2, "Using Innovation to Reduce Price Competition." One-size-fits-all can be used to simplify the purchase and delivery process. Real-time price variations may enable immediate responses to competitive price variations. Customer engagement pricing can be used to match price components with divergent customer value drivers. And finally, nonstandard revenue generation examines ways of generating new revenues or margins without directly dealing with product prices.

Business Brief 12.2

USING INNOVATION TO REDUCE PRICE COMPETITION

As always, one way to exit a price war is to innovate. Take Becton Dickinson's hypodermic needles. The company produces billions of them each year. Prices are generally flat. During one particularly painful period, a Japanese competitor began selling its wares for 7 cents a unit (significantly less than comparable products). In other words, you would not want to be stuck in the needle business. Then, Becton Dickinson got together with Baxter International, which had developed InterLink, a needleless needle.

The point to remember is that the needles doctors stick in your arm account for about 50 percent of the market. The other half is used to hook up intravenous lines to other IVs, which is where the Baxter-Becton team made its mark. InterLink looks like a regular syringe except the needle is replaced by a hard piece of tapered plastic tubing that ends in a blunt tip. Baxter created a new type of plastic and rubber seal that could be punctured and then would reseal around such a plastic spike. Baxter asked Becton to produce the spike.

Hospitals were willing to pay more for InterLink because the pointless needles lowered the risk of accidental needle sticks. At the time of launch, health-care workers reported about one million sticks, costing hospitals upward of $400 per incident in lost time and paperwork, excluding any legal or long-term health costs. "That's the attraction," says Gary Cohen, a marketing vice president with Becton Dickinson. "Even though InterLink needles cost about 25 cents, hospitals save money."

The innovation trend has also moved into consumer products, where companies have been struggling to win price increases. Procter & Gamble decided to jazz up humdrum brands by adopting Gillette's well-known razor-and-replacement-blade strategy, and by incorporating mechanical or electric features. The $14 Swiffer mop (with its $5.75 replacement pads) has been a profitable new product, generating both initial sales and follow-on sales. Tide StainBrush (a battery-powered brush), Mr. Clean AutoDry (a water-pressured car-cleaning system), and other gadget-related items accounted for about 8 percent of P&G's $54 billion.

Source: Andrew E. Serwer, "How to Escape a Price War," *Fortune* (June 13, 1994), p. 90. Robert Berner and William Symonds, "Welcome to Procter & Gadget," *BusinessWeek* (February 7, 2005). p. 76.

Customer Messaging

Now let's talk about having a conversation with your customers—not advertising, not communicating, but conversing. Think in terms of a dialogue rather than a monologue. What can you say, and how can you say it in a way that resonates with your customer? That's customer message management. It's more than coming up with a carefully crafted communiqué. It's more than a persuasive pitch to sell your product. Its shifting over to "their" side (the purchasing side) and helping customers make a purchase decision (hopefully in your favor).

There are often different audiences for a product that require subtly different messages. For example, a contractor may have one need for a garage door (e.g., to complete a job), a homeowner may have another need (e.g., ease of installation), and an architect may have still another (e.g., aesthetic fit with a building design). In addition, as mentioned earlier, for many products the user may be different from the purchaser or other influencers, and each may have different reasons for wanting a particular product. The challenge for the product manager is to decide on the primary and secondary audiences to target with a messaging strategy.

Profile your primary target customer in as much detail as necessary in order for you to visualize having a conversation with them. Some people refer to these profiles as archetypes or brand archetypes. If your primary purchaser is a plant manager, describe this person in both psychographic and demographic terms to aid in message strategy. For example, "Sam" is a 45-year-old plant manager who has worked for the same company for over 10 years. He is very interested in moving up the corporate ladder but worries that his lack of experience in other industries may be an impediment. He is an avid fisherman and enjoys occasional golf. He is married with two children and drives an SUV.

After you have profiled your target customers, try to really project yourself into their shoes. Why might they want this product at this time? How do they feel about the purchase? What objections might they have, and does your product pose any risk to them? What alternatives might they be considering? Does your product fit their need or application precisely? Where do your customers look for advice on making the purchase? Why should customers believe your product is better than that of the competition in satisfying their needs? How are customers buying the product (or getting their needs addressed) now? Remember what it is your customers want to know:

- What will your product (service) do for me?
- How will it do it?
- Why is it better than that of the competition?
- Who says so? Why should I believe you?
- What if I'm not satisfied?

Once you understand your defined target customer perceptions, the information can be used to write a creative platform for the product or service. The creative platform helps your marketing communications colleagues take your insights and convert them into customer messages. At minimum the creative brief should contain the following:

- Who—specifically—are you trying to reach? (Describe both the market profile and the "person" you are talking with.)
- What is the one main value proposition? (What is the one-word big idea you want customers to get from the conversation?)
- What is the product's positioning? (How is this superior to the competition?)
- What do you want the impact of the message to be on the audience? (How should the person feel—e.g., excited, relieved, energized?)
- Why should the customer believe you? (Do you have proof from beta tests, customer testimonials, third-party endorsements, or other "belief builders"?)
- What are the next steps the customer should take? (Set up a product trial, contact a salesperson, etc.?)

Most product managers are actively involved in deciding on the theme of the customer message, but the actual execution may be handled by the marketing or marketing services department. This means you must work in concert with them to determine the best way to reach the audience—and it might not always be through traditional means. Sometimes you have to be creative in breaking through to your audience, particularly for commodity products like mortgages. Arbor National Mortgage, a midsized company in Uniondale, New York, developed a database-building and positioning approach that has worked. By repackaging a standard mortgage into a bridal registry, the result was a distinctive identity.

Arbor takes a standard Fannie Mae mortgage and repackages it into the Arbor Home Bridal Registry. Couples register with Arbor instead of a department store so friends and families can contribute to the newly-weds' first home. "Running the registry is a lot of work, so we aren't as concerned with getting couples to register as we are in getting inquiries about purchasing a first home," says Boyles (Arbor's senior vice president of marketing). "Only three dozen couples have actually registered, but we've had over 5,000 couples call about the service. Their names are now in our database. We hope to have them as customers someday." Arbor also holds mortgage seminars for real estate brokers, accountants, and consumers. And the company plants a tree for customers who want one, either in their yard or in a public forest.[1]

Product managers might be involved in a variety of other promotional techniques, such as sampling, sales contests, and various incentive programs. These are referred to as "incentive programs" because they provide inducements to stimulate short-term incremental sales of the product as opposed to building long-run brand loyalty. Promotions are commonly used to introduce new products, influence the effectiveness of competitors' tactics, or tap into a new market.

Product sampling can be an effective technique for encouraging customers to try a new product. New products that require behavioral change by potential users generally benefit from the ability of customers to try them on a low-cost or no-cost basis. 3M's Post-it Notes, for example, required free sampling so that customers could experience using the product. Test drives are a method of sampling in the automotive industry. Rent-with-the-option-to-buy is a form of sampling that reduces cost (and risk) to both parties.

CHANNEL SELECTION AND SALES SUPPORT

Throughout this book I emphasize the criticality of end-customer knowledge. It might seem contradictory to now shift to the channel. But it's not. An effective first "sale" to salespeople, distributors, dealers, and retail buyers is often necessary to be able to implement a marketing strategy to reach end customers. Unless a company's go-to-market strategy is entirely through the Internet and wireless environments, most product managers need to consider direct and/or indirect sales channels in their plans and implementation.

Channel Knowledge

For many product managers the sales channel is a given. But for those challenged with new growth, selecting the right path to market can be the difference between success and failure. Unless a product manager's products are distributed differently from all other products in the company, chances are he or she will not have significant control over strategic methods of distribution. Most of the activities will be related to working with the existing distributors, dealers, or agents and perhaps expediting shipments as necessary. However, some new products will necessitate changes in the channel of distribution, or market and competitive forces will require changes for existing products. This could also be a critical element of the plan if a product manager is rolling out a product into new regions and/or expanding globally. As a result, distribution strategy should not be ignored as the product manager develops the product plans.

Whenever a product manager introduces a lower-priced or higher-priced product, or one that has a different image, it might be necessary to introduce new channels. A potentially successful product can be thwarted by the wrong channel decision, as Huffy found when it introduced its new Cross Sport bike.

Huffy Corp., for example, the successful $700 million bike maker, did careful research before it launched a new bicycle it dubbed the Cross Sport, a combination of the sturdy mountain bike popular with teenagers and the thin-framed, nimbler racing bike. Huffy conducted two separate series of market focus groups in shopping malls across the country, where *randomly selected children and adults viewed the bikes and ranked them. The bikes met with shoppers' approval. So far, so good. In the summer of 1991, Cross Sports were shipped out to mass retailers, such as the Kmart and Toys "R" Us chains, where Huffy already did most of its business. That was the mistake. As Richard L. Molen, Huffy president and chief executive, explains, the researchers missed one key piece of information. These special hybrid bikes were aimed at adults and, at $159, were priced 15 percent higher than other Huffy bikes, and therefore needed individual sales attention by the sort of knowledgeable salespeople who work only in bike specialty shops. Instead, Huffy's Cross Sports were supposed to be sold by the harried general salespeople at mass retailers such as Kmart. Result: "It was a $5 million mistake," says Molen. By 1992, the company had slashed Cross Sport production by 7 percent and recorded an earnings drop of 30 percent.[2]*

As markets fragment, different target customers—even for the same product—might seek alternative channels of distribution. Key accounts, for example, might best be served by going direct, whereas other customers can be more efficiently served through distributors. On the other hand, small customers might be handled by telesales, even if there are outside reps calling on larger customers in the same territory. Specialized distributors or agents might be more successful with certain segments than existing intermediaries, and that possibility should be periodically explored. Technology has changed the go-to-market strategy for many companies and products, as shown in Figure 12.2.

Effectively motivating intermediaries can have a positive impact on the bottom line. This starts by keeping a careful record of distributor or rep activity by product and assessing overall capabilities. Product managers should accompany regional or sales managers in routine visits to distributors or reps and might be expected to help prepare joint marketing plans. If there is an advisory council, the product manager should review the meeting minutes (at minimum the sections related to his or her product line) and react accordingly.

Manufacturers' and resellers' goals do not always match. Product managers sometimes tend to view resellers as the destination of their product. Resellers, on the other hand, view the receipt of a product as

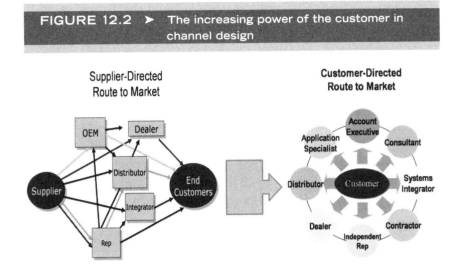

FIGURE 12.2 ➤ The increasing power of the customer in channel design

the beginning of a sales cycle. This can create unnecessary conflict, which could be reduced if information were shared more effectively.

Product managers spend a good deal of money and effort to understand end-user needs and how their products fit these needs. Resellers should also be given this information. Providing this education to resellers not only helps them work better, but it also enables them to provide valuable feedback to the manufacturer on product performance.

The channel is often involved in product support. Product support can encompass several things: installation, warranty follow-through, product upgrades, repairs, customer training, and so on. The product manager might not be directly involved in these activities, but he or she should be concerned about whether the policies and procedures are in place for them to happen. Customer satisfaction frequently depends as much on these factors as it does on the product itself. In addition, the product manager might be involved in developing services that optimize profit potential from various segments.

The cost of installation can be included in the price of the product or be an "optional" or unbundled component. The decision should be made in conjunction with the appropriate personnel (e.g., the service manager). If any significant changes are to be made, they should be mentioned in the marketing plan, and should include the impact on other marketing activities and on the bottom line.

A warranty or service contract can affect the salability of a product and should be examined along with other features. There are several questions to consider here:

- What do customers expect?
- Will there be a full or limited warranty?
- Can competitors match the warranty? Will they?
- Should the warranty be handled by the manufacturer, by the dealer, or by an independent organization?
- What are the advantages and disadvantages of service contracts and extended warranties?

Sales Support

The product manager will also interact extensively with the internal sales force. Product managers who have had sales experience will find it easier to understand the salesperson's "world" and provide the type of support the sales force really values. Too often the support and training product managers provide consist of technical product details and esoteric elements of the marketing plan. Sometimes what is missing are concrete tools and suggestions that help salespeople target the highest-probability customers and sell to them effectively. Collaborating with sales can be critical, as discussed in Business Brief 12.3.

Business Brief 12.3

THE IMPORTANCE OF MARKETING-SALES COLLABORATION

Managing the message being communicated to customers is a challenge in most organizations, including pharmaceutical companies. Product managers invest considerable effort in fine-tuning the key points, hoping to have the sales force deliver a single, carefully defined message. However, there is significant erosion in the message from product manager to salesperson to physician. Often the messages are not perceived as credible by the sales force, and the product managers as a whole are held in relatively low esteem.

Sometimes there should *not* be a single message, but rather different perspectives to fit different audiences. A criticism aimed at pharmaceutical companies by physicians was that there is too much marketing-speak in the information provided to them:

> *The physicians surveyed were looking for unbiased, evidence-based, scientific information about products, including head-to-head comparisons, as well as risks and side effects. Physicians are much more likely to ask for information regarding the benefits of the product compared with its rivals in that area and also details on side effects and risks. For others, cost-based information is key, while for yet others, an understanding of the holistic benefits for a patient's overall well-being is a top priority.*

If product managers are going to help salespeople develop more value-added relationships with customers, they need to create the right differentiated messages for the right subaudiences. And they must provide the right collateral and selling tools for the sales force to accomplish this. Collaboration between the two groups is required to accomplish these objectives:

> *It is crucial that sales and marketing work closely together to develop the message. Ideally, companies should be looking to build a cross-functional team led by the product manager. This not only makes the process more efficient, but ensures that all the requisite knowledge is included in the material. Such cross-functional collaboration ensures real buy-in from the sales organization.*
>
> *It is also best practice to factor customer input into the message development process. One of the best ways to do this is to use physician focus groups. These groups can be used to research and test new message options, as well as to help companies gain a deeper understanding of what physicians want to hear.*

Source: Alasdair Mackintosh, "Getting the Message Across," *International Journal of Medical Marketing* (April 2004), pp. 102–105.

A common mistake product managers make is to try to make the target audience appear as large as possible to create "excitement" among the sales force. Rather than focusing on the carefully honed target profile, they expand to secondary and tertiary markets. Unfortunately this dilutes the sales effort and reduces the probability of early wins. As a result, salespeople are less likely to believe in the product.

Salespeople are your first "customers," and they will have questions similar to the customer questions we listed earlier:

- What will your product (service) do for me? (In other words, how will this help salespeople earn commissions?)
- How will it do it? (Will you provide special incentives to entice customers to try it?)
- Why is it better than the competition? (What are the areas of competitive superiority, and how easy will it be to convince my customers?)
- Who says so? Why should I believe you? (Do you have any proof from customers or other salespeople? How is this different from products that were not successful?)

Be sure to build a network of salespeople you can trust and who are willing to help you. Ask them for help and advice on gaining commitment from the rest of the sales force. And be sure to follow through on the commitments you make to them.

CHAPTER CHALLENGE

Stop thinking about marketing from the single perspective of promoting and selling to customers. Rather, change your perspective to frame marketing as helping customers make purchase decisions in your favor.

INTERVIEW WITH GABRIELA SALDANHA BRINK: SOCIAL NETWORKING IN A SCIENTIFIC INDUSTRY

Gabriela Saldanha Brink, Global Product Manager, LSR, Promega Corporation

Gabriela, tell me about yourself and your career path starting with a biology degree from Brazil and progressing to a global product management position in the headquarters of Promega.

Okay. My name is Gabriela de Medeiros Saldanha Brink. By that very long name you can guess I'm of Portuguese descendent, but you are right, I'm actually from Brazil. When I was in high school in my hometown of Florianopolis and learned about DNA and the human genome project, I decided that was what I wanted to do. I'm very fortunate to have been able to follow my dreams and still today work in the same field. Even though I don't work in the lab any more, my science knowledge and understanding of the customer's pains and needs have provided me with the necessary tools to have a successful career as a global product manager at Promega Corporation. I have been with Promega for the last 11 years working with several different product lines, from short tandem repeat (STR) technology for forensic DNA and paternity testing to enzymes and kits that allow the study of nucleic acids through the polymerase chain reaction or PCR, the most widespread technique used by research scientists worldwide. Promega is a leader in providing innovative solutions and technical support to the life sciences industry. We have 2,000 products that enable scientists worldwide to advance their knowledge in genomics, proteomics, cellular analysis, molecular diagnostics, and human identification. I work at the company headquarters in Madison, Wisconsin, USA. However, we have branches in 15 countries and over 50 global distributors.

You've really embraced social networking and Internet technologies in your efforts to reach scientists. What are some of the tools, techniques, and strategies you've used?

I have always been an early adopter and with social media wasn't much different. Right away I saw the potential social media had, and I jumped on it immediately. But it was a slow start. I began reading articles and white papers, getting tips from other users, and participating in communities and forums. It was very important to learn from others. The field was in its infancy, and that meant trying new things and observing results. After understanding a little more about what social media really is, I was able to develop a plan and establish goals and objectives, as well as metrics to track. Social media is here to stay. It has changed the way we exchange information—the way we talk with family and friends and the way we talk with customers. Yes, we talk *with* them. We don't just disseminate information; we *exchange* information. It provides constant feedback, always changing and in motion. That's why it is so important to be attentive to what customers are saying about your company and products online. The information is out there for anyone to see. You have to be prepared. If you are not, you can be sure your competitor is.

What has worked exceptionally well for you, and what has not?

When something is in its infancy, you have to try a lot of things to see what works well and what doesn't, or what you have to change next time you try again. With social media we tried a few YouTube videos about specific products and wanted them to be funny and not necessarily too sales-oriented, but it didn't work as well as we thought, and they didn't go viral. As for what has worked, on the other hand, Promega developed a blog called "Promega Connections." Although I'm not directly involved in the project and don't have the details, this social media effort has been a success. The blogs are posted by R&D, technical services scientists, scientific writers, IT, and marketing. They are not product focused—the blogs may be about personal stories, scientific discovery, and so forth. It's not about Promega; it's about the community, and it's about the people. That's our new world. It's about people: who are they, what they do and want, but not about the companies.

Can you cite a couple of specific example of successes, as well as your analysis of why they were successful?

Well, the Promega Connections is a good example. We knew our scientists were online a lot, and we wanted to reach them where they already were. While Promega has a page on Facebook, that didn't seem to be the best venue to reach them yet, but that community is growing, and we will be able to continue to experiment. We preferred to create a community where our scientist customers could talk with each other. We were able to get out the Promega brand indirectly and serve as an information vehicle.

As you've advanced to your current position, what are a few of the most important things you have learned?

You have to be open and attentive to changes in your field. You need to know and understand your customers, their habits, likes and dislikes, pains, needs, and the solutions you are providing them. Social media may not work for everyone; it all depends on your understanding of your customer base. But it's important to try new things, different things. If you don't try, you won't know what works or what the results and consequences might be. Some customer bases may be more conservative and not jump into new things. I believe scientists are by nature curious, innovative, risk takers. Much research is trial-based, with resulting failure and success. Based on that profile of my customers I knew they would adopt social media. After all, we are all geeks.

PART IV

FINE-TUNING

CHAPTER 13

Establishing a Global Mindset

> **TRUE OR FALSE:** The majority of the world's cultures are relationship-focused.
>
> **TRUE.** This is a true statement. However, since most product managers from the United States and several Western countries come from task-focused cultures, they often find it difficult to adapt to the small talk and additional "get-to-know-you" time expected in relationship-oriented cultures.

COMMUNICATING ACROSS BORDERS AND CULTURES

A global product manager is not simply one who oversees products sold in other countries. The global product manager is one who thinks and plans with an appreciation of the global competitive arena. Even companies with a low percentage of foreign sales have competitors, suppliers, and customers that extend beyond domestic borders. Global thinking—not just sales—is important for these product managers. Whether or not a company has multinational locations, these product managers develop long-term product strategies on a global basis. They look for similarities across different world markets, standardizing whenever possible and customizing whenever necessary. This affords opportunities (proactively) for future foreign sales as well as for competitive strategies against global competitors.

Product managers will have different responsibilities depending on whether they are based in the country where their business resides (and sell to customers in other countries from the home office), or whether they are located in the country or region where sales take place. The first type is a *domestically based* global (DBG) product manager. The second is a *locationally based* global (LBG) product manager. Domestically based global product managers typically participate in the "upstream" product development efforts. Then they may be directly involved in go-to-market activities, or they may work with "downstream" managers in other countries.

Locationally based global product managers can fall along a continuum from downstream (tactical) to full-stream (both strategic and tactical) activities. Those involved solely in the tactical activities are given predesigned (and often premanufactured) products to sell in their countries of responsibility and are charged with the relevant marketing, sales, and distribution activities. The full-stream product managers create unique offerings for their markets, from design through sale. The locationally based managers may be expatriates who were transferred from another corporate location, or they may be native to the specific region. These product managers must have a thorough understanding of the customer needs in their particular countries. Business Brief 13.1 looks at some of the challenges for product managers in the China market.

Business Brief 13.1

BEING A PRODUCT MANAGER FOR THE CHINA MARKET

Shanghai, with its approximately 16 million people, is headquarters to numerous multinational organizations. This area is a fertile ground for many consumer products for two reasons. First, the millions of expatriates located there desire some familiar products and conveniences. Second, the rising middle class—a phenomenon closely linked to the growth of the multinationals—provides the "early adopter" market required for success. But it is far from the only market in China, and product managers must understand the different segments—both industrial and consumer—that exist there in order to be successful.

Industrial companies in different regions of China exhibit different types of buying behavior. There are fewer foreign enterprises in the northern districts of Heilongjiang, Jilin, Liaoning, and Hebei (which latter physically includes city provinces of Beijing and Tianjin). … Because they are less exposed to Western technologies, they are also less exposed to new ideas and less prepared to adopt new products. As a consequence, it is harder to make initial contact. The south contains many overseas Chinese-invested enterprises located in Guangdong and Fujian provinces. Since economic reform originated in this region, its companies are willing to try new things. Customers on the east coast (Shanghai municipality and Jiangsu and Zhejiang provinces) mainly operate in the Shanghai style. They have been the most influenced by Western culture.

There is a dramatic variety of terrain, dialect, custom, and cuisine in consumer markets. This results in potential markets as fragmented and diverse as those in Europe. Demographic and psychographic factors are becoming increasingly important. Teenagers in Shanghai and Xi'an may have similar budgets and aspirations. But differences in beliefs and attitudes will drive the Shanghainese to focus more on the emotional benefits of brands, while consumers in Xi'an will tend to focus more on functional benefits.

Whirlpool has also discovered the need to incorporate psychographic segmentation in order to sell their appliances in China. "For example, 19 percent of Chinese consumers fall into what Whirlpool has categorized as 'pragmatists,' people in lower income brackets who tend to live in more rural areas, who are less educated and older. Key touch points for these consumers are price, cost of ownership, and reliability. Another 20 percent of the Chinese market consists of the 'aspirational status seekers.' These people are younger, upwardly mobile, and more educated. They are people for whom price isn't the primary issue" (Drickhamer, 2004, cited below).

Product variety will be required to match segmented needs. As Austin Lally, P&G's general manager-marketing for beauty care brands in China states, "Winning in China depends on developing a deep understanding of who you are marketing to. If you start designing average products to meet the average Chinese consumer, you usually end up with stuff that isn't sophisticated or differentiated enough to win in Shanghai or Beijing, but you also end up with stuff that doesn't offer enough value for people in smaller cities and towns. What we ended up with is a much broader portfolio than we originally entered China with. Take a brand like Crest. We don't sell one tube of toothpaste in different flavors. We have different tiers of pricing and performance. Those different products we sell are not just cheaper versions of each other; they are designed against different groups of consumers."

Source: Adapted from Don Y. Lee, "Segmentation and Promotional Strategies for Selling CSRB Bearings in China," *The Journal of Business & Industrial Marketing* (2003, vol. 18, no. 2/3), pp. 258–270. George Crocker and Yi-Chung Tay, "What It Takes to Create a Successful Brand," *The China Business Review* (July/Aug 2004), pp. 10–16. Ann Chen and Vijay Vishwanath, "Expanding in China," *Harvard Business Review* (March 2005), pp. 19–21. "Navigating China's Ever-Changing Marketplace," *Advertising Age* (November 8, 2004), p. 12. David Drickhamer, "Appliance Envy," *Industry Week* (November 2004), pp. 24–30.

DBG product managers typically have strong input into the design of global products. Their products' success depends on their understanding of customer needs and local market requirements. Unfortunately, too many product managers spend limited time visiting customers in the countries they're responsible for and rely too heavily on statistical and secondary data. LBG product managers, primarily those focused on tactical activities, often feel powerless to affect change in product design that should reflect the needs of the market they serve. Their challenge is to influence upward, so that the most important and relevant features and benefits are built into their product offerings. Therefore, both DBG and LBG product managers should participate in global product strategy.

Where the P&L responsibility lies will also influence the role of global product managers.[1] Several years ago P&G adopted a system under which "managers of global business units are responsible for brand management and product development, and managers of regional market development organizations are responsible for sales, trade marketing, media, and multibrand marketing." P&L responsibility resides with the global managers. Unilever has a similar structure except that "profit-and-loss responsibilities lie with the regional presidents rather than the global category organizations that control marketing, product mixes, and strategy."

Product managers often lead or participate in cross-cultural product teams. This can pose several challenges, as discussed by Richard Gesteland in his Global Expert Advice Column.

GLOBAL EXPERT ADVICE COLUMN: MANAGING MULTICULTURAL PROJECT TEAMS

Richard R. Gesteland, president, Global Management LLC, Madison, Wisconsin

Practitioners have learned from experience that managing people who are at remote locations is difficult. They are also aware that cultural differences make managing project teams even more challenging. Our 18 years of training managers around the world have revealed that three cultural variables cause the most frustrations for Americans and many other Westerners who lead international project teams.

It happens that Chinese and Indians share these three trouble-causing behavioral characteristics and since most of our U.S. and northern European clients run project teams in China and India, the examples here focus on these two important business cultures.

Task-Focus versus Relationship-Focus

The United States belongs to a handful of task-focused business cultures found only in northern Europe and the Anglo-Saxon countries. In contrast over 90 percent of the world's cultures (including India and China) are relationship-focused, and project team members from those countries usually expect to be managed in ways that differ from the approach employed by task-focused managers. The resulting conflicts cause continuing frustration for both sides.

For example, Americans tend to assume that most communication with far-flung colleagues can be done via e-mail, phone, and videoconferencing. Relationship-focused team members, however, assume that complex, difficult, or painful issues will be handled in person, face to face. Relationship-focused Indians and Chinese also expect more small talk and more time devoted to developing personal rapport than task-focused companies expect.

Finally, matrix management, which is so often involved in project work, tends to confuse relationship-focused people even more than it does task-focused Americans. All these differences lead to friction and misunderstandings which reduce the project team's productivity.

Egalitarian versus Hierarchical Management Behavior

The second key behavioral difference also has to do with contrasting expectations and assumptions. Chinese and Indian team members, like the vast majority of the world's people, come from hierarchical, stratified societies where status differences are important. Employees defer to authority, learn to never challenge or contradict their boss, assume that higher-ups make all decisions, and tend to expect detailed instructions and close supervision.

So of course problems arise because egalitarian managers expect international team members to do their jobs with minimal direction, to use their initiative, and to openly express any disagreement they may have with the project leader's decisions. Those differences explain why experienced American project managers complain that their Chinese or Indian team members "lack initiative," "expect micromanagement," "avoid taking responsibility," and "can't make decisions on their own."

Direct versus Indirect Language

While, of course, no two individuals from any culture are alike, project team members from relationship-focused, hierarchical cultures tend to use indirect, vague language to avoid losing face or offending others. They especially learn to never say no to their boss. In contrast, most task-focused managers expect subordinates to use straightforward language and to express disagreement directly. Hence the most frequent comment we hear from Western participants in our China and India workshops is, "Why can't they say no?" and "Why do our colleagues say yes when they mean no?"

Bridging the Culture Gap

A number of U.S. and northern European companies have found ways to minimize the frustrations and improve communication between project leaders and their international team members:

1. Increase the frequency of face-to-face project team meetings, both at home and abroad.
2. Provide thorough interactive training for project managers and other home office staff.
3. As often as possible bring international team members to the home office for orientation, training, and cultural immersion.

These three proven steps have helped task-focused project managers create shared cultures with their international colleagues, thereby meeting the tough challenges of managing multicultural project teams.

TRANSNATIONAL PRODUCT STRATEGY

Global strategy for product managers means embedding both domestic and international standards into products and services at the point of design, not as afterthoughts. This implies meeting world standards while simultaneously acknowledging national differences and local norms. This approach has the obvious advantage of taking into consideration the needs of major markets right at the start, rather than having to retrofit a product developed for one national market only.

Product managers start by identifying globally strategic markets and then analyzing the needs of those markets. By searching for commonalities (as well as differences), product managers necessarily think in terms of platform design for global products. Product managers are wise to direct product design so that it meets the largest possible standardized core, while allowing for necessary customization at the same time. The main goal of the product development process is not to develop a standard product or product line but to build adaptability into products and product lines to achieve worldwide appeal.

The idea of a fully standardized global product that is identical all over the world is a near myth. Some of the benefits of global products (or services), however, can be achieved by standardizing the core product or large parts of it, while customizing peripheral or other parts of the product. In passenger automobiles, for example, product standardization comes primarily in the "platform" (the chassis and related parts) and to a lesser extent the engine. The auto industry has been talking about global cars for decades, but implementation has been difficult at best. Honda made progress with its 1998 Accord. By coming up with a platform that can be bent and stretched into markedly different vehicles, Honda saved hundreds of millions of dollars in development costs. By moving the car's gas tank back between the rear tires, Honda engineers discovered they could design a series of special brackets that would allow them to hook the wheels to the car's more flexible inner subframe. Rather than shipping the same car around the globe, only the underlying platform will be used worldwide.

Regardless of the attempt to standardize products or product lines globally, various levels of adaptation are required. Some products need only different language documentation. For example, in the 1990s when

Minolta cameras were shipped from Japan to New Wave Enterprise, a distribution center at the Port of Antwerp in Belgium, they were shipped without support materials. Language-specific documentation (e.g., French, Dutch, and German) was added when the products were shipped across land to other destinations in Europe.

Product strategy can vary across a continuum from (1) a near-universal product (with just labeling and language differences); to (2) a modified product where the core is standard with adaptations (such as voltage and color) made to reflect local differences; to (3) country-specific products where the physical product is tailored to the needs of each country or group of countries. Deciding on the approach to take depends on several variables. One argument for global brands is based on identifying high-tech and high-touch products:

> *High-tech products appeal to highly specialized buyers who share a common technical language and symbols. This is the case among computer and Internet users, tennis players, physicians using medical equipment, and musicians who all understand the technical aspects of the products. ... The mere existence of a common "shoptalk" facilitates communication and increases the chance of success as a global brand.*
>
> *High-touch products are more image-oriented than product-feature-oriented, but they respond to universal themes or needs, such as romance, wealth, heroism, play, etc. Many products, such as fragrance, fashion, jewelry and watches, recreation resorts and others are sold on these themes. ... [W]orldwide brand standardization appear[s] most feasible when products approach either end of the high-tech/high-touch spectrum.[2]*

Related research on global brands also suggests new perspectives on how consumers perceive them. A study based on surveys of 1,800 people in 12 nations, published in *Harvard Business Review* revealed that consumers all over the world associate global brands with three dimensions. The first dimension is a symbol of *quality*. Consumers believed that since transnational companies must compete more fiercely to develop new products and technologies faster than the competition, they offer more quality and better guarantees. It's interesting to note that this attitude was not directly related to the country of origin, but rather something simply being a global brand. The second dimension is a sense of a *global culture*. Consumers looked to the brands as "symbols of cultural ideals." The final dimension was *social responsibility*. The respondents in the study expected global firms to address social problems, to act as "stewards of public health, worker rights, and the environment."[3]

In other situations products could have their life cycles extended by having the best fit between market needs and product capabilities. For example, the current U.S. technology for anesthesia ventilators allows plus or minus a few milliliters of oxygen accuracy. However, many hospital operating rooms in developing countries are satisfied with plus or minus 100 milliliters of accuracy, with a commensurately lower price. A major supplier of anesthesia equipment found it could prolong the life of its "unsophisticated" ventilators by offering them in these markets at a much lower price than the "state-of-the-art" equipment.

This approach can apply to consumer products as well. Take basic flour as an example. India consumes about 69 million tons of wheat a year (compared to 26 million tons in the United States), yet almost no whole-wheat flour is sold prepackaged. Selling packaged flour in India is almost revolutionary, since most Indian housewives still buy raw wheat in bulk, clean it by hand, and on a weekly basis carry some to a neighborhood mill, or *chakki*, where it is ground between two stones. Pillsbury found it could increase the sales of basic prepackaged flour (a mature product in the United States) by appealing to this market and has modified the Pillsbury Doughboy to pitch this "old" product as something new in India.

Procter & Gamble's global marketing strategy is drawing from newly emerging marketing approaches, media, and technologies. A few concepts the company is working with include holistic marketing, permission marketing, and experimentation. *Holistic marketing* refers to gaining a thorough knowledge of consumers at the local level and how they prefer to receive information about products. *Permission marketing*, similar to its use in Internet applications, refers to getting contact information (like phone numbers) directly from consumers who indicate a willingness to hear from you. *Experimentation* refers to continually trying different approaches to reaching customers in new markets. Recently P&G has been using a lot of influencer marketing to get passionate consumers to "seed" the market for product introductions.[4]

With increasing competition able to react quickly when new products are introduced, worldwide planning at the product level provides a number of tangible benefits. First, product managers are better able to develop products with specifications compatible on a global scale. Second, they are able to more effectively and efficiently adapt products to local needs. And third, they are able to respond more quickly to the competitive moves of global companies.

GLOCALIZATION

Glocalization refers to the adage, "Think globally; act locally." Whether you are selling a unique product in every country or a standard product throughout the world, good product management still requires understanding local customers. There may also be a different set of local competitors than at the global level.

Start with the basics. How homogeneous is the country or region of interest? Segment the market into reasonable clusters of potential customers, and decide which one or which ones you will actively target. This could form the foundation of a product-line strategy for that area. Do the characteristics of any of the segments transcend national borders? Sometimes younger generations are more like their global counterparts than they are like other generations within their own country. If this is the case, they may be more open to a standardized global product.

Determine the *nonnegotiable* expectations of the local customers. Cultural mores and lifestyles may dictate changes even when other factors suggest that a global product strategy may suffice. Volkswagen learned this lesson in the United States:

> *Ever since the introduction of the original Beetle, VW has treated the U.S. as an automotive backwater. It used the country as a dumping ground for excess production and made little effort to understand American driving habits. A classic example: cup holders, which for years VW ignored.*[5]

When dealing with developing countries, price may be a bigger issue than multinationals have historically accepted. This can pose a challenge—especially for locationally based product managers who are expected to sell a relatively high-priced product that was designed in another country and can't hit the local price point expectations. These product managers have to (1) seek out thought leaders and innovators who may be willing to buy the product in the short term; (2) persuade corporate managers of the need to close the cost gap with local companies to be effective in those particular regions in the long term; and/ or (3) use reverse innovation. Reverse innovation refers to developing lower-cost products in and for developing countries and then finding applications for them in developed countries.

DISTRIBUTING TO OTHER COUNTRIES

Product managers will need to work with the sales function to determine the best method of distribution into the new market. Most firms initially enter other countries through either indirect or direct exporting. *Indirect* exporting refers to selling through a domestically based intermediary (e.g., agent or distributor). The major benefits of this approach lie in the ease of administration. Even companies with little or no experience in exporting can rely on the expertise of the channel partner without developing substantial multinational cultural skills. With *direct* exporting, the manufacturer deals directly with foreign intermediaries in the distribution of its products. While this approach requires a greater degree of cultural expertise, it also provides the product manager with more market knowledge and potentially greater control.

In addition to determining whether the best location for the intermediary is domestic or foreign, it is useful to examine the differences between agent, distributor, and other intermediaries. Agents, brokers, manufacturers' reps, and export management companies (EMCs) generally *do not* take title to the products they represent. Distributors, dealers, jobbers, wholesalers, and merchants generally *do* take title. Other partners may either have varied contractual relations with the manufacturer or provide specific differential functions. When licensing is used as an entry strategy, the manufacturer assigns the right to a patent or trademark to a foreign company. An advantage of this approach is that some governments may prefer it, thus allowing easier entry. The disadvantage is the manufacturer's dependence on the licensee. Franchising is a form of licensing agreement in which the manufacturer grants to the foreign company the rights to do business in a prescribed manner. This has similar advantages and disadvantages to licensing, but since the franchise agreement is more comprehensive than a licensing agreement, the manufacturer has somewhat more control. Under contract manufacturing, a company arranges to have its products manufactured by a foreign firm on a contractual basis. The manufacturing may involve assembly or fully integrated production, depending on the needs of the firm.

In his *Harvard Business Review* article, David Arnold states that the selection of international business partners is especially critical because of distances and cultures of the buying parties.[6] He elaborates on seven key points in selecting and working with international distributors and trading partners:

1. "Select distributors. Don't let them select you." The key point is to choose markets first and *then* select distributors and agents.
2. "Look for distributors capable of developing markets, rather than those with a few obvious customer contacts." Select partners who are willing to invest and grow the markets.
3. "Treat the local distributors as long-term partners, not temporary market-entry vehicles." Create an atmosphere that fosters appropriate goals, such as customer acquisition and retention, new product sales, collaborative inventory management, and replenishment.
4. "Support market entry by committing money, managers, and proven marketing ideas." Invest in product modifications and personnel support to meet the needs of local markets.
5. "From the start, maintain control over marketing strategy." Product managers should visit distributors and channel members to learn about the local markets.
6. "Make sure distributors provide you with detailed market and financial performance data." Develop relationships

and contracts that share detailed market data and financial performance.

7. "Build links among national distributors at the earliest opportunity." Just as in the United States, distributors meet and build relationships to share experiences. Help all parties improve their success in marketing efforts.

Once corporations understand that they can control their international operations through better relationship structures rather than simply through ownership, they might also find longer-term roles for local distributors with a regionalized approach to a global strategy.

When preparing go-to-market strategies in other countries, product managers should remember two ironclad rules of international business. First, the seller is expected to adapt to the buyer (when *you* are selling, you will need to do the adapting). Second, the visitor is expected to observe local customs. These rules compel an understanding of the different types of cultures that exist in different parts of the world. Richard Gesteland, in his book, *Cross-Cultural Business Behavior*, provides a thorough discussion of four types of cultural continua, as shown in Figure 13.1.[7] The book provides a clear explanation and case examples of working with business people throughout the world.

The first continuum deals with the business perspective ranging from deal-focused to relationship-focused. Distributors from relationship-focused cultures want to build a trusting relationship with a manufacturer prior to starting business, and they may perceive a deal-focused presentation as aggressive and pushy.

The second continuum is from informal to formal. *Informal* business managers typically come from relatively egalitarian cultures (like the United States) and sometimes make the mistake of not respecting the formality present in other cultures.

The third continuum is from rigid time to fluid time. Cultures that are driven by the clock may inappropriately perceive cultures at the other end of the continuum as lazy, resulting in tense and uncomfortable meetings.

The final type of continuum is from reserved to expressive. Reserved cultures demonstrate conservative communication both verbally and

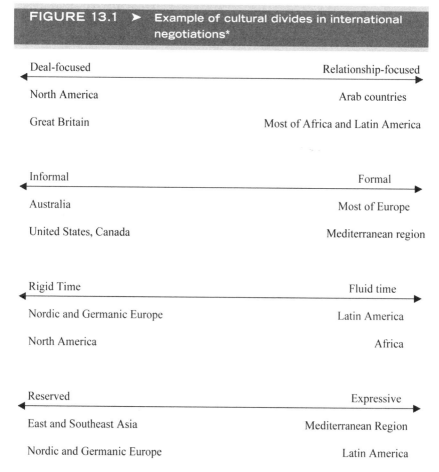

FIGURE 13.1 ➤ Example of cultural divides in international negotiations*

Deal-focused ◄──────────────────────────► Relationship-focused

North America   Arab countries

Great Britain   Most of Africa and Latin America

Informal ◄──────────────────────────► Formal

Australia   Most of Europe

United States, Canada   Mediterranean region

Rigid Time ◄──────────────────────────► Fluid time

Nordic and Germanic Europe   Latin America

North America   Africa

Reserved ◄──────────────────────────► Expressive

East and Southeast Asia   Mediterranean Region

Nordic and Germanic Europe   Latin America

*Condensed from Richard Gesteland, *Cross-Cultural Business Behavior*, Copenhagen Business School Press, 1997.

nonverbally and can therefore clash with people from expressive cultures. It is important that product managers who are establishing relationships with international channel partners understand and appreciate the cultural differences so that trust can be established and negotiations can run smoothly.

CHAPTER CHALLENGE

Make a conscious effort to understand the various cultural divides that exist in international relations and use the information to improve your global strategies.

INTERVIEW WITH MARK PHILLIPS: RAISE YOUR GLOBAL PRODUCT MANAGEMENT IQ

Mark A. Phillips, Chief Marketing Officer,
GE Healthcare Asia-Pacific,
http://www.linkedin.com/in/markalanphillips

Mark, when I interviewed you for the prior edition of this book, you were a downstream product manager for GE Healthcare in Asia; now you are the Asia-Pacific chief marketing officer. How has your job changed over that time period?

The role I have now is broader than when I was a product manager for one product group. However, many of the skills I learned as a product manager I use on a daily basis in my role as CMO for the region. One of the major changes is that now I need to work on the "white space" between our products and create a customer solution by combining multiple products to solve a customer need. An example of this is working across our MRI, ultrasound, and contrast agent product lines to address liver cancer. There are many stages of the disease, and our products play key roles across several buyers/users at different phases of the disease cycle. So the key is creating value for the customer by making $1 + 1 = 3$, or through combining products in a way that adds more value than the products have individually. This must go beyond giving a discount because a customer is buying more from you. You must create value by connecting the dots and filling in the white spaces with things like IT or services. The basic skills needed are similar to good product management:

- Understand the customer need and competition/alternative solutions in the market.

- Turn customer insight into a product or solution profile.
- Quantify market potential to build a business case.
- Use smart pricing methodologies based on the value (economic and intangible) to the customer compared with other possible substitutes and competition, both direct and indirect.
- Build a strong go-to-market plan.
- Pilot, test, and refine. Launch, excite, and train your distribution channels.

My role as CMO also requires that I lead or help to drive key company initiatives in my region such as in-country-for-country (ICFC) and reverse innovation. These initiatives involve designing product/solutions for a specific country need and in some cases taking that solution to a totally different market and using it in a new way.

Tell me more about ICFC and reverse innovation.

ICFC is a process we go through to define a specific country's needs for a particular product. In the past, we would design a product for the U.S. and then try to sell it to the rest of the world. Given the importance of emerging markets, BRIC [Brazil, Russia, India, China] and more, this model is not enough to stay competitive and drive growth. Thus we began to pay more attention to the needs of these markets and put processes and resources in place to be able to address those needs. In some cases this results in making the product in-country as well, but that doesn't have to be the case as long as the product is created and delivered to where the need is. Every year we go through the process of rolling up the local trends and customer needs along with business cases for the product requests we are making. Many times the product need will be similar to other markets, and it becomes part of a global product plan. Other times, the need may be particular to one country and the market is big enough to justify making the product for just that country. This is usually the case for only the biggest markets like India, China, the United States, etc.

Reverse innovation is a similar process but with a very different and often unexpected outcome. For most of the last century, innovation for many industries flowed from developed countries to developing countries. However, as we go through the process of ICFC, we end up developing new products and learning new business models from developing countries that can then be applied in a developed country. One example is an ultrasound product that was designed to meet the needs and cost points for rural China. Then later it was repositioned to fit a need in the U.S. market for use in clinics. I believe this will continue as we learn from emerging counties how to create more affordable, easier-to-use products faster and take them to market in new ways.

How transferable are these concepts to other multinationals and other types of products or services?

I think these concepts are very applicable to other companies as well as different types of products and services across markets. You see common trends across industries with local players from India and China emerging with products that are globally competitive. They often start by exporting to other value markets (South America, Eastern Europe, and Africa), build in sophistication and reach, and then go after the developed markets (U.S./Europe). They bring with them ideas and products that were designed for their home markets but eventually apply them in developed markets with success. Multinationals can compete by ensuring they have skills to understand customer needs in emerging markets and that leadership will listen and respond to them. One without the other will lead to failure.

What do you feel are the similarities and differences between a domestic product manager (where all operations are in one country) and a country product manager (who locally markets a global product)?

A domestic product manager often manages a product that has been specifically designed for his or her market. The products are designed to serve the domestic customer needs and combat the domestic and key global competitors. Product managers outside of the domestic market often "catch" these products "as is" and are charged with the task of launching them in international markets. This involves many challenges. Here again I'm going to give you my "laundry list" of bullets:

- While both domestic and international product managers face global competitors, the international product manager must also face local players. Combating local competitors—that specifically focus on local market needs—creates an additional battle front that domestic product managers do not face. Local players often have a better cost position, move faster, and are very focused on local needs. This creates big challenges in value markets where price is a major driver, or in markets with complex/specific needs such as Japan.
- Diverse markets. People refer to Europe or Asia as markets similar to the way they refer to the U.S. However, the U.S. is for the most part a homogenous market. Asia and Europe are a mix of several cultures and economies, each with its own unique characteristics. In Asia for example, there are huge socioeconomic disparities across the region coupled with diverse culture, language, and political systems. Asia itself spans numerous time zones and countries. There is usually not a one-size-fits-all strategy for Asia. This diversity of GTM (go-to-market) strategies makes the international product manager's role much more complex.
- There is an added task of localizing marketing materials that have been designed for a different country and culture. This can include basic translation to actually having to have your own photo shoots to ensure "local faces" are included in your collateral. This cuts into your local GTM budget that is often based on a global benchmark of GTM spending. Domestic product managers do not have to cover this extra cost and thus can apply the funds to more strategic activities.
- Size matters. While international product managers may represent markets that are growing faster than domestic

markets, the domestic markets are usually larger. Thus it makes getting the features and functions needed for local markets very challenging against the needs of the larger domestic markets.

■ Dealing with upstream teams in another time zone. This means early morning and/or late night conference calls to get the support you need. Product managers in Europe may have to stay up a little later than usual; Asia product managers are often squeezed at both ends of the day—both creating challenging schedules.

Since you were a product manager and continue to work with product managers on a daily basis, in your opinion, what separates the best from the rest?

I still strongly believe that product managers need to think of themselves as the CEO or entrepreneurial head of their products to succeed. This includes:

■ Going beyond purely product features to understand the distribution channels, manufacturing process, service processes, and detailed cost components of the product.

■ Working to acquire basic financial skills to be able to create clear business cases for their products.

■ Spending significant time in the field with the sales force and with users/buyers to hear directly from the market (not by just paying others to do market research) the feedback on the product.

■ Looking at customer needs beyond their specific product. Stepping back to understand what surrounds the before-and-after of how and when the product is used—a type of 360 degree observational exercise. This can lead to many insights for additional services and adjacencies for expansion.

■ Collaborating with others, either peers from other regions that own the same product or with product managers from other product lines. Dropping the insecurity and overcompetitiveness that is the downfall of many products managers can be key to get to the next level. Leadership in the organization will always promote those who can work across function and geographic lines to bring the entire organization forward. Look for ways to win together; that is what your leadership wants.

CHAPTER 14

Goal and Performance Alignment

TRUE OR FALSE: Companies are often disappointed in their product management structure when there is a mismatch between expectations and competencies.

TRUE. Many companies initiate a product management structure without a clear understanding of what they expect in terms of results and which product management skill sets will help deliver the results. Therefore it might be good to go back to the drawing board. Define expectations, determine what skills product managers do and should have relative to these expectations, and then establish a course of action to close the gap.

This chapter is a bit different from the chapters in the rest of the book because it is written as much for company leadership and human resource directors as it is for product managers. While I have compared product managers to entrepreneurs several times in the book, the reality is that they have to operate within the boundaries of an organization. Their product-line goals and strategies have to be linked to their business units and companies.

A PRODUCT MANAGEMENT PRIMER

Product management has long been viewed as an effective organizational form for multiproduct firms. The advantages are numerous and frequently documented. First, it provides a dedicated champion for a product, brand, or service. Second, product management can create a healthy internal competitive environment. Third, by championing a number of offerings, a firm can more quickly respond to shifting customer loyalties. And finally, it provides an opportunity to readily assess candidates for promotion to higher management levels.

Nevertheless, the effectiveness of product management is contingent upon several factors. If we expect product managers to truly champion brands, they must be engaged in both day-to-day decision issues and in developing the strategic future paths of their offerings. Product managers will play a major role in most product-related decisions, while they rely on specialists to carry out many of those decisions.

Once a structure is established, clarifying the roles of company personnel with whom product managers routinely interact is important. The product manager is the liaison with the functional departments within the company as well as with the company, the sales force, and the customers for all product-related issues. As a result, some understanding of mutual expectations is appropriate. Whether the mutual understandings are built into job descriptions, discussed in training programs, or informally determined, they will have an impact on product management success.

There has been an evolution in product management over the past few decades. Rather than declining in number and importance as had been forecast in numerous articles, product management (especially "nontraditional" product, market, and service management) has prevailed by encompassing customer management and value chain analysis, evolving into a more holistic position. The overall responsibility of a product manager is to integrate the various segments of a business into a strategically focused whole, thus maximizing the value of a product by coordinating the production of an offering with an understanding of market needs. To accomplish this, a product manager needs a broad knowledge of virtually all aspects of a company along with very focused knowledge of a specific product or product line and its customers. Product managers oversee not only products, but projects and processes as well.

Procter & Gamble has been credited with the creation of the product management concept. In 1931, Camay soap was languishing, while Ivory soap was thriving. A Procter & Gamble executive suggested that an individual manager be assigned responsibility for Camay, in effect pitting the brands against each other. This brand management system was so successful that it was copied by most consumer packaged goods companies.

There are both advantages and disadvantages to the product management approach. On the plus side, a product manager provides dedicated attention to a product line. This results in better information about the customers, competition, and strategic potential for that group of products. In addition, since the product manager must necessarily interact with the various operational units of a company, the position can provide a good training ground for young executives. On the other hand, a consequential criticism of the product management structure is that it is a fast-track or stepping-stone position, overemphasizing short-term results. It promotes the perception that product management skills are more transferable than product and industry knowledge. In addition, product management can cause conflict because the product manager has limited functional authority over many parts of the development, marketing, and sales of the product, but may nevertheless have bottom-line responsibility. Finally, product managers might focus on the product almost to the exclusion of the customer.

Companies have increasingly modified their approach to product management structure. Some service firms have created what is in fact segment management (even though the product manager title might still be used). For example, hospitals might have a product manager for women's services. Financial institutions might have a small business product manager or an "affluent market" manager.

Simply shifting the emphasis from products to segments, however, will not eliminate some of the problems that can exist in a matrix organization. A matrix organization is one in which people report directly to a specific functional area, but also report indirectly (through a dotted-line relationship) to other functional areas. Both—or neither—can result in an enhanced understanding of customers and an ability to satisfy their needs. It requires a commitment to make it work.

First there must be a clear understanding of the basic rationale for product management as an organizational form. Product management is generally most successful in companies with several products that have similar manufacturing but different marketing requirements, particularly when the same product cuts across several divisions or customer groups. Second, top management must be committed to the product management organization and provide the structure and tools to make it work. If the product manager is fundamentally a project coordinator position, it will not have the results discussed in this book. And finally, the right people must be selected and developed for the job.

Regardless of the organizational changes the position of product manager may undergo in the future, successful product managers must thoroughly understand the needs of various market segments, appreciate the corporate competencies in the company, and be able to leverage these competencies to meet market needs. In other words, the ultimate goal of the product manager will be customer satisfaction achieved by being a cross-functional leader in the firm.

Historically, the product manager's job has varied somewhat between consumer and business-to-business firms. Consumer product managers typically managed fewer products and spent more time on advertising and sales promotion. The target markets were generally larger (millions rather than thousands or hundreds), with a greater potential for diversity. Business product managers tended to be more involved in the technical aspects of the product or service and spent more time with engineering and the sales force.

However, the gap between the two types of product managers is narrowing. Fragmentation of consumer markets has escalated, resulting in greater product proliferation and parity products, for which consumers perceive little distinction in features or quality and usually make purchase decisions based on price. Trade satisfaction is becoming more critical as mass merchandisers and other "big box" retailers such as Walmart, Home Depot, and Office Max continue to gain momentum. As a result, consumer product managers are finding themselves more involved with salespeople and the trade (e.g., retailers). The ability to deal with the trade is likely to continue to escalate in importance. Although retail giants have existed for a long time, their clout has increased because of the emergence of powerful information systems that provide them with more data on consumers than manufacturers have. Consumer goods manufacturers are finding it necessary to organize around their customers (the retailers), invest in technology, and act more as a partner than was typical in the past. Vendors serving Walmart have to respond to a barrage of demands to get their product sold (or even on the shelves). Companies are also increasingly including retailer input at the early stages of product development. Black & Decker solicited input from several retailers, including Home Depot, when it introduced the DeWalt line of power tools. The president of Black & Decker's power tools group emphasized the group's involvement: "We talked to them about the name. We talked to them about the color. We talked to them about the warranty." Retailers' input was valuable not only in terms of product design, but also as a visible sign of their involvement as a partner.[1]

On the business-to-business side, product managers are finding a growing need to introduce marketing strategy to their firms and to establish a more solid position against an ever-increasing number of competitors. Market (as opposed to product) knowledge has become a key determinant of successful differentiation.

The use of product management teams (PMTs) to make product-related decisions has grown over the past decade. The specific role of the team, as well as its effectiveness, is still unclear. However, many larger firms are trying to assign specific finance and marketing individuals to specific product managers to increase the continuity of knowledge and relationships.

Globalization of brands is occurring in both consumer and business arenas. What does this mean for product managers and the companies that employ them? Many product managers will be challenged to understand market needs for their products beyond U.S. borders. The transition for some companies will be minor if few changes are required to the product or its marketing. In other cases, extensive market research, product adaptation, and promotional modifications will be unavoidable. The product manager may also be required to work with company personnel located at plants or offices in other countries, sometimes coordinating virtual teams through videoconferencing, faxes, and other electronic means. These cross-border business teams will be responsible for leveraging corporate capabilities throughout the world. Companies will need to make organizational decisions as to whether product managers are responsible for products around the world, whether upstream product managers will handle development in the home country with downstream (country) managers handling go-to-market strategies, or if another structure is more appropriate. They will also be charged with providing educational opportunities for product managers to learn cross-cultural skills.

TRANSFORMING THE PRODUCT MANAGEMENT ORGANIZATION

There are five steps involved in initiating a product management transformation. First, the company must assess whether product management is the appropriate organizational form and, if it is appropriate, decide what reporting structure (hierarchy) it will have. Second, the company must clearly specify the desired competencies and responsibilities of product managers as well as other integral members of the system. Third, gaps between desired and actual competencies must be defined. Fourth, there must be a system for hiring, developing, and evaluating talent. And, finally, the company must ensure continued alignment of goals, directives, and initiatives.

Assess the Fit of the Organizational Structure

Shifting from a functional (silo) organizational structure to any of a variety of team- or matrix-based organizational forms (including product management) requires careful planning. Job descriptions must be written to help the product managers understand their new roles, and other departments must understand what to expect from the new product manager positions. Product managers must rely on the support and performance of many others in the organization to achieve product performance goals, even though they have no control over those functions. For the successful introduction of a product management structure in an organization, it is imperative that objectives be clarified.

Product management can be an appropriate organizational structure when a company's product line has grown to the point where a functional structure no longer works. There might be more products than a single marketing manager can handle, even though the products could flow into a common market through the same channels. Or the company's products might be so different from each other in terms of competition and customer groups that they must be handled differently. Or technical or sophisticated product knowledge might be required to meet the needs of the market. In this case, the product manager might be involved in the development and marketing of a product line across various divisions or markets. (See Figure 14.1.)

On the other hand, there are subtle variations that might be appropriate under different circumstances. (See Table 14.1.) If the industry's products are primarily "parity" (essentially the same) in the minds of the customers, a traditional product manager structure might result in pressure to create artificial differences simply for the sake of differentiation. In this case, a market or segment management approach might be preferred. Market managers are used when a company needs to develop different markets for a single product line. Focus is on developing the *market* rather than on taking the product to market. The market manager would bundle and/or adapt combinations of a company's products to fit the needs of select market segments. There might or might not also be a need to have "special products" managers in conjunction with segment managers.

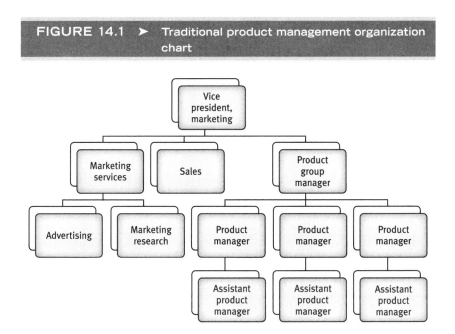

FIGURE 14.1 ➤ Traditional product management organization chart

Table 14.1

Organizational structures for various
product/market situations

Product/Market Characteristics	Possible Organizational Structure
Many products going to a limited number of market segments. The products require focused attention to be fully successful.	Product management.
The company sells to a variety of market segments with preferences for various product sets. The product might not require elaborate customization, but the bundling of products/ services is unique to market segments.	Market or segment manager.
The same situation as immediately above, but there is also a need to develop some new products for various market segments.	Segment management with "special products" managers or project managers.
The company sells to a few large customers with needs that differ from those of the rest of the customer base.	Key account managers.
New product efforts are time-consuming and critical for the company, to the point where a special position is created to handle new products exclusively.	Product development manager or new-products manager, possibly (although not necessarily) part of a technical department.
Shift from regional and/or country organization to strategic alignment with common customers/applications and distribution channels.	Global business units focused on major product categories.

A variation of market management is key account or national account management. With the emergence of "big box retailers," mass merchandisers, "category killers," and other large customers, key account managers are responsible for working with major accounts to determine how products can best be adapted to meet the needs of these accounts. If product managers are spending an inordinate amount of time handling special requests for major customers, a key account position could focus on the "special requests" and work with the product manager on product adaptation.

The last major consideration in organizational structure is related to new-product development. Although most product managers spend a significant part of their time on new product development activities, some companies choose to have a separate new product manager position to handle the specifications, design, and development of products, with the product managers following through with the marketing activities after the product launch. Although this is less common, it is an organizational form that can fit certain needs.

Most product managers are part of a marketing or marketing/sales department and usually report to a marketing or product management director, a marketing or product management manager, or a vice president of marketing. Product managers frequently have no one reporting to them. In larger firms, however, product managers might have assistants and associates reporting to them. They may also have authority over some functional subordinates. Some product managers may have eight or more people reporting to them directly. If there is to be staff reporting to the product manager, it's usually best for these staff members to be information processors, coordinators, or analysts rather than a proliferating pyramid of assistants and associates, which creates a hierarchy within a hierarchy.

Hierarchies are designed to prevent mistakes, but they also diminish individual responsibility, creativity, and risk-taking opportunities. That's why so many management gurus have espoused variations of the horizontal corporation, with an emphasis on providing better products and services for the end customer. Product managers and product management teams are consistent with this philosophy if they are linked to customer satisfaction (as they should be) and given the authority to make relevant decisions regarding their product lines.

Specify Responsibilities of Product Managers and Others in the Firm

To minimize the potential for miscommunication and misunderstanding and to increase the chances of a successful product management structure, management must thoroughly explain to key managers exactly how the organizational concept will work and what the underlying rationale is for changing to it. It's important to specify not only the roles of product managers, but also the roles of the individuals with whom the product managers commonly interact. Let's take a hypothetical example of a company with three product managers, a marketing services manager, a marketing research manager, and regional sales managers. (All these people might report to a marketing director or a vice president of marketing/sales.)

Typically, the product managers would recommend and establish strategic guidelines for their products; obtain market information about their customer segments and products; provide input to sales for the closing of selected accounts; and play a major role in product/ service development, modifications, and elimination. The marketing services manager would support the product managers by providing communication materials and handling companywide promotional and public relations activities. The marketing research manager would contract out or conduct marketing research activities that are necessary to fully understand customer needs and competitive capabilities and provide input into company growth and acquisition opportunities. The regional sales managers would provide the day-to-day motivation and management of the sales force and support the product managers in the introduction of new products.

Many product managers (particularly in business-to-business companies or in the service sector) are hired for their technical expertise with a specific product or service. Therefore, the roles of product management and the related operational functions need to be clarified. For example, the product manager might supply customer and competitor data in support of a recommended new product, but they must leave the actual design to the design staff.

Although these descriptions of responsibilities would not be appropriate for every organization, it's important to think through and define the related responsibilities and overlaps. Providing a summary of role responsibilities before introducing product management will reduce uncertainties about the organizational structure.

Where product managers are positioned in a company can also significantly influence their role, regardless of the responsibilities put in writing. A critical issue for management is to establish a balance between product managers' administrative and entrepreneurial functions. Product managers with a relatively low perceived status cannot become true change agents. On the other hand, product managers with a relatively high perceived status should have the skills and respect required to perform effectively.

A major service-sector firm, introducing product management for the first time, created a task force charged with establishing a model of product manager responsibilities along with the responsibilities of 10 support areas (plus senior and business unit management) as they related to product management. The product managers were charged with many of the specific activities listed in this chapter. An abbreviated summary of the responsibilities of the 10 support areas at one representative company is given in the list that follows. Once the structure of product management is installed, management must select the right people and monitor and coach their activities to make sure they stay on track.

Mutual Responsibilities of a Major Financial Services Firm

Senior vice president

- Setting overall direction and priorities of the organization
- Allocating overall resources

Business unit manager

- Approving annual product business plans and budgets
- Determining product resource allocations

Product development

- Conducting feasibility studies for new products or major enhancements
- Coordinating the development and introduction of new products

Market research

- Measuring, tracking, and reporting product market shares
- Conducting product research as requested

Marketing and communications

- Developing and coordinating product-related marketing and sales communication

- Assisting in the development of marketing plans
- Executing marketing plans

Sales

- Prospecting for new business opportunities
- Closing sales

Operations

- Providing routine customer support and service
- Providing product operational efficiency

Corporate relations

- Identifying new business opportunities and retention strategies
- Coordinating corporate business development plans

Personnel

- Developing and implementing a product manager professional development plan
- Conducting product manager specialized skill training

Quality assurance

- Assisting in the development and monitoring of quality standards
- Providing process management evaluations

Define Gaps between Desired and Actual Competencies

There is no ideal profile for a successful product manager. However, several traits, skills, and kinds of experience are often identified as relating to product management success. Frequently cited traits looked for in product managers include an entrepreneurial attitude, leadership, and self-confidence. Acquired abilities should include organizational, time management, and communication skills. Sales proficiency and technical competence are also important in many industries. The importance of prior experience depends on the particular needs of the product management position. If highly technical, engineering-oriented knowledge is required, a background in engineering is appropriate. If an understanding of customer applications is desired, a sales background in the industry is appropriate. If knowledge of large market trends and competitive positioning is important, marketing research and/or advertising experience are desirable.

The appropriate characteristics of a product manager also depend on the culture of the organization and the expectations placed on the position. Some product managers fill (and are expected to fill) a coordinator role; others may be more directive; and still others take on a leadership role.

Product managers who are coordinators primarily function as administrators to ensure deadlines are met and requests are carried out. Coordinative product managers are more likely to deal with budgets than plans. Product managers who are directive not only coordinate projects but also develop product plans. Product managers who are leaders are more entrepreneurial and become more active in the strategic planning of products and services for the company.

Part of the difference among desired product manager characteristics depends on whether they work for consumer or industrial product manufacturers. A study of senior marketing executives from Australian companies with a product management organization found differences in management expectations between consumer and industrial firms. Marketing executives from consumer goods firms tended to view product managers as coordinators or implementers of strategy to a greater degree than was true for industrial firms. On the other hand, a greater importance was placed on forecasting and competitor intelligence for industrial product managers than was the case for consumer product managers. This is partly because of the wealth of syndicated data available about consumers that is absent in many industrial channels.

This same study highlighted some problems with the product management concept (PMC):

Those companies that expressed dissatisfaction with the PMC were asked in an open-ended question to explain their reasons. The range of reasons embraced the following: product managers spent too much time on day-to-day matters and not enough on planning and searching for new opportunities; product managers were not sufficiently entrepreneurial; product managers did not have enough authority over the sales department and had poor communication with the sales force (the most frequently mentioned responses); there was poor understanding of the product manager role; product managers were inexperienced; and there was an authority-responsibility mismatch.[2]

Evaluate and Coach Product Managers

Product managers need different kinds of knowledge, including product/industry knowledge, business knowledge, and interpersonal skills/management knowledge. Since beginning product managers typically spend most of their time gathering and organizing information on the product, its customers, and the competition, product knowledge is paramount. As they gain experience, the focus shifts to more comprehensive business knowledge, including finance, marketing, and strategic planning. At the same time, they develop team-building, negotiation, communication, and leadership abilities. Companies use both formal and informal approaches to developing product managers, as discussed in Business Brief 14.1, "Skill and Knowledge Development for Product Managers."

Business Brief 14.1

SKILL AND KNOWLEDGE DEVELOPMENT FOR PRODUCT MANAGERS

Product managers typically have job descriptions that list duties and responsibilities such as competitive analysis and new product development. But discovering—and enhancing—the skills and knowledge required can be challenging. Identifying competencies is a process of discovery. Many companies start by analyzing top performers to uncover the "secrets" to their success, and/or they compile general information from outside sources. An *internal* analysis is useful for industry-specific competency requirements, whereas the *external* analysis allows a broader benchmarking perspective. In either situation, the competencies should be truly related to effective performance as a product manager.

The process of developing product managers can be formal or informal. Unilever has a relatively formal program with its Marketing Academy, a global pseudo university for its employees that is focused on enhancing marketing capabilities. The curriculum forms the focal point of the way the organization develops brands, and it ties training into business objectives. The approach also increases the transfer of knowledge. Resources consist of books, booklets, an intranet, and workshops and courses.

Given the importance of cross-functional knowledge and the need to create the right culture and atmosphere, informal processes are also important. Paula Sneed, senior vice president of global marketing resources for Kraft Foods, found that listening to and appreciating colleagues at all levels during her career at General Foods and Kraft—a tool she referred to as a *mentoring mosaic*—provided a significant developmental boost.

Source: Linda Gorchels, *The Product Manager's Field Guide* (McGraw-Hill, 2003) provides a product manager competency model, along with alignment exercises for each competency. "Unilever: The Marketing Academy," *Brand Strategy* (May 2004), p. 28. "Dreaming Big, Preposterous Dreams Gives Vision for Success," *Chicago Tribune* (October 25, 2005), p. 5.

Many companies believe it takes from three to five years to develop an effective product manager. According to Bill Meserve, a principal at the management consulting firm of Temple, Barker & Sloane Inc., training and motivation are critical at this time, and career development must be an obligation: "The formal approach used at one 3M division is based on a written career development document and scheduled annual reviews, which are separate from performance appraisal. Primary responsibility for monitoring career development rests with senior marketing management or a separate marketing council."[3] It's a good idea to develop a product manager competency model, similar to the one shown in Figure 14.2. Define the desired competencies and their relative weights and then use the tool to evaluate and coach individual product managers.

For product managers to be effective, they need to build bridges throughout the company and be cross-functional leaders. Therefore, in the selection and development of product managers, this ability to transcend functional lines must be considered. The downfall of several product or brand management systems was the establishment of a product manager as caretaker of the product, with an emphasis on "safe" results. Product managers were charged with immediate results rather than the creation of long-term customer value. When this happens, product managers focus on improving their own position rather than on that of the company's product. According to William Weilbacher in his book *Brand Marketing,*

FIGURE 14.2 ➤ Product manager competency model

Drive business results	Deliver results through people	Create strategies	Ensure market-driven direction	Guide product fit and function	Manage multiple priorities	Exhibit entrepreneurial traits
Financial aptitude	Leadership	Ability to spot trends	Market analysis and segmentation	Technical know-how	Project management skills	Self-discipline
Selling knowledge and skills	Influence and motivation	Product portfolio building	Competitive intelligence	New product development knowledge	Time management skills	Visionary
Business planning	Team management	Long-term foresight	Go-to-market knowledge	Quality assurance	Organized	Risk tolerance
Forecasting	Decision making	Ability to deal with ambiguity	Customer champion	Product line fit	Ability to execute plans	Can-do attitude
Process know-how	Perceptive	Partnerships	Brand and message fit	Prototype validation	Ability to say no when necessary	Results-oriented
Total Weighted Scores						

Weight of the specific competency

Rating of product manager on the specified competency

Scores based on the sum of the weight x rating numbers

Skill level ratings:
1. *Deficient.* Product manager lacks some of the necessary experience, skills, or abilities related to this competence.
2. *Basically competent.* Product manager is able to perform these competencies on a fundamental level and understand the knowledge to be able to participate in decision making.
3. *Proficient.* Product manager is able to perform these competencies on a fully operational level and understand them well enough to teach others, if necessary.
4. *Advanced.* Product manager is not only proficient in these competencies, but also pushes the competency to a higher level.

In the end, the brand manager is forced by the brand-management system to pay more attention to career management than to brand management. Brand championship and brand advocacy are replaced by actions that make the brand manager look good to management, no matter what the long-term effect upon the brand or the perceptions of the consumers who buy it.[4]

Ensure Continued Alignment of Goals, Directives, and Initiatives

Appropriate evaluation criteria depend on the performance expectations of management. Sales and/or profit goals are fairly common measures of performance. However, if profit is a measure, it's important to distinguish between profit contribution and bottom-line profit. Profit contribution is the amount of product revenue remaining after subtracting all of a product manager's direct, controllable, or relevant expenses. This contribution to overhead (CTO) figure is a fairer assessment of performance than is fully allocated profit, because CTO minimizes the concern over the validity of the allocation methodology. Obsessive attention to allocating overhead against each product often consumes effort that could be better spent elsewhere. This isn't meant to imply that total overhead doesn't need to be covered. The CTO goal is established to cover anticipated overhead allocations but doesn't hold product managers responsible for overhead increases beyond their control.

Some companies that implement quality management principles have opted to minimize individual performance measures and focus on company performance. This does not have to be an either/or decision. Metrics can be designed to measure both individual and corporate performance. Companies can weigh these metrics differently depending on their corporate philosophies on performance measurement.

In addition to financial measures, product managers may be evaluated on some combination of other factors, such as the following:

- Successful introduction of new products
- Market share defense or growth
- Customer satisfaction indexes
- Attainment of company-specific goals

CHAPTER CHALLENGE

Study the top product managers in your company (or industry) to identify "expected" competencies associated with success. Match the competencies most aligned with your corporate goals and direction. Use the resulting competencies to design a competency for improving product management success.

INTERVIEW WITH STAN KOPEC AND JOHN LUSZCZEK: PRODUCT-LINE MANAGEMENT TRANSFORMATION

Stan Kopec, Intellectual Property Portfolio Manager, Nortel, skopec @charter.net

John Luszczek, General Manager, MSS Business Unit, Nortel

Stan and John, you've both been with Nortel for some time. What have your current and past positions been with the firm?

JOHN: I'm currently the general manager with the Nortel MSS Business unit. Prior to that, I was the leader of the Product Line Management (PLM) Transformation Project across Nortel. And of course I held positions in product management and engineering earlier than that.

STAN: I am managing Nortel's portfolio of intellectual property license agreements right now. I had previously worked with John on the PLM Transformation Project, and before that I worked in various product portfolio, project management, and competitive/market intelligence positions.

Nortel has faced some challenges over the years. One of the steps taken to progress forward was the Product Line Management (PLM) Transformation Project you both mentioned. Can you talk a bit about that process?

JOHN and STAN: Nortel had initiated various business transformation projects across numerous functional areas to develop best practices across the corporation. PLM was one of those functional areas. We took a pretty structured approach to the overall process.

First, we interviewed the executive team and the functional groups that worked with PLM to understand what was expected as key accountabilities and objectives from the PLM organization. This became an important foundation to framing the expected product management competencies.

We also identified the demographics (such as years of service, education, previous work experience, and other factors) and current mode of operation of each of the product management groups. This gave us a good look at the status quo.

Next we defined the major pillars of accountability of market planning, portfolio management, business planning, and lifecycle management—and developed that into an overall accountability model. We realized that for people to be accountable for certain results and outcomes, they need to have baseline skills. The model helped us identify and define those skills—that is, the competencies and levels of proficiency we needed from product managers to fulfill the pillars of accountability.

The next step was to look for areas of potential skill improvement. We conducted a skills assessment of the total PLM organization to identify general and specific skills (what we called implementation skills) that could be enhanced. Based on that information, we worked with leading universities to define the training required to enhance those skills.

The final step in the process—rolling out training—was not completed because of the financial restructure of Nortel at that time. Recommendations from the PLM Business Transformation team were provided to the various business units.

What was the most surprising thing you learned as you went through this?

STAN and JOHN: There were actually three key areas. One, we realized that most PLMs were ex-R&D individuals and consequently focused very strongly on product capabilities. Two, we discovered that most of the PLM training had been done on the job and by working with mentors. And three, there were very few off-the-shelf courses available for our specific PLM development.

Can you cite a few accomplishments of the transformation process?

JOHN and STAN: Sure. The process really helped us define a PLM accountability model that was applicable across all PLM roles at Nortel. In particular the model covered all aspects from hardware to software (applications)—as well as services. It also covered all major areas of activities throughout the life cycle of the product—specifically market planning, portfolio management, business planning, and life-cycle management.

I think there are a few other accomplishments as well. We obtained better skills definition for PLMs—skills that matched the accountability model—and that enabled a skills assessment and the resultant recommended training requirements.

There were a couple of other things that didn't come up in our previous answers. As part of the training efforts, we created a development handbook that guided individual PLMs through the defined course offerings and made clear which courses addressed which skills. We also identified a priority list of tools that needed to be enhanced to perform the PLM role.

What advice can you give to other firms striving to strengthen their product management organization?

STAN and JOHN: There are actually several things. You absolutely need to get alignment on what the executive team is expecting from the PLM organization and get corporate-level buy-in. Be sure you understand the current capabilities of the PLM organization and customize the skills development and training to address the skill areas that most need enhancement. And finally, recognize that implementation skills (that is, specific product-related skills such as VOC and go-to-market) are needed to accomplish the PLM role, but excellent general skills (leadership, strategy, innovation) are required to get to the next level.

Notes

CHAPTER 1

1. G. M. Naidu, A. Kleimenhagen, and G. D. Pillari, "Is Product-Line Management Appropriate for Your Health Care Facility?" *Journal of Health Care Marketing* (Fall 1993), p. 8.

CHAPTER 2

1. Robert W. Koehler, "Triple-Threat Strategy," *Management Accounting* (October 1991), p. 32.

2. Some executives are working with writers, directors, producers, and actors to gain better skills at storytelling. Screenwriting coach Robert McKee discusses this phenomenon in "Storytelling that Moves People," *Harvard Business Review* (June 2003), pp. 51–55.

3. Camille H. James and William C. Minnis, "Organizational Storytelling: It Makes Sense," *Business Horizons* (July–August 2004), p. 29.

4. Social scientists refer to this as the principle of authority, a critical component of persuasion. For more detail refer to Robert B. Cialdini, "Harnessing the Science of Persuasion," *Harvard Business Review* (October 2001), pp. 72–79.

CHAPTER 4

1. Peter Burrows and Ben Elgin, "Why HP Is Pruning the Printers," *BusinessWeek* (May 9, 2005), pp. 38–39.

2. Numerous trend-watching publications follow nanotechnology. *The Futurist* (a publication of the World Future Society) has covered it in several issues. One such article is "Molecular Nanotech: Benefits and Risks," by Mike Treder, *The Futurist* (January–February

2004), pp. 42–46. This was also the *BusinessWeek* cover story in the February 14, 2005, issue.

3. Rich Tomaselli, "Pharma Replacing Reps with Web," *Advertising Age* (January 24, 2005), p. 50.

4. John A. Nolan, "It's the Third Millennium: Do You Know Where Your Competitor Is?" *Journal of Business Strategy* (November/ December 1999), pp. 11–15.

5. Theresa Howard, "Glen Ellen Reformulates to Go Upscale," *Brandweek* (May 1, 2000), p. 78.

6. Julie Schlosser, "Looking for Intelligence in Ice Cream," *Fortune* (March 17, 2003), p. 115.

7. Liz Torlee, "The Perils of Segmentation," *Marketing* (August 23– August 30, 2004), p. 31.

8. Industries were previously grouped according to the Standard Industrial Classification (SIC) codes. Refer to census.gov for the translation to NAICS.

9. Refer to Niraj Dawar, "What are Brands Good For?" *MIT Sloan Management Review* (Fall 2004), pp. 31–37 for a discussion on replacing brand management with customer management.

10. Alan W. H. Grant and Leonard A. Schlesinger, "Realize Your Customers' Full Profit Potential," *Harvard Business Review*, vol. 73, no. 5 (September–October 1995), pp. 61–62.

11. Kelly Greene, "Marketing Surprise: Older Consumers Buy Stuff, Too," *Wall Street Journal* (April 6, 2004), pp. A1–A12.

CHAPTER 5

1. "Hyundai Steers for the Top," *Wall Street Journal* (April 27, 2005), p. B3.

2. Chad Terhune, "In Switch, Pepsi Makes Diet Cola its New Flagship," *Wall Street Journal* (March 16, 2005), p. B1.

3. Amy Barrett, "DuPont Tries to Unclog a Pipeline," *BusinessWeek* (January 23, 2003), pp. 103–104.

4. Betsy D. Gelb, "Why Rich Brands Get Richer, and What to Do About It," *Business Horizons* (September–October 1992), p. 46.

CHAPTER 6

1. James Carbone, *Purchasing*, vol. 136, no. 4 (March 15, 2007), p. 30.
2. Geoff Colvin, "Here It Is. Now, You Design It!" *Fortune* (May 26, 2008), p. 34.
3. Vanessa Wong, "Co-Creation: Not Just Another Focus Group," Bloomberg *BusinessWeek* special report (April 1, 2010).
4. Regina Fazio Maruca, "The Right Way to Go Global," *Harvard Business Review*, vol. 72 (March/April 1994), p. 143.
5. Christopher Power, Kathleen Kerwin, Keith Alexander, and Robert D. Hof, "Flops," *BusinessWeek* (August 16, 1993), p. 79.
6. Janet Guyon, "CEOs on Managing Globally," *Fortune*, the 2004 Global 500 special insert (July 12, 2004).
7. "The Knowledge Creating Company," *Harvard Business Review* (November–December 1991), p. 101.
8. A more complete listing of screening (or business case evaluation) criteria can be found in Philip A. Himmelfarb, *Survival of the Fittest* (Prentice Hall, 1992), pp. 107–111.
9. Peter Strub and Steven Herman, "Can the Sales Force Speak for the Customer?" *Marketing Research*, vol. 5, no. 5 (Fall 1993), pp. 32–35.

CHAPTER 8

1. The section on heavyweight product managers was adapted from Kim B. Clark and Takahiro Fujimoto, "The Power of Product Integrity," *Harvard Business Review* (November–December 1990), pp. 107–118; Christopher Power et al., "Flops," *BusinessWeek*, (August 16, 1993), pp. 76–82; and Jean E. LeGrand, "A Product in Need of Management," *Bankers Magazine* (November–December 1992), pp. 73–76. While the product managers in the automotive industry described in this section were generally part of engineering, most product managers in other industries are in marketing, marketing/sales, or product management departments.
2. Clark and Fujimoto, p. 108.
3. Clark and Fujimoto, p. 109.

4. Clark and Fujimoto, p. 110.

5. LeGrand (1992), p. 73.

6. R. Madhavan, "From Embedded Knowledge to Embodied Knowledge: New Product Development as Knowledge Management," *Journal of Marketing* (October 1998), pp. 1–12.

7. Faye Rice, "Secret of Product Testing," *Fortune* (November 28, 1994), pp. 88–95.

8. Preston G. Smith and John S. Farnbach, "Avoid Costly 11th-hour Project Dilemmas by Preparing for Change," *PDMA Visions* (December 2010), pp. 24–26.

CHAPTER 9

1. C. Merle Crawford, *New Products Management*, 4th ed. (Richard D. Irwin, 1994), p. 351.

2. Wayne Koberstein, "Master Launchers," *Pharmaceutical Executive* (May 1998), p. 45.

3. Bruce Nussbaum and Robert Neff, "I Can't Work This Thing!" *BusinessWeek* (April 19, 1991), p. 60.

4. Fernando Suarez and Gianvito Lanzolla, "The Half-Truth of First-Mover Advantage," *Harvard Business Review* (April 2005), pp. 121–127.

5. C. Merle Crawford, *New Products Management*, 4th ed. (Richard Irwin, 1994), pp. 351–353.

6. Mary Jo Feldstein, "How Do You Take a New Product, Create a Need for It and Sell It?" *St. Louis Post-Dispatch* (April 19, 2005), p. D1.

CHAPTER 10

1. James R. Rindall, "Marketing Established Brands," *Journal of Consumer Marketing* (Fall 1991), pp. 5–10.

2. Jason Stein, "What's Brewing?" *Wisconsin State Journal* (May 15, 2005), p. C10.

3. Paulette Thomas, "Case Study: Narrow Markets Need Cultivation to Thrive," *Wall Street Journal* (November 23, 2004), p. B8.

4. Steve Varon, "Filling in the Gaps," *Medical Marketing and Media* (June 2004), pp. 52–56.

5. Jeremy Main, "How to Steal the Best Ideas Around," *Fortune* (October 19, 1992), p. 103.

6. Ibid.

7. Alexandra Jardine, "Next Generation," *Marketing* (November 24, 2004), pp. 31–36.

8. Refer to Youngme Moon, "Break Free from the Product Life Cycle," *Harvard Business Review* (May 2005), pp. 87–94, for a discussion of reverse positioning, breakaway positioning, and stealth positioning concepts.

9. Staci Sturrock, "Time Not on Our Side," *Wisconsin State Journal* (May 15, 2005), p. I8.

10. Ralph Ruark, "Innovation Matters," *Ceramic Industry* (May 2004), pp. 38–41.

11. Nirmalya Kumar, "Kill a Brand, Keep a Customer," *Harvard Business Review* (December 2003), pp. 86–95.

12. David M. Anderson and B. Joseph Pine II, *Agile Product Development for Mass Customization* (Times Mirror, 1997), pp.75–83.

CHAPTER 11

1. From the dictionary on the American Marketing Association Web site, http://www.marketingpower.com/.

2. Kevin Lane Keller, *Strategic Brand Management* (Prentice-Hall, 1998), p. 4.

3. http://www.brandchannel.com/education_glossary.asp.

4. Beth Snyder Bulik, "Apple Hires HP Star to Bring Stronger Marketing Punch," *Advertising Age,* vol. 76, no. 8 (February 21, 2005), p. 4.

5. Joseph Weber, "He Really Got Harley Roaring," *BusinessWeek* (March 21, 2005), p. 70.

6. David Rocks and Moon Ihlwan, "Samsung Design," *BusinessWeek* (December 6, 2004), pp. 88–96.

7. Kevin Helliker, "In Natural Foods, a Big Name's No Big Help," *Wall Street Journal* (June 7, 2002), pp. B1–B7.

8. "Leaders: Brand New," *Consumer Electronics*, (January 15, 2005), p. 10.

9. Todd Wasserman, "Marketers Extend Kudos to Jeep, Apple," *Brandweek* (October 11, 2004), p. 4.

10. Kevin Lane Keller, *Strategic Brand Management*, p. 132.

11. Steve Butler, "Product Range Brands: A Frequently Overlooked Source of Value in the Chemical Industry," *Chemical Market Reporter* (December 9, 2002), p. 26.

12. Betsy McKay and Suzanne Vranica, "How a Coke Ad Campaign Fell Flat with Viewers," *Wall Street Journal* (March 19, 2001), pp. B1–B4.

CHAPTER 12

1. Andrew Serwer, "How to Escape a Price War," *Fortune* (June 1994), p. 84.

2. Christopher Power et al., "Flops," *BusinessWeek* (August 16, 1993), p. 79.

CHAPTER 13

1. The information in this paragraph is derived from Jack Neff, "Unilever Reorganization Shifts P&L Responsibility," *Advertising Age* (February 28, 2005), p. 13.

2. Salah S. Hassan, Stephen Craft, and Wael Kortam, "Understanding the New Bases for Global Market Segmentation," *The Journal of Consumer Marketing*, vol. 20, no. 4/5 (2003), p. 454.

3. Douglas B. Holt, John A. Quelch, and Earl L. Taylor, "How Global Brands Compete," *Harvard Business Review* (September 2004), pp. 68–75.

4. John Galvin, "The World on a String," *Advertising Age* (February 2005), pp. 13–19.

5. Alex Taylor III, "Can America Fall in Love with VW Again?" *Fortune* (May 16, 2005), p. 130.

6. David Arnold, "Seven Rules of International Business," *Harvard Business Review* (November –December 2000), pp. 131–137

7. Richard R. Gesteland, *Cross-Cultural Business Behavior,* 5th ed. (Copenhagen Business School Press, 2011).

CHAPTER 14

1. Zachary Schiller, Wendy Zellner, Ron Stodghill, and Mark Maremont, "Clout!" *BusinessWeek* (December 21, 1992), p. 70.

2. P. L. Dawes and P. G. Patterson, "The Performance of Industrial and Consumer Product Managers, *Industrial Marketing Management* (February 1988), pp. 73–84.

3. Bill Meserve, "The Changing Role of Product Management," *Electronic Business* (January 9, 1989), p. 146.

4. William Weilbacher, *Brand Marketing* (NTC Business Books, 1993), p. 123.

Index

Accounting, 37, 87
Action maps, 133
Activity charts, 206–209
Activity networks, 133
Adjacency growth, 153–154
Administrative expenses, 42
Administrators, 363
Advertising, 230, 303 (*See also* Marketing)
Advertising agencies, 28–29
Advisory councils, 317
Aflac, 297
AIPMM (Association of International
        Product Marketing and Management),
        100
Air Liquide, 164
Airline industry, 67
Aligning goals and performance, 351–371
        and development of product managers,
                364–367
        gaps between desired and actual
                competenecies, 362–364
        and organizational structure, 356–359
        and performance measures, 367
        primer for, 351–356
        responsibilities to others in the firm,
                359–362
        steps in, 356
Allied Signal, 154
Alpha testing, 161
Alternative positions (branding), 292
American Airlines, 67
American companies, 334, 335
American Heart Association, 240
American Marketing Association, 284, 304
Anderson, David, 278
Annual product business plans, 106
Anthropology, 101–102
Apple Computers:
        branding by, 285, 286, 288, 290, 294
        pricing by, 308–309
        product launches by, 247
Aramark, 79
Arbor National Mortgage, 315

Arm & Hammer, 154
Arnold, David, 341
Association of International Product
        Marketing and Management
        (AIPMM), 100
Assumptions, in business cases, 178–179
AT&T, 169
Attribute positioning, 292–293
Automobile industry, 92, 200
Average rate of return, 46–47

Bank of America, 140
Banks, 5, 80
"Batting average" culture, 140–141
Bayer, 154
Beckman Coulter, 8
Becton Dickinson, 311–312
Benchmarking, 272, 365
Bennis, Warren, 15
Best practices, 17, 105
Beta testing, 161, 209–212, 221
"Big box" retailers, 354, 358
Big-lot segments, 82
Black & Decker, 247, 355
Bleustein, Jeffrey, 291
Booth, Kevin, 192–197
Boston Consulting Group, 253
Brainstorming, 163
Brand(s), 283–299
        core, 254–255
        customers' perceptions of, 285–287
        defined, 284, 300
        elements of, 283, 295–298
        flanker, 154–156, 289
        function of, 284
        global, 337–338
        and growth, 35–36
        hierarchy of, 287–289
        and launches, 230
        line extensions of, 293–295
        in marketing programs, 298–299
        as part of product plan, 136
        umbrella approach to, 28

Brand advocacy, 11
Brand equity, 284–286
Brand image, 285
Brand management:
   and career management, 367
   and customer's perception, 284, 285
   product management vs., 283
   Mark Rothwell on, 10–14
Brand Marketing (William Weilbacher), 366
Brand positioning, 284, 286, 289–293
Breakeven analysis, 39, 40, 48–50, 306
Breakthrough growth, 156
Breakthroughs, 150
BRIC countries, 345
Briggs & Stratton, 225–228
Brink, Gabriela Saldanha, 322–325
Bristol-Myers, 66, 234
B2B companies (*see* Business-to-business
   companies)
B2C companies (*see* Business-to-consumer
   companies)
Bubble charts, 149
Budget competition, 68, 69
Bundle books, 112–114
Burke, Sean, 34
Business cases, 175–191
   accuracy of, 175
   approval of, 209
   building solid, 41
   company components of, 188–191
   defined, 176, 193
   development of, 7, 193–194
   framing and selling, 191
   importance of, 176–178
   industry components of, 188
   market components of, 179–187
   and planning, 106
   presentation of, 161
   product components of, 187–188
Business competencies, 37–54
Business plans (*see* Business cases)
Business-to-business (B2B) companies:
   brands of, 287
   business-to-consumer vs., 4, 12–13,
      300–301, 354
   and customer contact, 29
   and levels of customers, 103
   market segmentation for, 78
   and marketing strategy, 355
   and salespeople, 106

Business-to-consumer (B2C) companies:
   brands of, 287
   business-to-business vs., 4, 12–13,
      300–301, 354
BusinessWeek, 291
Buyer power, 61, 62
Buy-in, 31
Buying behavior, 255
Buying factors, 81
Buzz, generating, 220

Cadillac, 238–239
Canon, 163, 260
Capital equipment, 305
Cascadian Farms, 289
Cash flow projections, 176
Castle & Cooke, 154
Category competition, 66, 69
"Category killers," 358
Caterpillar, 115–116
Causal forecasts, 124, 126
Celebrity endorsements, 292
Centers for Disease Control and
   Prevention, 240
Change, 16
Character icons, 296–298
Charters, product, 156–157
Checklists, 133, 222–223
Chesbrough, Henry, 150, 165
Chief marketing officers (CMOs), 37
China, 330–332
Chinese companies, 334, 335
Christensen, Clayton, 180
Chrysler, 237–238
CI (competitive intelligence), 64–66, 74–75
Circuit City, 247
Clark, Kim, 200–202
Clorox, 155
CM (*see* Contribution margin)
CMOs (chief marketing officers), 37
Coaching, 364–367
Coca-Cola, 298–299
Cocreation, 151
COGS (cost of goods sold), 48
Cohen, Gary, 312
Cole, David, 237
Colgate-Palmolive, 112–114
Commercial Federal, 80
Common costs, 44
Communication, 22–23, 165, 166, 329–335

Community banks, 80
Company components, of business cases, 188–191
Company culture, 117, 140–141, 205
Company size, 78
Compaq, 215
Competencies:
   assessment of, 118
   business, 37–54
   and business cases, 193
   for decision making, 17–19
   desired vs. actual, 362–364
   for influencing stakeholders, 30–33
   for leadership, 15–17
   with matrix structures and cross-functional teams, 19–20
   for stakeholder relationships, 20–29
Competition:
   in Colgate-Palmolive's bundle books, 114
   existing, 61, 62
   taking customers from the, 273, 274
   threat of new, 61–64
   and timing of launches, 233
Competitive analysis, 64–75
   competitive intelligence process in, 65–66, 74–75
   defined, 64
   ideas from, 150
   identifying competition in, 66–70
   information required for, 71–73
Competitive intelligence (CI), 64–66, 74–75
Competitive matrix, 255–256
Compiled forecasts, 124–126
Complacency, 17
Comstock, Beth, 35
Concept testing, 189, 190
Consumer protection, 266
Consumption pricing, 309
Continental Airlines, 67
Contingency plans, 242
Continuous competitive intelligence, 74
Contract manufacturing, 341
Contribution income statements, 43–46
Contribution margin (CM), 40, 44, 50–51
Contribution to overhead (CTO), 367
Control plans, 242, 243
Control systems, 208
Cooper, Robert, 158
Core brands, 254–255

Core growth, 153–154
Corel, 66
Corporate brands, 287–289
Correlation-based forecasts, 126
Cost classifications, 41–43
Cost drivers, 46
Cost of goods sold (COGS), 48
Cost reduction projects, 26
CPM (critical path method), 207–208
Cradle to Cradle (William McDonough), 271
Crest, 297
Critical path method (CPM), 207–208
Cross-Cultural Business Behavior (Richard Gesteland), 342
CSRs (customer service representatives), 26–27
CTO (contribution to overhead), 367
Culture(s):
   "batting average," 140–141
   communicating across, 329–335
   company, 117, 205
   expressive, 342
   global, 338
   relationship-focused, 329, 334
   reserved, 342, 343
   task-focused, 329, 334
Culture gaps, 335, 343
CUNA Mutual, 266–269, 275–277
Curet, Am, 99
Customer analysis, 83–88
Customer engagement pricing, 311
Customer messaging, 313–315
Customer satisfaction, 25
Customer service department, 25–27, 150, 236
Customer service representatives (CSRs), 26–27
Customer value chain (CVC), 269–270
Customers:
   acquisition of, 88–89
   contact with, 29
   existing, 76–77
   firing your, 90–91
   gathering information on, 75–82
   ideas from, 150, 163
   market input from, 179–181, 183
   mindset of, 152–153
   needs of, 7, 24, 348
   perception of brands by, 284–287
   retention of, 88–89

Cutter, 240
CVC (customer value chain), 269–270

Daimler-Chrysler, 294
Data, secondary, 179
Database programs, 88
Davis, Scott, 33–36
DBG product managers (*see* Domestically
    based global product managers)
Dealerships, 237–239
Decision making:
    categorizing products for, 253
    by leaders, 17–19
    and learning, 139
    by management teams, 195
    and new product development, 159
Decision reviews (*see* Gate reviews)
Delivery, product, 270
Dell, 297
Delphi technique, 126
Demand innovation, 164
Demographic trends, 92
Design Concepts, Inc., 169–170
Design thinking, 170–171, 173–174
Development costs, 190
Development readiness appraisal, 211
DiCillo, Greg, 280–282
Digital Equipment Corporation, 215
Direct competition, 66, 69
Direct costs, 44
Direct exporting, 340
Direct labor costs, 42, 43
Direct language, 335
Direct materials, 41, 43
Directives, 367
Discounted contribution, 191
Discounts, 37, 309
Distribution:
    to other countries, 340–343
    strategy for, 110–111
Diversification, 122
Do-it-yourself competition, 67–68
Domestically based global (DBG) product
    managers, 330, 332, 346–347
Dow, 273
Downstream product management:
    functions in, 8–9
    and globalization, 356
    (*See also specific headings*)
DuPont, 121
Dynamic stability, 137

Early indicator chart, 232
Eco-friendliness, 270
Economic Value Estimation (EVE),
    39, 52, 306
Economic value modeling, 52–53
Economic value spreadsheets, 37
Egalitarian management, 334–335
80/20 (Pareto) rule, 253
E-Lab, 102–103
Elderly people, 92
Electronic self-testing modules, 242
Electronics industry, 30–31
Emotion, 19
Entrepreneurial mindset, 6–8, 10
Entry-level positions, 3
Epson, 131
Estimated sales, 125
Ethnography research, 94, 101–102,
    150, 151
Evaluation:
    of launches, 242, 243
    PERT technique, 207, 208
    of product line, 257–263
    of product managers, 364–367
    of product performance, 254–257
EVE (*see* Economic Value Estimation)
Events, 91–93, 111
Excedrin, 290
Execution, of plans, 19
Expenses, administrative, 42
Experimental research, 94–95
Experimentation, 338–339
Exponential smoothing, 125
Exporting, 340
Expressive cultures, 342

Facebook, 29, 151
Face-to-face meetings, 335
Fact books, 111, 112
FACTS (planning), 132–134
Failure, 33, 157–158
Faith, 196
Farnham, Laura, 214–218
Fast-moving consumer goods
    (FMCG), 203
Fazes, 355
Federal Reserve Board (FRB), 266
Federal Trade Commission, 234
Finance, 38–48
    and annual product business
        plans, 106

cost classifications, 41–43
cost drivers, 46
financial statements, 46–47
relevant costs for pricing decisions,
    48–54
segmented reporting, 43–46
Finance department, 27, 38–41
Financial analysis, 188–191
Financial reporting, 43–47 (*See also specific
    financial statements*)
Financial services industry, 266–269
First-mover advantage, 219
Fisher Space Pen, 264
Five forces analysis, 61–62
Fixed costs, 43, 48
Flanker brands, 154–156, 289
Flowcharts, 132, 133, 149
FMCG (fast-moving consumer goods), 203
Focus groups, 29, 93, 163
Ford Motor Company, 25, 92, 272
Forecasting, sales, 22, 124–126
Formal business managers, 342
Franchino, Dave, 151, 169–174
Franchising, 341
FRB (Federal Reserve Board), 266
Fujimoto, Takahiro, 200–202
Functional structures, 356
"Fuzzy front end" of development,
    120, 121

Gallo, 70
Gate reviews, 209–212, 216
GE Healthcare, 8, 34, 164
General Instrument Corp., 30
General Mills, 289
Geographic strategy, 235
Gesteland, Richard, 333–335, 342
Glad, 155
Glassman, James, 122
GlaxoSmithKline, 234
Glen Ellen, 70
Global culture, 338
Globalization, 329–343
    and communication, 329–335
    distributing to other countries, 340–343
    effects of, 355–356
    and glocalization, 339–340
    and product manager responsibilities, 106
    transnational product strategy, 336–339
Glocalization, 339–340
GM (gross margin), 40

Goals:
    corporate, 188
    for directives and initiatives, 367
    (*See also* Aligning goals and
        performance)
Google Alerts, 74
Governance, 139
Gray, Paula, 100–104, 151
Green, Gloria, 96
Gross contribution, 190
Gross margin (GM), 40
Growth, 35–36, 153–156

Harley-Davidson, 149, 284–287, 290–292
HDTV (high definition television),
    181, 182
Health care industry:
    brand management in, 11–12
    product management in, 6
Heavyweight product managers,
    200–201, 204
Hess, Jon, 234
Hewlett-Packard:
    acquisition of Compaq by, 215
    brand of, 294
    competitors of, 60–61
    medical product groups of, 157–158
    product development at, 30, 258–260
    repositioning of DeskJet by, 130–131
Hierarchical management, 334–335, 359
High definition television (HDTV),
    181, 182
Hill-Rom, 300
Historical sales patterns, 124
Holistic marketing, 338
Home Depot, 355
HoMedics, 245
Honda, 117, 201–203, 336
Honesty, 11, 32
Hospitals, 6
Huffy, 316–317
Hyundai, 117

ICFC (in-country-for-country), 345–346
Ideas:
    generation of, 161–169
    sharing of, 32
    (*See also* Innovation)
Ideation, 149–150
IDEO, 151
Image (brand), 284, 285

Incentive programs, 315
Income statements:
    contribution, 43–46
    importance of understanding, 56
    net income on, 42–43
    SG&A line on, 42
    traditional, 43–44
In-country-for-country (ICFC), 345–346
India, 338
Indian companies, 334, 335
Indirect exporting, 340
Indirect language, 335
Industrial products, 82
Industry components, of business cases, 188
Industry knowledge, 61–64
Influencers, 128
Informal business managers, 342
In-home testing, 210
In-house advertising, 28
Initiatives, 367
InnoCentive, 151
Innovation, 162–169
    breakthroughs and incremental changes,
        149–151
    demand, 164
    open, 150–151, 165
    reverse, 272, 340
Installation, product, 270, 318
Insurance industry, 5–6
Intel, 62, 258
Intelligence gathering, 59–100
    competitive analysis in (see Competitive
        analysis)
    on customer retention and acquisition,
        88–89
    of customer segment information, 75–88
    and decision making, 17
    on events and trends, 91–93
    and firing your customers, 90–91
    of industry knowledge, 61–64
    from internal data, 95–99
    market and customer analysis in, 83–88
    of technology information, 60–61
    types of information in, 59
    types of research in, 93–95
Intention to buy, 184–185
Interbrand, 299
InterLink, 312
Internal assessments, 113
Internal intelligence, 95–99

Internal rate of return (IRR), 47, 191
Intrapreneurs, 7
Inventory access, 270
Investments, 54
Invoice price, 53
iPods, 68, 75, 288, 308–309
IRR (internal rate of return), 47, 191

Japanese cars, 92
Jingles, 296
Job descriptions, 356, 364
Jobs, project management, 3–5
Johnson & Johnson, 66, 234
Jong-Yong, Yun, 119
Journal of Health Care Marketing, 6

Katz, Gerry, 94
Kaye, Elyse, 244–248
Keebler, 297
Keller, Kevin Lane, 284, 295
Kenny, David, 260–262
Key accounts, 23–24, 358
Kindel, Sharen, 114
Kohler Plumbing, 68
Komatsu, 115–116
Kopec, Stan, 368–371
Kotter, John, 16
Kraft Foods, 365
Kumar, Nirmalya, 278

Labor costs, 42, 43
Lally, Austin, 331–332
Lanzolla, Gianvito, 233
Launches, 219–243
    activities during, 162
    costs of, 264
    crafting strategy for, 219–220
    documentation for, 157, 224–232
    evaluation of, 242, 243
    geographic strategy for, 235
    and market testing, 221–222
    and marketing communications,
        239–242
    sales training for, 235–239
    timing of, 233–234
    and "what if?" questions, 222–224
LBG product managers (see Locationally
        based global product managers)
Lead user research, 150
Leadership, 15–20

and decision making, 17–19
    genetic component to, 15
    in industry, 129
    and matrix structures, 19–20
    as skill of product manager, 15–17
    of teams, 205–206
Leaduser.com, 150
Learning, 33
LeGrand, Jean, 203
Licensing, 340
Life-cycle management, 251–279
    and portfolios, 251–252
    product categorization in, 253–254
    product line evaluation in, 257–263
    product performance evaluation in,
        254–257
    rationalization decisions in, 278–279
    reinforcement and protection strategies
        in, 263–265
    and relaunches, 274–277
    renewal and revitalization strategies in,
        265–274
    retirement strategies in, 278–279
Line extensions:
    branding for, 293–295
    flowcharts for, 159
    market input on, 179
    successes and failures with, 260–263
Linens-N-Things, 247
LinkedIn, 6
Lipitor, 222, 239–240
Locationally based global (LBG) product
        managers, 330, 332, 346–347
Logos, 295, 296
Long-term plans, 115–116
Luminaries, 150–151
Luszczek, John, 368–371

Mac mini, 308–309
"Magical thinking," 195
Maintenance accounts, 23–24
Manuals, 230
Manufacturing, 25, 158
Manufacturing costs, 25, 41–42
Market analysis, 83–88, 114
Market conditions, 59
Market managers, 357
Market profiles, 224, 225
Market requirements document (MRD),
        176, 185–187

Market segments:
    finding new, 273–274
    grouping products by, 120
    information on, 75–82
    and planning, 129–130
    segmentation example, 83–88
    (See also Target markets)
Market size, 166
Market testing, 210, 221–222, 235
Marketing, 303–321
    advertising vs., 303
    costs of, 42, 190
    and customer messaging, 313–315
    defined, 304
    ethnographic insight in, 101
    holistic, 338
    for launches, 239–242
    and manufacturing, 25
    need for, 355
    permission, 338
    plans for, 189
    pricing strategies in, 306–312
    product manager's relationship with,
        28–29, 359
    readiness for, 224
    relevance of, 24
    and sales channels, 316–319
    and sales support, 319–321
    to target customers, 305–306
Marketing research, 29, 93
Markets, 179–187
Marriott, 154
Marvin Windows, 129
Mass merchandisers, 358
Matrix organizations:
    defined, 353
    key players in, 139–140
    leadership in, 19–20
    product manager's role in, 5
    in relationship-focused cultures, 334
    switching to structure of, 356
Maytag, 297
MBA programs, 3
McDonald's, 36, 294
McDonough, William, 271
Medical products industry, 265
Mellon Bank, 272
Mentoring mosaic, 365
Merck, 229
Meserve, Bill, 30, 31, 365–366

Metrics:
  and business cases, 187
  design of, 367
  measuring progress with, 137
  reliance on, 196
Mikula, Jeff, 299–302
Milestone activities chart, 230
Miller Brewing, 68
Minolta, 337
Mission statements, 72, 205
Molen, Richard L., 317
Motorola, 148, 149, 287
MRD (market requirements document), 176, 185–187
Muda, 97
Multinational companies, 346

Nabisco, 260
Nagle, Tom, 52
NAICS (North American Industry Classification System), 78
Nanotechnology, 61
National account management, 358
Negotiator segment, 82
Net contribution, 190
Net income, 42–43
Net present value (NPV), 47, 191
New Glarus Brewery, 264
New Line, 246
New product charters, 156–157
New product development (NPD), 25
  cost implications of, 37
  criteria for, 167
  goal of, 336
  ideation as separate from, 150
  in organizational structure, 358–359
  overseeing (*see* Project management)
  as part of product management, 4–5
  and planning, 106
  previewing processes in, 158–162
  in product-line management, 258–260
New products:
  distribution of, 316
  plans for, 136
  sales training for, 73
Newsletters, 236
"Next practices," 17
Niche concepts, 129
Nike, 290
NineSigma, 151
Nissan Motors, 92

Nokia Group, 164
Nonmanufacturing costs, 42
Nortel, 368–370
North American Industry Classification System (NAICS), 78
NPD (*see* New product development)
NPV (net present value), 47, 191

Objectives:
  accomplishing your, 134–136
  setting, 127–128
Observational research, 93, 94
Open innovation, 150–151
Operations:
  product manager's relationship with, 24–26
  results of, 43
Opportunities, identifying, 123–124, 180–181
Order-size discounts, 309
Organic growth, 153
Organizational competition, 68–69
Organizational structure, 356–359 (*See also* Matrix organizations)
Overhead costs, 190, 367

Packaging, 136, 230, 296
Pampers, 273
Pareto (80/20) rule, 253
Past performance, 46
Patent expiration, 234
Patents, 341
Payback period, 47, 191
Payment, 270
PepsiCo, 120
Perceptual map, 255–256
Perdue Farms, 67–68
Performance evaluation, 254–257, 367
Performance history, 108, 114
Performance measurements, 196, 367
Performance objectives, 23 (*See also* Aligning goals and performance)
Periodic competitive intelligence, 74
Permission marketing, 338
PERT (program evaluation and review technique), 207, 208
Pfizer, 234
P&G (*see* Procter & Gamble)
Pharmaceutical industry, 75, 222, 229, 234, 320
Phillips, Mark A., 38–41, 344–349

Picaridin, 240
Pillsbury, 338
Pitney Bowes, 68
P&L (profit-and-loss) responsibilities, 333
Planning, 105–137
    and assessment of current state, 108–114
    difficulty of, 196
    FACTS of, 132–134
    framework for, 106–107
    and metrics, 137
    objectives in, 127–128, 134–136
    positioning statements in, 130–132
    problems and opportunities in, 123–124
    product vision in, 115–123
    purpose of, 105
    and road maps, 147–149
    and sales forecasting, 124–126
    strategic, 139
    and target markets, 128–130
    tools for, 18–19
PLM (Product Line Management), 369–371
PMC (product management concept),
    363–364
PMTs (product management teams), 355
Pocket price waterfall, 53–54
Porter's five forces analysis, 61–62
Portfolio reviews, 159, 212
Portfolios:
    defined, 122
    investing with, 122–123
    in life-cycle management, 251–253
    types of, 120–121
Positioning, brand (see Brand positioning)
Positioning statements, 130–132
Prelaunch period, 161–162, 221–235
Present value, 47
Press kits, 240
Press releases, 240
Price leakage, 307
Price to contribution margin, 40
Price to gross margin, 40
Price waterfalls, 39, 53–54
Price–value positions, 289
Price-volume analysis (see Breakeven analysis)
Pricing:
    assessment of current, 109–110
    and launches, 230
    policies for, 224
    relevant costs for, 48–52
    strategies for, 39–41, 306–312
    target prices, 187

Primary research, 93
Problems, identification of, 123–124
Procter & Gamble (P&G):
    and creation of product management,
        352–353
    and globalization, 333
    growth of, 278
    innovation at, 164–165, 180
    marketing by, 91, 312, 338–339
    relationship with Walmart, 87
    research and development at, 151
Procurement departments, 25
Product categorization, 253–254
Product charters, 156–157
Product fact books, 111, 112
Product launches (see Launches)
Product Line Management (PLM), 369–371
Product lines:
    and brands, 293–295
    evaluation of, 257–258
    management of, 258–263
    (See also Line extensions)
Product management, 3–8
    advantages of, 351–352
    approaches to, 353–355
    entrepreneurial mindset for, 6–8, 10
    evolution in, 352
    in organizational structure, 356–359
    for services, 5–6
    types of jobs in, 3–5
    (See also specific headings)
Product management concept (PMC),
    363–364
Product management teams (PMTs), 355
Product managers:
    desired vs. actual competencies of,
        362–364
    evaluation of, 364–367
    and reliance on specialists, 19–20
    responsibilities of, 359–362
    roles of, 21
    (See also specific headings)
Product plans:
    presentation of, 136
    purpose of, 134
    resource requirements in, 188
    strategic, 160
    typical components of, 135
Product rationalization review committees,
    278
Product review committees, 257–258

Product sampling, 315
Product scaling map, 256–257
Product support, 318
Product support services department, 26–27
Product versioning, 273
Product vision:
    communication of, 31–32
    development of, 115
    in planning process, 115–123
    strategic, 118–123
Productivity, 26
Products:
    assessment of current, 108–109
    in business cases, 187–188
    new (see New products)
    questions about, 22
    risk with, 153
    value analysis of, 26
Profit and loss statements, 136
Profit-and-loss (P&L) responsibilities, 333
Program evaluation and review technique
    (PERT), 207, 208
Project management, 199–214
    gate reviews and beta testing in, 209–212
    as part of product management, 200–203
    responsibility for, 199
    and scope creep, 199, 213–214
    shift from product management to, 161
    team structure and composition in,
        203–209
Project-based competitive intelligence, 74
Projected financial analysis, 188–191
Promega Corporation, 322–324
Promotional campaigns, 110, 315 (See also
    Marketing)
Proof of quality, 6
Prophet, 33–34
Proposals (see Business cases)
Protection strategies, 263–265
Prototypes, 161–162, 190, 210–212
Public relations, 239–240
Publicity, 239–240

Quad Graphics, 67
Qualitative research, 94, 101
Quality:
    brands as symbols of, 337
    proof of, 6
    standards for, 25
Quantitative information, 196

Quantitative research, 94
Quelch, John, 260–262
Questionnaires, 94
Quinn, Steven, 34

Ranking products, 257–258
Rationalization decisions, 278–279
R&D (see Research and development)
Red Bull, 273
Reengineering, 272
Regression analysis, 124
Regulatory approvals, 222
"Reinforce" products, 254
Reinforcement strategies, 263–265
Relationship-focused cultures,
    329, 334
Relaunch products, 254
Relaunches, 242, 274–277
Renewal products, 254
Renewal strategies, 265–274
Repair services, 270
Repositioning, 273
Research and development (R&D):
    as contributor to product planning,
        158
    costs of, 190
    ideas from, 150
    product manager's relationship with,
        24–26
Research projects, 93–95, 150 (See also
    Intelligence gathering)
Resellers, 236–237, 317, 318
Reserved cultures, 342, 343
Resource allocation, 139
Resource requirements, 208
Respect, 19
Resurrect products, 254
Retirement strategies, 278–279
Return on investment (ROI), 25
Revenue, 190
Reverse innovation, 272, 340
Revitalization strategies, 265–274
Reynolds, 155
Risk, 153
Road maps, 147–149
Roche, Dan, 225
Rogers, Brad, 137–143
ROI (return on investment), 25
Rollout strategies, 224, 235
Rothwell, Mark, 10–14

Sales, 303
Sales channels, 316–319
Sales force:
　　and B2B product managers, 106
　　collaboration with, 319–321
　　collecting information from, 72–73
　　communicating with, 22–23, 165, 166
　　effectiveness of, 109
　　ideas from, 150
　　and prelaunch, 224
　　training of, 23–24, 73, 235–239, 241
Sales forecasting, 22, 124–126
Samsung, 119, 285, 294
Schedules, 134
Scope creep, 199, 213–214
Screening tools (product ideas),
　　167–169, 209
Secondary associations, 292
Secondary research, 94, 179
The Secret Code of the Superior Investor (James
　　Glassman), 122
Segment management, 353
Segmented reporting, 43–46
Selling costs, 42
Serial entrepreneurs, 8
Service contracts, 319
Services:
　　design thinking for, 173
　　market segmentation for businesses
　　　offering, 79
　　product management for, 5–6
7-Up, 260, 292
Sharper Image, 247
The Shift (Scott Davis), 34
Silo structures, 356
Simplicity, 62–63
SKUs (stockkeeping units), 5
Slogans, 296, 297
SMART objectives, 127
Sneed, Paula, 365
Social media, 247–248, 323
Social responsibility, 338
Social trends, 91
Soft benefits, 177
Software as a service, 272
Solutions segments, 82
Sony, 91–92, 287, 294
Specialists, 20
Spreadsheets, 37–39, 306
Springs Window Fashion, 95–99

Sprint Corporation, 68
Stage-gate processes, 133, 158
Stakeholders:
　　emotions of, 19
　　influencing, 30–33
　　on product review committees, 258
　　relationship between product manager
　　　and, 20
　　(*See also specific stakeholder groups*)
Standard costs, 42
Steelcase, 102–103
Stihl Inc., 62
Stockkeeping units (SKUs), 5
Storytelling, 32
Strategic planning, 139
Strategic product managers, 8
Strategic product thinking, 152–156
　　customer mindset in, 152–153
　　growth in, 153–156
The Strategy and Tactics of Pricing
　　(Tom Nagle), 52
Streamlining purchases, 270
Street price, 53
Suarez, Fernando, 233
Substitute competition, 61, 62, 67–69
Success:
　　learning from, 33
　　understanding past, 157–158
Superior Clay Corporation, 274
Supplementary contribution, 190
Supplier power, 61, 62
Supply chain partners, 150
Supply chains, 62
Support services, 111
Surveys, 93, 94, 150, 225
Symbols, company, 296
Syndicated research, 93, 94
Synergy sessions, 26

Tables, in road maps, 149
Tactical product managers, 8
TAGs (trend analysis groups), 91
Target accounts, 23–24
Target markets:
　　and brands, 286
　　descriptions of, 28
　　marketing to, 305–306
　　and planning, 128–130
Target prices, 187
Task forces, 26

Task-focused cultures, 329, 334
Teams:
  cross-functional, 169, 204, 209
  product management, 355
  productivity of, 26
  size of, 204
  structure of, 203–209
  virtual, 355
Technical feasibility, 25
Technology:
  convergence and disruption in, 68
  gathering information about, 60–61
  and operations, 26
Templates, 133–134
3C development, 159, 160
3M, 32, 315
Time, 194
TIME clock, 59–60, 108
Time series forecasts, 124–125
Time zones, 348
Timing, of launches, 233
Torless, Liz, 77
Toshiba America Medical Systems, 180
Toyota Motor Company, 68
Track record, 32
Trade shows, 163
Trademarks, 341
Training:
  of customer service representatives,
    26–27
  interactive, 335
  of sales force, 23–24, 73, 235–239,
    241
Transactional leadership, 16
Transformational leadership, 16
Transnational product strategy, 336–339
Trend analysis groups (TAGs), 91
Trend-fitting, 124
Trends, 91–93, 111, 114
Tri-Tech Corporation, 80
Trust, 32–33

Umbrella approach, to branding, 28
Uncertainty, 193, 213
Underhill, Paco, 103

Unilever, 113, 278, 365
University of Wisconsin–Madison, 288
Upstream product management:
  functions in, 8–9
  and globalization, 356
  (See also specific headings)
U.S. Congress, 266
Usage positions, 290

Value:
  adding new, 265–266
  in customer value chain, 269–270
Value analysis, 26
Variable costs, 43, 48
Vaughan, Doug, 47, 54–57
Videoconferencing, 355
Videos, 242
Virtual teams, 355
Voice-of-customer (VOC) requirements,
    213, 226
Volkswagen, 339
Von Hippel, Eric, 150

Walmart, 62–63, 87, 355
Warranty programs, 222, 319
Wasson, Christina, 102
WBSs (work breakdown structures),
    206–209
Weilbacher, William, 366
Wettemann, Rebecca, 75
"What if?" questions, 222–224, 271–272
Whirlpool, 158, 331
Whitmus, Wade W., 266, 275
Whitwam, David, 152–153
Wier, Jim, 63
Work breakdown structures (WBSs),
    206–209
World Health Organization, 240
World Wide Web, 61, 95, 247

Yet2, 151
Yoder, Stephen Kreider, 259
YourEncore, 151

Zebra Technologies Corp., 308